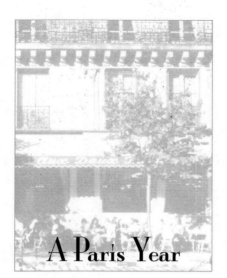

# A Paris Year

# A Paris Year

*Dorothy and James T. Farrell, 1931–1932*

Edgar Marquess Branch

*Ohio University Press*
*Athens*

Ohio University Press, Athens, Ohio 45701
© 1998 by Edgar Marquess Branch
Printed in the United States of America
All rights reserved

Ohio University Press books are printed on acid-free paper ⊗™

02 01 00 99 98    5 4 3 2 1

*Book design by Chiquita Babb*

Library of Congress Cataloging-in-Publication Data

Branch, Edgar Marquess, 1913–
    A Paris year : Dorothy and James T. Farrell, 1931–1932 / Edgar
Marquess Branch.
        p.    cm.
    Includes bibliographical references and index.
    ISBN 0-8214-1236-1 (cloth : alk. paper)
    1. Farrell, James T. (James Thomas), 1904–1979—Homes and haunts
—France—Paris. 2. Farrell, James T. (James Thomas), 1904–1979—
Marriage. 3. Paris (France)—Intellectual life—20th century.
4. Americans—France—Paris—History—20th century. 5. Novelists,
American—20th century—Biography. 6. Authors' spouses—United
States—Biography. 7. Married people—France—Biography.
8. Farrell, Dorothy. I. Farrell, Dorothy. II. Farrell, James T.
(James Thomas), 1904–1979. III. Title.
PS3511.A738Z635  1998
818'.5203—dc21
    [B]                                                98-21295

In Memory of

James T. Farrell

# Contents

# Illustrations

# Preface

In April 1931, native Chicagoans James and Dorothy Farrell, twenty-seven and twenty-one years old, sailed for Paris and remained there one year. They had been lovers two and a half years, married four days, and were expecting a baby. Their destination, the "city of dreams,"[1] had lost many leading members of its well-publicized "lost generation." Americans still there, smelling war in the air and feeling curbed by the Great Depression, had sobered down. Hard times were drying up funds for the "remittance men" of Montparnasse, *la crise* was spreading through France, and the value of the U.S. dollar was threatening to tumble. In April 1931, that exodus was still under way.

But the Farrells breasted the current—seemingly, a brash and surprising action to take. Neither of them had been to Paris. Their concept of Parisian culture was naive, their French elementary. In many respects, Chicago, their only home, had been good to them. Dorothy loved the city. Her family ties were close, and she lived in comfort. Jim knew that Chicago had given him invaluable, virtually inexhaustible material for his fiction. He had already completed many Chicago tales and a first draft of volumes 1 and 2 of his future trilogy *Studs Lonigan*. Other Chicago novels were taking shape in his mind. The city remained a vital source of inspiration. Moreover, his studies at the University of Chicago had liberated him from what he believed to have been the banal authoritarianism and spiritual emptiness of his youthful training in school and church.

Yet both of the Farrells had compelling reasons to put Chicago behind them, and both saw Paris as the land of promise. Dorothy's reasons were intimately personal, Jim's professional. Spurned by U.S. publishers and bedeviled by censorship curbs, Jim felt constrained, impotent. Each had heard good reports from their University of Chicago professors and student friends about life on the Left Bank. They believed that Montparnasse offered the freedom to live as they chose and, for Jim, the opportunity to flourish as a writer. Paris offered desirable solutions to their problems. Chicago—both its constraints and its advantages—gave them a push, a running start, for their jump to Paris.

What follows is the story of their Paris year, a flowering from desires and needs that sprouted in Chicago soil. It is a tale of joy and sorrow, struggle and growth, failure and success, and tragedy.

Farrell's year in Paris set him moving as a writer. There he won a measure of recognition and respect for his work. He proved to himself he could successfully write as he chose. There, too, he and Dorothy fended off poverty and dealt with the wrenching fact of death. The rigors of that experience tested the strength of their personal relationship and brought their values and characters into strong relief. Years later, Farrell accurately observed: "Paris was very important in my development. . . . It was there that my youth ended. . . . [That year] was the beginning of an adventure in living, in writing, in feeling, in seeing, and in thinking which has not yet ended."[2]

What was it like for a young, relatively unknown American writer and his wife, grappling with severe conditions, to make their way in literary Paris in 1931–32? To answer that question, this story conveys a sense of the texture of their daily lives, the normality of what being a Parisian expatriate meant for these Chicagoans. Their Paris was not a Paris of glamor, of hijinks, of fame and rumors that attended celebrities, of ideological aesthetic wars. Usually it was a Paris of anonymity, day by day plugging, struggle on all fronts, a search for support systems and survival strategies, and yet a fun-filled, exhilarating, expansive Paris, constantly bringing new friends and experiences. The story that emerges is compelling and moving.

# Acknowledgments

I want to acknowledge James T. Farrell's longstanding help given while he was alive. He authorized my use of the papers in the Farrell Collection, Department of Special Collections, University of Pennsylvania Libraries (a collection that includes his Paris notebooks and memoirs) as well as his writings in other depositories. He granted interviews and packed his conversations with informative details. His letters willingly answered my questions and liberally volunteered additional information. He wanted his biography to be written and indicated a special interest in the Paris period. Above all, I am grateful for the friendship he offered me during his lifetime.

Dorothy Farrell, too, was a reliable friend. She was always ready to talk with me. She permitted me to use her words and the information she supplied, all of which enriched this story of the time she shared with her husband in Chicago and Paris. I thank her for her friendliness, her concern, and her willing cooperation, which has continued up to the present.

Cleo Paturis has known of this book almost from its inception and she welcomed its coming. She made the book possible in its present form by supplying me with available copies of Farrell's unpublished, partially completed long fictions about his Paris year with his wife. These provided useful background material. Their portrait of the Farrells' activities and of the people they knew helped to fill out the picture. I will always be grateful to her for her friendship of many years.

I want to thank the Guggenheim Foundation and the National Endowment for the Humanities for their senior fellowships, which made it possible for me to undertake research in Paris. This aid enabled me to acquaint myself with the places where the Farrells lived and played during their residence there.

My special thanks go to the Farrells' Chicago friend Edward Bastian. He graduated from the University of Chicago in June 1931, then went to Paris to study history at the Sorbonne. He became the Farrells' closest Paris friend, a constant visitor, and a participant in many of their doings. In his weekly letters from Paris to his mother, to his uncle, and to friends, he became the Farrells' Boswell. Intelligent and perceptive, he recorded what Jim and Dorothy did and his feelings about them and what happened to them. Bastian gave me three lengthy interviews and let me copy and freely use the letters he wrote to the United States from France in 1931–32. The result is a contemporary, first-hand record of Jim and Dorothy in Paris.

The acceptance of Farrell's *Young Lonigan* and *Gas-House McGinty* by the late James Henle of Vanguard Press, while the Farrells were in Paris, made it possible for them to remain there an entire year. Wanting to promote the study of his friend, a major Vanguard author, Henle gave me access to his voluminous correspondence with Farrell. He let me copy whatever letters I needed and offered them for use in my publications on Farrell. As I have done before, I want to express my gratitude to the memory of this exceptionally able editor.

Michael Ryan, Nancy Shawcross, and their staff in the Department of Special Collections, University of Pennsylvania Libraries, once again have generously satisfied my need for information and unpublished material, including letters to and from Farrell, in the Farrell Collection. I thank them for helping to make this book possible. Unless otherwise recognized, unpublished material written by or to Farrell and cited in this book is located in the Farrell archives at Pennsylvania.

It is a pleasure to acknowledge my huge debt to the entire staff of Miami University's King Library, directed by Dean and University Librarian Judith A. Sessions, ably assisted by Elizabeth Brice and Richard Pettitt. In particular, for expert guidance in research problems, I most often turned to William Wortman, and I often relied on the help provided by Richard H. Quay, and by C. Martin Miller and his staff in Special Collections. Ruth Miller and Elizabeth Ping stood by me in the sometimes frustrating task of searching microfilm reels. Scott Van Dam, Ronald Brown, and Mary Hubbard of Access Services, and Ed Via, James Bricker, and Monica Sweeney of the Interlibrary Loan Department, were always ready to obtain what I needed when it was needed. When my computer frustrated or failed me, Library Systems experts Stan Brown, Belinda Barr, John Fink, Andy Farler, John Millard, Lisa Santucci, and Bonnie Neiswander-Fannin set it, or me, straight, and in unexpected crises I often called on Jean Sears, Kenneth Grabach, Margaret Lewis, and Judy Austin, all of whom were within easy reach from my library office. Janet Stuckey, Susan Wortman, Jenny Presnell, Mary Malone, and Karen Clift also stood ready to solve one problem or another.

Marcy Powell, professor emeritus of French and my longtime friend at Miami University, read the typescript of this book. To it he brought his extensive knowledge of Paris, French culture, and the French language, as well as his experience as a professional proofreader. I thank him for the invaluable service he so willingly offered. Likewise, my thanks go to my sister, Beverly Branch, now a retired professor of French, who was on ready call to answer my questions about many things Parisian or French.

I fondly remember and thank the seminar members, exceptionally able students, who joined me in exploring the Farrells' Parisian experience.

Once again I want to recognize the indispensable help of my wife, Mary. While writing this book, I relied heavily on her critical skills and her well-founded understanding of Jim and Dorothy Farrell's personalities.

## Credits

I wish to thank the following people and organizations for permission to quote unpublished material from numerous letters:

Letter from Alf to Jacob Schwartz. Patricia C. Willis, curator of the

Yale Collection of American Literature, Beinecke Rare Book and Manuscript Library, Yale University.

Letters from Kay Boyle to James T. Farrell and Edgar M. Branch. Stacy Schwandt, agent for the estate of Kay Boyle, and Karen D. Drickamer, curator of manuscripts, Kay Boyle Papers, Special Collections/ Morris Library, Southern Illinois University at Carbondale; also, the Department of Special Collections, University of Pennsylvania Libraries.

Letters from George Brodsky to James T. Farrell and Edgar M. Branch. George Brodsky; also the Department of Special Collections, University of Pennsylvania Libraries.

Letters from Robert Carlton Brown to James T. Farrell. Karen D. Drickamer, curator of manuscripts, Philip Kaplan Collection, Special Collections/Morris Library, Southern Illinois University at Carbondale; also, the Department of Special Collections, University of Pennsylvania Libraries.

Letters from Margaret Butler to Dorothy Butler Farrell and James T. Farrell. Dorothy Farrell; also the Department of Special Collections, University of Pennsylvania Libraries.

Letter from Malcolm Cowley to James T. Farrell. Robert W. Cowley; also Diana Haskell, the Malcolm Cowley Papers, the Newberry Library.

Letters from Clifton Fadiman to James T. Farrell. Clifton Fadiman; also the Department of Special Collections, University of Pennsylvania Libraries.

Letters from James T. Farrell to Robert Carlton Brown. Michael Plunkett, Special Collections and Manuscripts, Alderman Library, University of Virginia.

Letter from H. L. Mencken to James T. Farrell. Averil J. Kadis, public relations director, Enoch Pratt Free Library (quoted by permission of the Enoch Pratt Free Library of Baltimore in accordance with the terms of the will of H. L. Mencken).

Letter from Peter Neagoe to James T. Farrell. Carolyn A. Davis, reader services librarian, and Mark Weiman, curator of special collections, Peter Neagoe Papers, Syracuse University Library, Department of Special Collections; also the Department of Special Collections, University of Pennsylvania Libraries.

Letter from Stanley Newman to Edgar M. Branch. David S. Newman.

Letters from Ezra Pound to James T. Farrell and Samuel Putnam. Copyright © 1998 by Mary de Rachewiltz and Omar S. Pound (used courtesy of Declan Spring and New Directions Publishing Corporation).

Letters from Samuel Putnam to James T. Farrell and J. G. Grey. Hilary Putnam; also the Department of Special Collections, University of Pennsylvania Libraries.

Letters from Jacob Schwartz to James T. Farrell. Patricia C. Willis, curator of the Yale Collection of American Literature, Beinecke Rare Book and Manuscript Library, Yale University.

Letters from Isabel Simpson to Dorothy Butler Farrell. Dorothy Farrell; also the Department of Special Collections, University of Pennsylvania Libraries.

Letters from Lloyd Stern to James T. Farrell. Gerald Stern and Eric Stern; also the Department of Special Collections, University of Pennsylvania Libraries.

Letter from William Carlos Williams to Charles Henri Ford, as quoted in a letter from Ford to James T. Farrell (copyright © 1998 by Paul H. Williams and the estate of William Eric Williams; used by permission of Declan Spring and New Directions Publishing Corporation); also, Robert J. Bertholf, curator (quoted with the permission of the Poetry/Rare Books Collection, University Libraries, State University of New York at Buffalo).

I wish to thank the following people and organizations for permission to reproduce photographs:

Photo of Kay Boyle. Stacy Schwandt, agent for the estate of Kay Boyle; also Karen D. Drickamer, curator of manuscripts, Kay Boyle Collection, Special Collections/Morris Library, Southern Illinois University at Carbondale.

Photo of Dorothy Farrell. Courtesy of Dorothy Farrell.

Photo of Ezra Pound. Courtesy of New Directions Publishing Corporation, agent for Mary de Rachewiltz and Omar S. Pound; also the Library of Congress, Prints and Photographs Division, Arnold Genthe Collection: Negatives and Transparencies, #LC-USZ62-44966.

Photo of Samuel Putnam. Karen D. Drickamer, curator of manuscripts, Samuel Putnam Collection, Special Collections/Morris Library, Southern Illinois University at Carbondale.

Photographs of Wambly Bald, Kay Boyle, Bob Brown, James T. Farrell, Virginia Hersch, Peter Neagoe, and Samuel Putnam, as marked, are from *Americans Abroad: An Anthology,* ed. Peter Neagoe (The Hague: Servire Press, 1932).

The author photographed the Paris and Sceaux scenes in 1979, and, in 1995, the South Shore homes of the Dalys and the Cunninghams.

# A Paris Year

Early in 1927, James Farrell determined to become a writer of fiction, and almost immediately he began composing short stories. He lived with his family in the Washington Park neighborhood across the park from the University of Chicago, where he had matriculated in the summer of 1925. In midsummer 1927, after completing six quarters of course work at the university, he went to New York City hoping to advance his fortunes as a writer. He returned to Chicago after six months, having published none of his stories.

# Gearing Up for Paris

## In Chicago and New York

IN JANUARY 1928 Farrell returned to Chicago from the East, carrying with him a satchel of short-story manuscripts. He had spent nearly six fruitless and daunting months in New York City. Almost twenty-four years old, he had published nothing and, while in New York, had floundered helplessly in the dry bottoms of commercial salesmanship. Now, back in Chicago, he fought depression and struggled to overcome a sense of revulsion for his family (reflected in his first published tale, "Slob"). He was going through a period he described as one of temporary "drifting and disintegration." Rather than returning to live with his family, the Dalys, until June he "lived around" and "grubbed one way or another," writing where and when he could.[1] With his friends Paul Caron and Jack Sullivan, he lingered in Uasia, later rechristened the Slow Club, a group of would-be bohemians who met regularly in the Hotel Drexel at Fifty-seventh and Cottage Grove Avenue.[2] His writing fell off. Once, without cash, he hocked his typewriter until he scraped up five dollars to redeem it.

In May, the Dalys—Farrell's Grandmother Julia, Uncle Tom, and Aunt Ella—moved out of the Washington Park neighborhood where, earlier, from the age of eleven, he had lived with them. They rented an apartment at 7136 East End Avenue on the northern edge of the South Shore district and hoped Jim would join them there. His uncle had urged him to become a salesman, but Jim was now doubly sure that after his failure in New York he must plunge right in and write. "The notion of writing honest stuff," he later asserted to his friend Ed Bastian, "but having to delay it while one makes money is just so much hooey."[3] In June, deciding that he needed greater security and more opportunity to write, he moved back in with the Dalys. He was now assured of shelter, food, cash handouts from his uncle or his grandmother, and, best of all, the time and a comfortable place in which to write. Some thirty years later, Farrell remarked that what kept him turned around at this time was his love affair with Dorothy Butler, which began after their meeting in July.[4]

He wrote long hours at home. But on many mornings he walked a block to the Bryn Mawr station of the Illinois Central Railroad's South Shore branch to take a train to the University of Chicago campus. He was no longer an enrolled student there, but many recognized him as a familiar and shabby hanger-on usually lugging a briefcase bulging with papers. In the Harper Library reading room, he wrote short stories and read. He relaxed by walking on campus or talking with friends in the university's coffee shop. Nearby in the library's periodical room, he read the files of little magazines, including the Paris journal *transition*, which opened his eyes to the Parisian literary scene. Later in the year, he praised that quarterly in the student newspaper, the *Daily Maroon*, for its interest in "literary experiments and novelty" as seen in such writers as Ernest Hemingway, Gertrude Stein, Hart Crane, and Kay Boyle.[5]

The thought of living and writing in Paris some day absorbed him. Years later, he portrayed Eddie Ryan, an autobiographical character, in Harper Library brooding about Paris. Eddie is "dissatisfied with the present conditions of his life. Would he ever get there? Would he ever see Paris? He might never even get to New York again."[6] The July 1927 number of *transition* contained "This Is No Conclusion," an excerpt from a novel under way by his campus friend Ruth Jameson. Soon Ruth would be off to spend a year in Paris with her husband, Jim's friend Vladimir Janowicz. Janowicz was a public-school art teacher and a painter who had trained at the Chicago Art Institute and was currently studying for his bar examination.[7]

Jim envied Ruth and Vlad; he, too, wanted to be on the Left Bank. His character Eddie Ryan, shown sipping coffee in the café Sélect in Paris, remembers his days in Harper Library "thinking about Paris, about being here, and sitting in a café like the café Sélect, talking about books."[8] Ruth's success in placing her story with *transition* was an early signal to Jim that perhaps he should look to Paris for recognition—U.S. magazines had routinely rejected his stories, often for fear of censorship. He revised a group of stories and, beginning in the autumn and continuing for several months, he submitted them to *transition*. He received no replies: neither returned manuscripts nor rejection slips. It was discouraging, but he laid plans for besieging other Paris magazines, including Harold Salemson's *Tambour*. The lure of Paris remained.[9]

In *transition*, Farrell also read James Joyce's "Work in Progress," the emerging *Finnegan's Wake*, of which he already had seen portions in Ernest Walsh's and Ethel Moorhead's *This Quarter*.[10] The writing was puzzling and difficult, but intriguing. It led him that spring to the Harper Library's Rare Books room. There he found Sylvia Beach's Shakespeare and Company edition of Joyce's *Ulysses*, a work he knew by reputation. He signed it out and kept it several weeks.[11] In 1927, while in New York, he had read Joyce's *Dubliners*, *Exiles*, *Chamber Music*, and *A Portrait of the Artist as a Young Man*, the last bringing with it the familiar "shock of recognition."[12] He now judged *Ulysses* to be the greatest twentieth-century novel he had ever read. When the university bookstore promoted a student contest for the best list of five books submitted as a library nucleus, he chose *Ulysses*, Yeats's *Collected Poems*, Nietzsche's *Thus Spake Zarathustra*, Bertrand Russell's *Essays in Mysticism and Logic*, and Dostoyevsky's *The Brothers Karamazov*. The contest judges were Professors James Weber (Teddy) Linn, T. V. Smith, and Edward Sapir. They awarded his list and accompanying essay honorable mention. They commented: "James Farrell's list is an example of insight, grasp, and critical facility."[13] Jim saw in the person of Joyce an independent Irish writer self-exiled from his urban roots who bucked censorship to succeed magnificently in Paris.

He enrolled in three courses in the spring quarter of 1928, but quickly withdrew without penalty in order to concentrate on his writing.[14] About this time, he began going to the Chicago Art Institute, beginning a life-long interest in painting. A few months later, after he had met his future wife, Dorothy Butler, he collaborated with her on an article for the *Daily Maroon* about the institute's exhibit of leading American artists, although her name alone was on the byline.[15] Farrell, in fact, was far more interested in the art institute's French painting than in its American exhibits. While in Paris four years later, on 12 January 1932, he wrote to his sister Mary Farrell in Chicago: "If you go to the Art Institute look mainly for pictures by Cézanne, Matisse, Van Gogh, Gauguin, Monet, Manet, a Picasso there, also a Titian, the El Greco assumption, a boy on a donkey by Goya, a portrait of a saint by Velásquez, both in the same room with the big El Greco—also Forain, Daumier (I think there is [*sic*] one or two of his there), Courbet, Corot, and almost above all Renoir."[16] He came to believe that the French impressionists he had learned to love in Chicago exerted a major influence on his fiction.[17]

Many of Farrell's friends at this time, including Emil Armin and other painters, lived in the Hyde Park art colony. Its center was a string of small shops built on Fifty-seventh Street during the World's Columbian Exposition. The immediately surrounding area was Chicago's South

Side bohemia, enjoying a renaissance in the 1920s. The shops stretched for several blocks just east of the main campus, and many of them were rented dirt cheap by the "free spirits" of the colony.[18]

On 16 February 1928, a little theater named the Cube opened in one of the shops, located at 1538 East Fifty-seventh. It became the center for authors' readings, modern-dance programs, musical evenings, and play productions.[19] Stanley Newman, a contemporary and friend of Farrell's at the university and, along with his wife, a habitué of the Cube, remembered "the Cube Crowd" as "an assorted bunch of writers, painters, sculptors, and advanced thinkers or hangers-on, all of us strongly influenced by the Nathan and Mencken atmosphere of maintaining gaiety in the process of tearing down idols."[20] The Cube's founder and impresario was Farrell's friend Nick Matsoukas, known as the "campus aesthete" and art critic.[21]

The Cube's play director was Mary Hunter, the well-educated, sophisticated niece of Mary Austin.[22] Jim was constantly drawn to her. In Farrell's "The Distance of Sadness," when Eddie (Jim) is with Joan (Mary), he finds her "charming" and wants "to reach his arms out and kiss her." Farrell wrote the text of his tale "Studs" in Mary's apartment in the spring of 1929, and he turned to her for advice when he first mapped out a novel on Studs. One night in 1929 he made love to her. It was a one-time affair, but it was the occasion for writing his first published poem, "The Sacrament of Marriage," which appeared in the little magazine *Poetry World*.[23]

In the Cube on a July evening during a poetry reading by Maxwell Bodenheim, John Howe, the university's assistant director for public relations, introduced Jim to Dorothy Butler.[24] Dorothy lived nearby with her mother, Margaret (Maggie) Butler, her younger sister Virginia, and Beatrice Timmins, a long-time family servant, then friend, who had helped bring up the two girls from babyhood.[25] Dorothy was an extremely pretty, red-haired eighteen-year-old, then in her fourth quarter at the university. "I didn't go there [to the Cube] for acting," Dorothy remembered. "I went there because I was taking a [modern] poetry class with James Weber Linn. And on my way home from school I saw a poster in front of Woodworth's bookstore that Maxwell Bodenheim was going to speak at the Cube. And I knew where the Cube was. . . . I thought, Well, I will go there, and listen to him speak and write my term paper on that, because it was modern poetry. And I told Linn, and he said—that was more modern than we were considering, but go ahead. So I went, and I heard Maxwell Bodenheim, and that's where I met James."[26]

Years later, Jim vividly recalled the attractive strawberry blond with the round, fresh face whom he met that night. She was wearing a wide-brimmed straw hat with a band of flowers around it, and an ankle-length chiffon dress splashed with red flowers. He walked her home that evening to her big apartment at 5600 Blackstone Avenue, only four blocks from the Cube and near the campus.[27]

Dorothy had grown up in Hyde Park and gone to the University of Chicago kindergarten, John Dewey's school. For three years she went to St. Thomas Grade School. Then, because her father Patrick wanted her to go to a public school, she transferred to the Ray Public School. After graduation, she attended St. Xavier's, the best Roman Catholic high school for girls in the neighborhood. Because she took French both in high school and in college, she was more expert in that language than was Jim (who had learned little in high school during his sophomore and junior French classes),[28] although her fluency was still severely limited.

At the university, Dorothy was a prelaw student who was actively interested in theater and dancing. Along with Katherine Dunham and other students, she attended Mark Turbyfill's dancing class in a studio in the art colony on Fifty-seventh Street across from the Cube. She also had acted in Zona Gale's "The Neighbors," staged by the university Dramatic Society.[29] Returning to the Cube after having heard Bodenheim, she auditioned for, and secured, the role of Mrs. Solness in Ibsen's *The Master Builder*, directed by Mary Hunter.[30] Jim Farrell was there that night, too. He was encouraged to act in a dramatization of Hemingway's

"Today Is Friday." Dorothy remembered that he was "a terrible actor. To tell the truth, he only did it to hang around, that's all. . . . And we had fun at the same time."[31]

In the Cube, Dorothy heard much chatter about Paris. For years she had dreamed of going there, having listened to enthusiastic tales told by four of her aunts—her mother's sisters—of Paris visits with their husbands. Her Aunt Grace, in particular, was a regular visitor to the annual Paris fashion shows. Her husband, John Roney, had made millions through the sale of his 450 grocery stores in the Consumers and Hi-Lo chains to Kroger's of Ohio.[32] After John and Grace lost their only daughter Marian, who died at eighteen, Dorothy became their favorite niece.[33] Dorothy was a girl whom almost everyone liked. She was socially adept and loved good times. She was inclined toward happiness. She reminisced: "I was not born with much except a happy disposition. My grandmother said when I was born: 'This child will not want for anything.' And I have never wanted, because I've been happy. Within myself. . . . Not having things never bothered me. . . . I was happy, whatever I had. If we had an ice-cream cone I was happy."[34] She knew that one day she would go to Paris. Unlike Jim, who worked with consuming intensity and often saw the future as gloomy or threatening, Dorothy was rarely morose or over-burdened with heavy fears and worries. But both she and Jim were ad-venturous and welcomed change. She and Jim "merged" in their desire to go to Paris, each for their own reasons.[35]

Jim, always restless, and revolted by his Aunt Ella's drunken binges at home, started hitchhiking in July to New York with his friend Paul Caron and Jack Selby, who claimed to have been an instructor at the University of Michigan. On 19 July, from Gary, Indiana, he wrote Dorothy a long, respectful letter encouraging her to continue working on Bodenheim's verse. After Paul Caron went his own way, Jim and Selby ran out of money in Indianapolis. Stranded in their hotel, and ducking out without paying his bill, Jim was temporarily reduced to panhandling before catch-ing rides home. Tired, hungry, and dirty, he straggled into the art colony at night and cleaned up in a friend's apartment.[36] After this unnerving episode, he sought predictability by registering for the second summer term at Chicago. He took two composition courses, one from Martin Joseph (Tom) Freeman, who became a close friend, and the other from Llewellyn Jones, literary editor of the *Chicago Evening Post.* He did not enroll again until the spring quarter of 1929, his last.[37]

He resumed his writing and picked up with Dorothy. They often met in the university's coffee shop and took their evening meals together in nearby restaurants, with Dorothy paying the tab. As she rightly claimed, "It was my money for quite a while before we went to Paris, that was sort of keeping him going, even though he did live at home with his aunt and uncles, you know. He didn't have money otherwise, until he got the job for a while on the paper [the *Chicago Herald-Examiner*]."[38] Dorothy had money left to her by her father Patrick, an attorney who had died in 1925, as well as money put in her name by her mother. She also shared in money given her family by her wealthy uncle John Roney.[39]

The two went to campus lectures: Clarence Darrow, John Dewey, Bertrand Russell, Ole Rolvaag, Sherwood Anderson, and Irving Babbitt. They heard Carl Sandburg sing ballads, Vachel Lindsay read his poetry, and Paul Robeson give a recital.[40] They saw plays on campus, in the Chicago Loop, and at the Goodman Theater. They went to Jack Jones's and Slim Brundage's Dill Pickle Club at 10 Tooker Alley on the Near North Side; to Ben Reitman's Hobo College; to the Art Institute; to see the Isadora Duncan dancers; to see Mae West in *Diamond Lil*, then on tour at Chicago's Apollo Theater; to movies; and, as the craze developed, to dance marathons.[41] Dorothy paid most of the bills. By September, they were lovers. They met where and when they could: in Dorothy's apartment, in friends' Hyde Park apartments, in hotels, and in the 633 North Michigan Avenue boardinghouse run by the painter Charles Colahan and his wife Gene, a friendly couple.[42]

They were able to keep their affair secret from Dorothy's mother, Maggie, a practical, able, and gregarious "family" person of limited education. Although lacking the religiosity of Jim's mother, Mary, she was a conventionally minded Roman Catholic who disapproved of sex before marriage. She actively promoted the social life of her two daughters, Dorothy and Virginia, encouraging them to bring their friends—including Jim Farrell—to the apartment, where she could meet and talk with them. On special occasions, she helped the girls give parties. She did not begrudge the money spent on their education and for their pleasure. Relatively well off, Maggie had income from a trust, and like all her relatives she had held stock in John Roney's grocery stores and had shared in his profits. After the death of her husband, for five years she successfully ran a delicatessen on Fifty-fifth Street, a few blocks from home;[43] recently, she had made profitable investments in the Avon Company.[44]

Jim and Dorothy continued their affair during the two and one-half years before their marriage. Along the way, as we shall see, they endured a series of sexual mishaps.[45] Throughout, Jim worked on his writing at every opportunity and sprayed out his tales to numerous magazine editors.

In the notebooks he kept during those years, Jim recorded his reactions to his reading and his experiences, his ideas for short stories and articles, and sometimes early versions of them. In "Happy Sunday" he tried to express in poetry the new-found eroticism and the deeper understanding of female sexuality that his love for a woman had given him:

> Like a woman laughing fulfilled,
> The spring moves over the indolent Sunday street,
> A string of sun about her hair,
> A band of green hiding her feet.
> She has drained into her womb,
> The secrets of winter's seeds,
> And she comes
> Laughing and fulfilled.
>
> ("Notebook and Diary for 1930," p. 46. Published
> in *College English* 24 (March 1963): 480)

He had been rejected by girls in the past, but he was now ardently embracing a girl who reciprocated his affection.

In January 1929, acting on a tip from John Howe, the university public relations man, Farrell was hired by Duffy Cornell, the managing editor of the *Chicago Herald-Examiner,* to replace Milton Mayer as the paper's campus correspondent. He was given a press card, an expense account, and space rates. He telephoned in his stories to Harry Jordan on the city desk or George Morgenstern on the rewrite desk.[46] Hustling on campus to find story ideas for his newspaper items, he cooperated—sometimes stormily—with George's brother, William V. Morgenstern, the university's director of publicity from 1927 to 1942.[47] For the first time since he had quit a remunerative job as a service-station attendant in 1927, he had a fairly regular, though modest, income.

Meantime, Dorothy enrolled in the winter 1929 quarter, after which she withdrew from the university with near failing grades.[48] Her main interests had shifted away from academic studies to Jim Farrell and the happy social life she was leading. She knew that dropping out of school would hurt her mother and be censured by her wealthy, conventional uncle John Roney and Grace, his wife. For two years, she carried on a remarkably successful deception. She kept her mother and the Roneys from knowing what she had done, by occupying herself outside her apartment and on campus during class hours. She used her tuition money of $100 a quarter as spending money for herself and Jim.[49]

During the year, Jim kept a steady flow of manuscripts going to magazines and newspapers, sometimes as many as twenty at one time. He reported many items for the *Herald-Examiner.* He published fifteen feature articles in the *Daily Maroon,* and book reviews in leading New York and Chicago publications. His ambitious article "Liberals in Chicago" in *Plain Talk* was based on interviews with Clarence Darrow, Jane Addams, Paul Douglas, Julius Rosenwald, and others.[50] With these successes, the possibility of working in Paris came more clearly into view.

He even saw himself there, especially after talking with Vladimir Janowicz and Ruth Jameson, who had returned to the Fifty-seventh Street art colony after their year in France. Ruth told him how inexpensive food and lodging were. She and Vlad told him tales of American expatriates in Montparnasse—how free they were to express themselves in their conduct and in their art. They were accepted. When Jim did get to Paris, he remembered how Vlad had told him of the engrossing chess games he had played there with the writer Peter Neagoe—who became Jim's friend—in the Paris headquarters of PEN at 4, rue de Chevreuse.[51]

Try as he might, and despite his success with articles, in 1929 Farrell succeeded in publishing only one story, the tale "Slob" in Charles Henri Ford's struggling little magazine *Blues*, put out in Columbus, Mississippi. Encouraged, he submitted eight other stories to Ford before the year was out. The editor liked his writing but urged him to take more time and care in its composition.[52] Among the stories Ford read was "Scene." Concerned about censorship, he sent it to William Carlos Williams for his judgment. Williams replied: "'Scene' is amusing and realistically convincing but I do not think it is worth going to the mat with the authorities about. You would certainly be suppressed because of it if it were used, [but] . . . my wife and I were much entertained."[53] Ford especially liked the manuscript of "Calico Shoes," but afraid of being censored, he wanted Jim to send it to Eugene Jolas at *transition*. Jim replied, "I practically foreknow its fate" there. Still, encouraged, he persuaded Ford to submit it, because "if someone who knows them sends the story, it would be given a better break." There was no reply from Jolas.[54]

On 10 March 1929, William (Studs) Cunningham, the model for the character Studs Lonigan, died in his parents' South Shore home less than a mile from where Farrell lived.[55] The death of Jim's former friend, and enemy, was the happening, above all others, that triggered the chain of events ensuring Jim's and Dorothy's departure for Paris two years later. At the time, Farrell was taking Teddy Linn's course in advanced composition. With his friend Joe Cody, he went to Studs's wake and came to see in that experience the germ of the story "Studs" that he soon wrote for Linn's class. Leaving the wake, he was struck by the unbridgeable gulf in values that now separated him from the life Studs symbolized.[56] Linn approved the tale enthusiastically, and Jim discovered that the images and impressions that went into the story remained with him so vividly he could not let them rest.[57]

In June, he unexpectedly heard from Clifton Fadiman, an editor at Simon & Schuster who had read and liked Jim's story "Slob" in *Blues*. Fadiman was enquiring about the possibility of the author producing a longer work.[58] His letter jump-started Farrell into action: he took "Studs" to Professor Robert Morss Lovett of the English Department, who encouraged him to develop his story and its milieu in greater detail and to submit the result to Fadiman—who, Lovett assured him, had a reputation for picking winners. He set to work immediately, dredging up memories of the intricate experience he, Studs, and others had shared in the Washington Park neighborhood. To Fadiman, he laid out his plans for what he then called his "corner gang novel."[59]

That same summer, Fadiman read thirty-six of Farrell's rough, first-draft pages of this novel-in-progress and, understandably, was disappointed. "To tell the truth," he explained in August, "I don't believe the method you have employed is capable of producing anything like a mature fictional effect. . . . I think the prose is wordy, disorganized and a bit hysterical."[60] Toward the end of the month, his job as campus reporter behind him, Jim again hitchhiked to New York, this time with Sam Rose, an aspiring playwright. He planned to see Fadiman and hoped to find a niche for himself in the city. "I hoped to stay in New York in 1929, but couldn't make it," he explained.[61] With only thirty cents in his pocket on arrival, he put up at the Twenty-third Street Chelsea Y and later at the Mills Hotel at thirty-five cents a night. During the month he was there, he and Dorothy exchanged twenty long letters. Dorothy sent him small sums of money, cookies, fudge, and a pair of glasses left behind.[62]

On 2 September, the day after his arrival in New York, he picked up $100 from G. D. Eaton of *Plain Talk* for his article "Liberals in Chicago."[63] Two interviews with Fadiman proved futile, and he began making the rounds of book-review journals, armed with a letter of introduction from Professor Lovett.[64] He saw Amy Loveman of the *Saturday Review of*

*Literature,* Bruce Bliven of the *New Republic,* Irita Van Doren of the *Herald-Tribune Book Review,* William Soskin of the *New York Post,* and others.[65] When not furiously reading books given him for review—at one time five in tandem—he turned to his own manuscript. "I'm getting a little start on the book," he wrote to Dorothy on 16 September. But writing book reviews, some of them merely unsigned notes, was unprofitable and discouraging. He confided to Dorothy: "I do not think that I shall remain much longer. . . . I find that I ought to get some more education, before I try and make myself any sort of an ambitious literary person in N. Y."[66]

A damaged typewriter and a persistent cold finally put an end to his effort. He was taken in by his friends Paul and Sarajo Caron, and Osborne and Ann Andreas, all sharing a Riverside Drive apartment. They nursed his cold and fed him.[67] There, he visited with his friend the black poet Donald Jeffrey Hayes. He also had dinner with Mary Hunter, then in New York, but she refused to renew their brief Chicago affair. He headed for home early in October, using money for bus fare sent to him by Dorothy.[68]

Back in Chicago, Jim put most of his energy into writing his "corner gang" novel. He wrote at home, in Harper Library, and in the Chicago Public Library downtown at Randolph and Michigan. Rejection slips for his short stories continued to mount and he felt mired in unproductive effort. Farrell portrays his character Eddie Ryan as extremely unhappy with his life in Chicago at this time: "Both of the times that he had gotten out of the city, he had been glad, and getting out for good had been in his mind as an aim ever since he had returned here from New York in the fall of 1929. . . . He didn't belong in Chicago. He belonged in New York. And beyond New York there was Paris. . . . But how would he ever be able to get to Paris and live and write there, and be able to support himself[?]"[69] Marion Healy (Dorothy) comforts and encourages him. She sees the intensity with which he works and believes that writing is his future. She hints that there may be a way for both of them "to go to

New York, or to Paris, to wherever it was that you thought you'd like to go." Eddie suspects that Marion is about to propose they leave Chicago by getting additional money dishonestly from her mother. He dislikes the idea and does not respond.[70]

During 1930, Farrell published a dozen book reviews in New York and Chicago journals and three articles that revealed much of his intellectual development up to that time: "Half Way from the Cradle," in *Earth*, "Thirty and Under," in the *New Freeman*, and "John Dewey's Philosophy," in the *Saturday Review of Literature*. He continued to submit short stories to U.S. magazines with no success. At one time in June, he had thirty-four manuscripts out to magazines.[71] He entered "Studs" in a prize contest sponsored by V. F. Calverton's *Modern Monthly*. The editor returned it in early June and announced that none of the submitted short stories merited the prize, which was not awarded.[72]

Farrell had better luck with Paris magazines in 1930. In the spring, Harold Salemson's *Tambour* published two of his sketches, "In the Park" and "My Friend the Doctor."[73] He also began submitting stories to *This Quarter*, which had been owned and edited by Edward Titus since mid-1929. Late in April, he heard from Sam Putnam, hired in 1930 by Titus as associate editor. Putnam was then overseeing the preparation of the April–May–June 1930 number, the "Italian issue" containing Putnam's translations of many Italian authors he was interested in. "I like your work very much. I think it's swell," Putnam assured Farrell. He saw in Jim's tales his "own Chicago that was coming to life." Ignoring Titus's verdict that "This is rot! Why, this fellow can't even write," Putnam called for more manuscripts, and they arrived by every ship. Among them were excerpts from the "Young Lonigan" portion of Jim's long manuscript that Putnam especially liked: the playground scene, Lucy and Studs in Washington Park, and Marion Shires and Weary Reilley dribbling the soccer ball. In July, Jim sent a final batch, including "Studs." Putnam later reminisced: "I had never seen such an output and with the quality standing up so well to the quantity."[74]

Both Jim and Dorothy were excited by Putnam's letters. The enthusiastic praise of his fiction was the first he had received from an editor. Who was this man who was familiar with his Chicago? He asked his friends in the Fifty-seventh Street artists' colony and was told that Putnam's Chicago credentials were genuine. He learned that Putnam, born in Chicago, had gone to the University of Chicago. Then he had worked in the city for a decade as a journalist on various newspapers and had contributed poems and essays to Midwestern magazines. On the *Chicago Evening Post,* he wrote feature articles, book reviews, and literary and art criticism. Dissatisfied with life in Chicago, he and his family settled in Paris in 1927. He was known as a skilled translator of literary works in several languages. A year before he and Farrell met, he published *François Rabelais, a Spiritual Biography.* It was true, Jim realized, that he and Putnam had a common background in some respects.[75] Later, he learned that his own growing disillusionment with Chicago's cultural life was more than matched by Putnam's.

Hoping to learn more about Putnam, Jim turned to the current number of *This Quarter* in Harper Library. There he saw Putnam's signed editorial, "The Truth about Fascism." It expressed the opinion that "Fascism is a reaction against Renaissance individualism, that it is a form of pragmatic relativism (page [sic] the late William James), and, lastly, that it represents a revolution against the decadent liberal state and, as such, is a challenge to Democracy . . . with which our watery-eyed liberals of the *Nation* and the *New Republic* stamp in America are, naturally, not quite capable of dealing." The Fascist state, Putnam continued, was "merely a reflection of something that, in Italy, is 'in the air,' something that contemporary literature, so to speak, is catching out of the air." "Impressed by the manner in which the present régime is being backed up by writers and artists generally," he cited as examples Pirandello, Marinetti, and Bontempelli.[76]

Jim was familiar with the rationale for Fascism, which he had studied in his political science courses at the University of Chicago.[77] He disagreed with Putnam and agreed with his instructors that Fascism was dictatorial and a dangerous fraud. He believed it would lead to war. He was perplexed by Putnam's linking of Fascism with the pragmatism of William James.[78] Nevertheless, as he always conceded, here was a professional who was the first to stand foursquare behind his fiction, a rare bird indeed.

Jim was unaware that Putnam's developing aesthetic predisposed him toward the psychosocial realism of Farrell's fiction. By 1930, Putnam was a leader of the Directions group in Paris, which opposed the tenets of "The Revolution of the Word" expressed in Eugene Jolas's *transition*. He called for "content and lucidity" in literature, "as opposed to a verbal experimentation which, carried far enough, becomes a philosophic game rather than literature." He deplored the overstress on form and on autonomous subjectivism championed by prominent expatriates associated with *transition*. They had proclaimed: "The writer expresses, he does not communicate. The plain reader be damned"; and what the writer expressed, they believed, was an "absolute that seeks an a priori reality within ourselves alone." Putnam sensed a "new spirit" in the air, a swing away from dehumanized symbols and empty forms toward "objects." "The object," he wrote, "means reality, and reality is what is wanted —reality and direction"—particularly in a troubled United States undergoing a social crisis, a country that did not need "a badly translated and badly garbled European carry-over" in its literature. Putnam found in Farrell's fiction the new spirit he sought.[79]

Farrell was also unaware that Putnam had grown deeply dissatisfied working as an underling to Titus. Associate editor Putnam already had planned to start his own magazine, and the disagreement with Titus over the merits of Farrell's tales sealed his decision. Writing to Farrell on 23 July 1930, Putnam promised to publish one of Jim's stories—which one he did not say—in *This Quarter*; then, as a final thumbing of his nose at Titus, he quietly slipped "Studs" into the July–August–September number, the "Russian issue" of the magazine. Titus did not notice it: the story was buried in the final nine pages. Nor did Putnam let Farrell know.

Only when Jim received a letter from Slater Brown, formerly a Parisian expatriate who was then working as an editor for the *New Republic* in New York, where he had seen *This Quarter*, did he learn of "Studs's" appearance. He and Dorothy arranged a private celebration. After a double exchange of letters with Titus, Jim received twenty dollars in payment.[80]

In a December letter to Farrell, Putnam spoke of his break with Titus. He enclosed a copy of the *New Review*, his own, newly founded journal, and stated his intention to publish Farrell in a future number. In his reply, Farrell asked Putnam if the *New Review* would consider bringing out a volume of his tales. Putnam answered that he wanted to do a series of booklets. "There is no one I'd rather start with than you." But he doubted he could do a large volume.[81] Farrell depicts his character Eddie Ryan showing the letter to Marion (Dorothy) and several of his friends. One of them, Jan Varsky (Vladimir Janowicz), responds: "'You belong in Paris, Eddie.'"[82] The remark sinks home. Like Marion, Eddie had been wishing to go to Paris, but Jan's remark "fixed the desire in his mind." In Farrell's novel *Boarding House Blues*, he shows Anna Brown (Dorothy Butler), Danny O'Neill (Farrell), and their friend Ed Lanson (Paul Caron) talking about their plans for the immediate future. Ed speaks vaguely about his plans to go to Paris. Anna uses the occasion to again let Danny know she definitely wants to go there.[83]

Late in January 1931, a few days after Jim received Putnam's encouraging letter, his friend Bus Stern read Farrell's bulky manuscript on Studs Lonigan.[84] Stern argued that the novel was "too real, and too long for the burden of reality it would lay upon the reader."[85] Why not, Bus asked, divide the enormous manuscript into two parts and make the first section, which was about young Studs, a kid novel? Jim immediately agreed. His division formed the nuclei of what would become *Young Lonigan* and *The Young Manhood of Studs Lonigan*.[86]

In his response to Putnam, Farrell revealed that he had finished a novel of forty thousand words. It "deals with kids after the manner of those fragments you saw. Originally, I planned to have it six hundred typewritten pages. But then I decided that that style would not carry so long a volume without repetitiveness, so I made it a kid novel, and if I can get it printed, I'll do a sequel three or four years hence." He explained that he was sending the manuscript of the kid novel to Fadiman at Simon & Schuster.[87]

Back came Fadiman's reply. He could not "cotton" to the writing. It still was too crude, done with "both hands."[88] In a letter of 4 February to Sam Putnam, Jim mentioned the rejection with some bitterness: "Fadiman . . . summed his opinion up with 'Your material is very genuine, but you go at it with two hands.' Also, he found overstressed irony, where I didn't know there was any irony at all. I have the feeling that he, like several others, picked me up and wrote more or less patronizing letters to the young writer who might be promising, and, then, dropped me coldly and hurriedly. Naturally, he has a perfect right to reject what he pleases, and to dislike what he pleases, but he certainly, in my opinion, did so with empty platitudes."[89] He informed Putnam he would try Covici-Friede, and then, if necessary, Brewer & Warren, Coward-McCann, and finally Jonathan Cape-Smith. But, he added, the novel "will probably bump right square into most people's prejudices. . . . I'm in a tough spot, and have my back pretty much up against the wall. If something doesn't break for me soon I'll probably have to let all my writing go hang."[90]

He knew that Dorothy was pregnant again and that she did not want an abortion. He also knew that probably she would defer to whatever his decision about it might be, but he, too, refused to consider an abortion. He remembered the termination of her pregnancy in 1930. It was performed, he said, by the second-best abortionist in Chicago, to whom he paid the fifty dollars he had received for "Thirty and Under." He had paced up and down alongside Jackson Park in front of the Jackson Park hospital where the procedure was taking place. Utterly distraught, he had tried unsuccessfully to distract his mind by reading *The Charterhouse of Parma* as he walked.[91] After Dorothy was released, he had nursed her in the Colahans' boardinghouse, where supposedly she was spending a few days with her friends. Never again, he had vowed then—never again an abortion. Now, without a job, he was faced with supporting a wife and child in a depression-ridden Chicago he wanted to leave behind him.

Fighting off desperation, Jim mailed his manuscript to Covici-Friede. Harry Block, an editor, responded that his firm could not handle it. Jim then tried Brewer & Warren, recommended to him by Harold Salemson. After one week, Joseph Brewer advised Farrell that although he liked some things about the novel, it would invite censorship from John S. Sumner's Society for the Suppression of Vice. He could not afford the resulting lawsuits. Moreover, the novel needed direction, a formal plot, and a discernible moral. And Jim should remember that the modern trend was toward romance. But Brewer left some hope that the novel might be salvaged. He would be happy to meet with Farrell in New York.[92]

In Paris, in the meantime, Sam Putnam had forwarded Farrell's tales "Jewboy" and "The Scarecrow" to his associate editor Ezra Pound in Rapallo. Pound responded with a resounding endorsement of the two tales: they were "certainly the stuff we are here to print. You can say over my signature. A contribution to l'histoire morale contemporaine. It lacks a dedication to the sponsors of the 18th Amendment. E.P." His praise continued. Print them, he urged, even if blank pages must be substituted in copies of the magazine "sent through the Jewnited States post." Of the two tales, "'The Scarecrow' is much the more important. I should print them BOTH together. Effect cumulative, and shows that a new writer is here (I don't know how much more he has to say,) but this much ought to be printed." "The Scarecrow," he concluded, is "an attempt of literature to keep up with American life as lived under the shadow of the 18th amendment, the baboon law (art. 211) and a dead system of education." It is "an answer to several questions asked by the late Henry James."[93]

Putnam forwarded Pound's letter to Farrell and enclosed a copy of his own letter to Pascal Covici urging the publisher to accept "Young Lonigan." He promised Jim "some sort of spread in the near future."[94] Putnam, an ex-Chicagoan, taking his cue from Farrell's weary dislike of that city, confided: "Personally, I hate the goddamned provincial hellhole! . . . I had good opportunity to get fed up with the pettiness of the dawdlers and publicity seekers about town; and if you will stand for a bit of fatherly advice, don't waste your time on 'em. You've got something."[95]

With Putnam's advice ringing in his head, a promise of publication freely given, and, above all, the unexpected surge of exhilaration flowing from Ezra Pound's solid backing, Jim knew that the decision about his and Dorothy's immediate future was not in doubt. They would go to Paris, the "world center" that for two years had been "a city of dreams" to him.[96] On 21 March, he wrote to Putnam: "I am in hopes of leaving here within a month." Ten days later, Farrell had his passport in hand—the very day Joseph Brewer wrote his letter rejecting "Young Lonigan."[97] About this time, Farrell saw Robert Morss Lovett and told him that if he had no luck in placing his novel in New York, he might try Sylvia Beach's Shakespeare and Company in Paris.[98]

Dorothy already had concluded they should go to Paris soon. Her counterpart in "Innocents in Paris" hints that she had a plan at this time to get them there.[99] John and Grace Roney had recently stayed in Paris, at the Hôtel Crillon, and this had reawakened her interest in going abroad; in addition, her pregnancy added a note of urgency. Dorothy did not see how she, a favored child now unwed and pregnant and a covert college dropout, could face her mother and the Roneys when the truth came out. In 1994, Dorothy reconstructed her state of mind at the time as having been forthright and decisive: "The fact that we went off to Paris . . . was in itself a little eccentric at the time. . . . Considering I was still just a kid and he was pretty conventional in a lot of ways, you know? . . . I wanted to go, that's all. . . . At that time there was so much stuff in the newspapers about Paris. . . . I wanted to go to Paris, so I said, Come on, we'll go. . . . And off we went, without any hesitation."[100]

Together they plotted an elaborate scheme, which came off without a hitch. She would enlist her mother's support for going to Paris by telling her she wanted "to go there and study." As she explained: "You see, my uncle and aunt and all my other aunts had been in Europe. They had all been there, and she was happy for me to go to study a little. I was going to go to the Sorbonne and study."[101] Farrell filled in the picture: his friend Charles Coe, a close campus friend and fellow student in a political science course, agreed to steal some stationery from the dean's office of the university's undergraduate division. Jim forged a letter on it saying Dorothy had won a scholarship in music to the Sorbonne, to begin in April, and he mailed the letter to Dorothy. Upon reading it, Maggie told her daughter to accept the scholarship. Dorothy returned the letter to Jim, who destroyed it. In the meantime, Farrell was keeping their plan to himself. He was spreading the story, at home and to his friends, that soon he was leaving Chicago to live in New York City in order to write and get published. His mailing address would be the office of the *New Masses*, a magazine to which he had unsuccessfully submitted reviews and tales for some time.[102]

Writing about this period of his life, Farrell later asserted that he had become "more and more alienated from my own Chicago past. My own differences were symbolized by books," for books "were doorways to a larger world. And that larger world had come to mean Paris."[103] Dorothy saw Paris as a temporary solution to her problems, but she also knew that for Jim it was the best place for him to do what he was impelled to do. As she observed, "It was perhaps very important for him to be there [in Paris], to remove himself from Chicago at that time, because he was being sort of repressed there, not being allowed to develop, to say, 'Look, I can do this, I'm doing it.'"[104] Yet, ironically, while writing in Paris, he was not removed from Chicago. "During that year in Paris," he recalled in 1976, "I wrote several thousand pages, perhaps, set in Chicago. My mind didn't leave Chicago for Paris."[105]

Farrell knew that he and Dorothy "couldn't have stayed in New York [even] if I sold 'Young Lonigan.' Publishers didn't give big advances . . . and Dorothy was already pregnant."[106] He believed that Paris, rather than New York, offered the better opportunity to get his family and his career started. New York, like Chicago, he informed Sam Putnam, was a "hellhole."[107] The depression had not yet seriously hit France. But in the United States, he observed, it "had been severe for well over a year. There were Hoovervilles, and men selling apples on streets. . . . Fellows whom I knew were out of work. There were a few news stories of men jumping out of windows because they had been wiped out. . . . There were many beggars and panhandlers on the streets." Jim witnessed evictions. In March 1931, he "marched in an unemployment Parade, organized by the Communist Party, and led by Clarence Hathaway," then the Communist Party's district organizer in Chicago.[108]

Every sign pointed to Paris as the place to be. Two of their acquaintances from Chicago's bohemia recently had taken that plunge: Reuben Menken (whom Farrell called Rue) and his wife Ginny, a University of Chicago student. The Farrells first knew Rue as a radical soapboxer in Bug House Square and at the Dill Pickle, then later at the Cube. His family owned and managed expensive North Side real estate. A strongly built man in his twenties, with a stiff, black mustache, like Farrell he was an aspiring writer who worked as one of a publisher's team preparing a history of art. Ginny was a vivacious, black-haired girl whose good looks were marred only by slightly crossed eyes. If the Menkens could cast off for Paris, why not the Farrells?[109]

In early April, Dorothy made the final travel arrangements, keeping the details secret from her mother. She purchased three railroad tickets to New York, for her mother, Jim, and herself; and two tickets on the Red Star liner *Pennland*, sailing from New York to Cherbourg on 17 April. Dorothy explained the source of her funds this way in 1992: "It was my mother's money. I just lifted it . . . so I was a bad girl. . . . It wasn't all that much money. I mean it was a thousand dollars or so, maybe a little more." But the money really had been left for her benefit by her father. "So I wasn't really stealing from her. I was just helping myself a little early to my own money."[110] Her mother was to accompany her to New York. Maggie knew nothing of the train and steamship tickets bought for Jim.

Farrell had his tickets in hand at least by 8 April, the day he wrote to Sam Putnam giving his sailing and arrival times. He cautioned Sam to reveal to no one that he would be in Paris rather than New York. On 13 April, he and Dorothy took the Illinois Central train to the Cook County Building in Chicago's Loop. There they were married by the clerk for Cook County.[111] "We just got married," said Dorothy, "because we were going to Europe together. . . . I guess we were naive."[112] With them was Ted Marvel, the best man, who would become a top executive at CBS News. Jim and Ted had been friends since summer 1927, when they were staying at the Chelsea YMCA in New York.[113] Ted, like Jim, soon returned to Chicago, where he earned his degree at the university. He, Jim, and Dorothy often were together. Standing before the clerk, Jim had no ring for Dorothy. She pulled a hairpin from her hair, bent it, and he put it on her finger.[114] As the three walked out of the building, they met Felix Kolodziej, Jim's best campus friend, who guessed what was going on. Felix and Ted were in on the newlyweds' marriage and their true destination, as were Jim's younger sister and brother, Mary and Jack, his longtime friends Joe Cody and Jack Sullivan, Martin Joseph (Tom) Freeman, and Dorothy's younger sister Virginia. All of them were pledged to secrecy.[115]

That same evening, Farrell left alone for New York. He wanted several days in which to look up people and possibly arrange for the publication of "Young Lonigan" before sailing on 17 April. When he boarded the train in Chicago, he was wearing an old, bluish suit, the badly worn, frayed overcoat he had owned since 1925, and a floppy Stetson. He was carrying an ancient Royal portable typewriter and a shoe-sample case, given him by his Uncle Tom, stuffed with clothes and a few books. Like Dorothy, he had already shipped a trunk; hers was filled with clothes, his with books and manuscripts and his one good suit, a gray-flannel cast-off given him by Paul Rosenfels, a wealthy Oak Park, Illinois, friend.[116] Two days later, Dorothy and Maggie, seen off by Dorothy's cousin Isabel Simpson, boarded the Twentieth Century Limited to New York. The new bride wore a brand-new, expensive suit and a beret. She and Jim had carefully planned for Jim to board the *Pennland* well before Dorothy and to keep out of Maggie's sight. In New York, he stayed at the Chelsea YMCA, Dorothy and Maggie at a fashionable hotel.[117]

His first day in New York, Farrell lunched with Joseph Brewer and George Dangerfield, a reader for Brewer & Warren. Brewer still thought "Young Lonigan" would not do in its present form. He wanted a longer novel, one with more sex, more romance, something Macy's shopgirls would devour as they rode home on the subway after work. Jim refused to revise it to order.[118] He headed directly to see Slater Brown at the *New Republic*. The magazine had published his reviews, and he had been friendly with Brown ever since Slater had alerted him to the publication of "Studs" in *This Quarter*. He explained his need to get a quick reading of his manuscript. Slater persuaded Jonathan Cape and Harrison Smith to have a reader look at the novel overnight. Jim dashed off to hand-deliver his manuscript.[119]

Early the next morning, he learned that Jonathan Cape-Smith had rejected his novel. He then took his manuscript to the office of the *New Masses*. Walt Carmon was the managing editor, under editor Mike Gold, who left nearly all the daily work to Walt. Walt, from Gary, Indiana, had been a southpaw in the Three Eye League until his arm went dead. In Chicago, he became a Communist Party member and later in the 1920s was assigned to the magazine's staff in New York, where he and Farrell had met in 1927.[120] At Carmon's request, in 1929, in return for a small fee for every copy sold, Farrell agreed to distribute the *New Masses* around the University of Chicago campus.[121] But "I could not give them away," Farrell confessed. "I understood why. The magazine was poorly edited, and for the most part, badly written. The spirit of the magazine was unfair and its tone was coarse. The level of thought was sub-mediocre." In New York in September 1929, Farrell and Carmon had met again. Carmon urged him to submit tales and articles to the *New Masses*, which Jim did.[122]

Since 1928, Farrell had corresponded with Carmon about getting review assignments and about his own writing. Now, to help Jim, Carmon telephoned Jesse Carmack at Coward, McCann Publishers, who agreed to read *Young Lonigan* that evening. Jim delivered the manuscript to Carmack and learned the next morning that Carmack "liked it immensely, but one of the firm members has two sisters who are devout Catholics. And so on. The literary game here is a goddamn racket."[123]

From Walt's office, he went to see Suzanne La Follette and Ernest Boyd at the *New Freeman*, which had published his "Thirty and Under" the year before. They gave him sympathy but nothing else. He had once offered to review Horace Gregory's latest collection of poems for the *New Freeman*. The offer had been refused, but it had put him in touch with the poet. Jim now telephoned him and was invited for dinner at Horace and Marya Gregory's home in Long Island City near Sunnyside, Queens. The three spent a pleasant evening together, the beginning of a long friendship. Horace also invited Jim to go with him the next night, 16 April, to the now famous meeting of intellectuals and writers in Theodore Dreiser's apartment. The two men were to meet in Columbus Circle, but somehow missed connection, and Jim went back to the YMCA.[124]

He returned to the *New Republic* office the morning of the sixteenth and met Malcolm Cowley, the literary editor. Cowley gave him a list of Paris hotels, and Slater Brown provided a letter of introduction and recommendation.[125] From there, Jim returned to the *New Masses* office and persuaded Walt Carmon to forward all of Farrell's incoming mail to American Express in Paris. Walt also introduced him to Mike Gold, who Jim felt was "a nice guy."[126]

It became obvious to Jim that both Carmon and Gold ardently believed that the future of American literature belonged to proletarian novelists and poets, to writers who championed the workingman. While speaking with them, he remembered he had written about workingmen he knew intimately. In Teddy Linn's 1927 creative writing course, he had submitted a story "Harry and Barney" that exposed the stressful working conditions in the American Railway Express Company, where he had been employed.[127] As he wrote to the Vanguard Press's James Henle two months later, "I told him [Carmon] I planned to do a novel on the American Express that might be almost proletarian in nature," an allusion to *Gas-House McGinty*, his second novel, which he already had in mind and most of which he wrote in Paris that summer and fall.[128] Carmon, increasingly interested, agreed to act as Jim's literary agent. He would immediately try to place "Young Lonigan" and a sheaf of short stories Jim handed him. He suggested they try Vanguard Press for the novel. Walt knew the firm's bookkeeper, Eva Ginn, who was then visiting the Soviet Union. He also knew that Vanguard had a tradition of publishing "radical" writers such as Peter Kropotkin, Tolstoy, Jack London, the anarchists Sacco and Vanzetti, and Thorstein Veblen. Furthermore, he liked James Henle, Vanguard's present owner, formerly a newspaperman on the *Socialist Call* and the *New York World* and the editor of *McCall's Magazine*. Farrell agreed.[129]

Farrell spent the remainder of the day, the final one before he sailed, with his and Dorothy's friends Chuck and Gene Colahan, then living in New York and preparing to open their Knife and Fork restaurant, in Greenwich Village.[130] He had failed to find a publisher, but he was determined to continue trying by breaking new ground abroad. The day before he sailed, he wrote Tom Freeman: "Going to try and bring out either my novel or a volume of short stories in Paris."[131] The next morning, he and Dorothy, safely together on the *Pennland*, were bound for Paris. Their cash, he later claimed, was about eighty-five dollars. Sam Putnam had been his European mentor for several months. Jim half expected Sam to meet them in Paris at the Gare Saint-Lazare to offer help and advice.

Farrell's autobiographical character Eddie Ryan, in "Innocents in Paris," reflects on his bride as they embark for Paris:

Marion was twenty-one, small, beautiful with a look of utter innocence on her round face. She had long, thick Titian red hair. She loved me, trusted me, and felt with an uncomprehending sense of need and desperation that she must be with me. Her father, Mr. Healy, had died when she was fifteen, and she was not completely out of the trauma which this had caused. She was a girl with great warmth, and a desire never to offend people. Rather than offend others, she would hurt herself. And she was much less worried than I. Hers was a childlike faith. Things had always turned out well for her, and she could not conceive of disaster.[132]

The *Pennland* was one-class, except for a small steerage section. Many of those aboard were older and wealthier than Jim and Dorothy. The passengers dressed for dinner, which was accompanied by music and dancing. Jim had no tuxedo, only his old suit. "I felt out of it, different from many of the other passengers . . . especially the younger ones who danced at night. . . . I was shy about my literary aspirations, and because of them, I felt myself set off and different. More deep than this in my character, I had not as yet learned to feel any confidence about my personality. People and money and security in the world were like strangers to me."[133] During the voyage, Dorothy was often seasick and confined to their cabin, so Jim frequently found himself alone on deck or with other passengers.[134]

On their third day out, on a cold Sunday morning, the *Pennland* stopped at Halifax. Jim and Dorothy went ashore and took an old trolley into town. They walked the hilly streets of Halifax, then visited the ancient Nova Scotia fort, escorted by a Cockney soldier who showed them the dark cells in the dungeon.[135] During the next week on the boat, Jim read books and wrote book reviews that he hoped would be accepted back home. He spoke briefly with a University of Chicago professor, Paul MacClintock, also a passenger. He enjoyed talking with General H. D. Styer, who had been attached to the Russian army during the First World War. "James used to talk to him all the time," Dorothy said, "especially because it was pre–Russian Revolution, you know."[136] These conversations initiated his interest in military strategy.

On the following Saturday morning, the *Pennland* briefly docked at Plymouth, then pulled out across the English Channel in a choppy sea, arriving at Cherbourg in the early afternoon of 25 April. They were shepherded by a fellow-passenger, a stranger named Nielsen,[137] a tall, blond American who claimed to be familiar with Paris and to have worked in hotels there. After passing customs, all three entrained across Normandy to Paris, arriving at the Gare Saint-Lazare at 11:30 P.M.[138] Shortly after midnight, Nielsen led Jim and Dorothy into the Hôtel de l'Ouest on the rue des Deux-Gares, between the Gare du Nord and the Gare de l'Est on the Right Bank.[139]

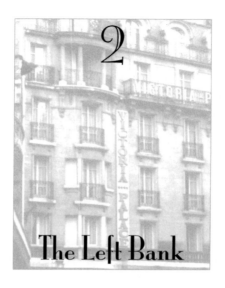

**The Left Bank**

Jim and Dorothy were out on the streets early that morning. He later wrote: "In awe and in a mood of childlike naiveté, I first came to Paris."[1] He was apprehensive, too. The uncertain future weighed on him. Sam Putnam had not met them, even though he knew of their uninformed, precarious situation. But Dorothy was bubbling over with happiness. "We saw those trees — beautiful trees, you know, that were just coming out . . . those wonderful chestnut trees that they have around. And the boulevards! — I think we went along . . . the boulevard Haussmann to the Bastille section or the rue de Saint-Antoine, which is a very wide street with lots of trees on it. And I was flabbergasted, because it was very much like the Chicago Loop, but it had trees on it. That was different, and that intrigued me. And then we saw for the first time the little cafés, the chairs outside, the people sitting. Oh! That was tantalizing. I loved it."[2] They were fascinated by the myriad of cyclists flashing by and the web of intersecting streets, each one a small adventure.

At the Hôtel de l'Ouest, Dorothy lost no time writing a carefully thought-out fiction to her mother, her aunt Matie, and her cousin Isabel Simpson, to assure them that all was well. She was rooming, she said, with a professor's daughter, a nice girl happily met on the boat, but she didn't like Paris as much as expected. After a week, Dorothy informed her family she was taking two courses at the Sorbonne. She had been asked to teach beginning English to French students and was very busy, having a stack of papers to grade each week. Dorothy's story was convincing.[3]

During their four days at the Hôtel de l'Ouest, Jim and Dorothy haunted the American Express office at 11, rue Scribe, hoping to hear from Sam Putnam. They wanted to get settled. Twice Jim traveled to Sam's home at 42 bis, rue de Plessis, in Fontenay-aux-Roses, a suburb south of Paris where Sam lived with his wife Riva and son Hilary. Twice he found no one. Later, he was told that Sam occasionally went on a drinking binge. He learned that not long before he and Dorothy had arrived in Paris, Sam and his *New Review* staff had thrown a party for Ezra Pound, who was visiting Paris from Rapallo. Had it been a long hangover for Sam?[4] Several letters brought no response from him.[5] As they waited, they walked the streets of Paris. They went to the Bois de Boulogne and stumbled onto the popular Pavillon d'Armenonville. There they ate, drank, danced, marveled at the aplomb of the gigolos, and were outraged by the bill.[6]

Failing to hear from Putnam, Jim looked up Edward Titus, the owner and editor of *This Quarter*, in his bookstore at 4, rue Delambre. Titus, who as we have seen had once denied to Farrell that his journal *This Quarter* had published "Studs," slipped in by his assistant Sam Putnam; later, he apologized for his mistake and paid Jim twenty dollars for the tale. Now, speaking with Jim in Paris, he was cordial but did not want to buy another story. He introduced Jim to Lawrence Drake (formerly known as Samuel Pessin), who had replaced Sam Putnam as Titus's assistant. Drake was slender, dark, and Jewish, a young American who had come to Paris as a feature writer for the *New York World*. Earlier, he had written a novel, *Don't Call Me Clever* (1929) and had published the *Milwaukee Arts Journal* and the magazine *Prairie*.[7] Drake suggested they have coffee at the nearby Café du Dôme, which, when compared with other cafés, Jim came to value mainly for the quality of its mashed potatoes. There, he peppered the voluble Drake with questions about the American "colony."

On 29 April, Jim and Dorothy moved to the Left Bank. Nielsen, their shipboard acquaintance, shepherded them again, this time to the Victoria Palace Hotel in a small square off the rue de Rennes at 5, rue Blaise-Desgoffe. They paid ninety-three francs (about five dollars) a night, a price they would soon learn was inflated. Jim believed Nielsen had taken a rakeoff.[8] A note from Riva Putnam addressed to him at the American Express office came the next day, and the Farrells met her and a business companion at the Café Aux Deux Magots. Riva and her friend Ernest Baldwin worked in the office of the *Business Weekly* at 7, boulevard Haussmann. They helped the Farrells locate in the nearby Hôtel de l'Académie on the rue des Saints-Pères, two blocks from the café Deux Magots and one block toward the Seine from the boulevard Saint-Germain. Their third-floor room cost twenty-five francs, or about one dollar, a night.[9]

Dorothy recalled that "it was a little hotel right on the corner. . . . There was a bidet there, and I had never seen a bidet. . . . That intrigued me. I didn't know what it was. And then, we had a basin in the room. It was quite a large room with . . . three—which was a lot—of those long windows, you know, with a little balcony. Oh! I liked it. It was very pleasant there. I liked that little place. Then we finally arranged to cook there on a Sterno stove, and stuff like that."[10] Dorothy, who had never cooked in her twenty-one years, learned a few rudiments on that stove. She shopped at a nearby Félix Potin, and they ate their breakfasts and lunches in their room. One day, the sink drain got plugged with macaroni. Jim, not an expert with tools, won a small victory by unplugging it with a borrowed monkey wrench.[11] Sam Putnam, who came by later, saw their situation as a bleak one: "Lodged in a barren *chambre meublée*, they lived out of tins and on coffee and rolls."[12]

Now in their third hotel, they soon found a restaurant just off the boulevard Saint-Michel and there purchased weekly meal tickets for thirty francs—excellent dinners for six nights a week at five francs per meal.[13] The magic of Paris was beginning to take hold. In his "Innocents in Paris," Farrell pictures Eddie Ryan and Marion Healy walking on the boulevard Saint-Michel. They felt alive, "and merely to walk on it stirred and stimulated them, gave them the expectation that something important, dramatic, and even wonderful would happen at almost any moment. They felt themselves part of a group, a throng of young people who would one day accomplish and achieve in the world. . . . There was an international flavor. . . . They felt that they had escaped from Chicago into a world that was large and wide and free."[14]

The date with Riva at the Deux Magots introduced the Farrells to their favorite Paris café—that is, along with the Sélect. The Deux Magots was near their hotel. From the Académie, they could walk a block to the boulevard St.-Germain, then a block to the café. Or they could follow a shortcut along the rue Bonaparte, past the religious stores with crucifixes and statues in the windows. The Deux Magots was more intimate than the Dôme and was on a square with trams conveniently running to the Porte d'Orléans and to Sceaux, where they would find a new home in a few weeks. At the Deux Magots, the other customers, the turbaned Oriental rug merchants, vendors of peanuts and oddities, and distributors of *poule* sheets (lists of registered prostitutes) captured their interest. Here, too, they got to know Eve Adams, a friend of Emma Goldman and an anarchist who had been deported from the United States for her lesbian publications. A young woman in her thirties, she was small, thin, and girlish-looking. Familiar and well liked in the cafés, the impoverished Eve made her rounds selling magazines, books, the *Paris Herald* and the *Paris Tribune,* and almost anything to earn a few sous.[15] Finally, the Deux Magots was memorable for the view it afforded from its café tables of the Saint-Germain-des-Prés tower.[16]

The tower awoke feelings in Jim like those of Bernard in Farrell's undated manuscript "Paris." Bernard is a political radical, a rationalist, and an artist. Sitting in the Deux Magots café one evening with his bride Elizabeth, he looks across the square at the abbey tower.

> It stood against an empty sky. The sky was a deep blue, and it was gradually growing darker. . . . Bernard stared at the old tower, solid and magnificent with its aged stones, its dark and mellowed coloring. Its beauty lay in its utter simplicity. . . . There it was, straight, and solid, with its flat sides, fixed as though forever against an empty sky. It was unlike the Gothic towers of Notre-Dame which seemed to soar as though they did not fully belong to this earth. This tower rose out of the earth, and belonged to it . . .
>
> This tower was growing into him. It had endless meaning for him. . . . Here was something perfect, old and perfect . . . Looking at it now, he wanted to feel more. He wanted to rush home and to write. . . . He had come here to find nourishment from the works of the dead. And there . . . stood that old tower, a signature, a memorial, a reminder of the dead.

When Bernard tries to explain his feelings to Elizabeth, she teases him by responding, "Bernard do you know what I think? I think there is some religious feeling in you." Bernard is quick to reply, "rather stiffly": "There is not. My appreciation of that tower is purely aesthetic."[17]

Sixty-four years after looking at "that old tower" with Jim, Dorothy explicitly stated what Elizabeth had implied in her comment to Bernard. "You know, James was a staunch Catholic inside himself. He didn't know it. He was more Catholic when we were married . . . than I was. . . . I used to think to myself, 'James is so much more Catholic than I am.' You know, I was baptized a Catholic, but neither one of my parents went to church."[18]

The day following their meeting with Riva, Jim and Dorothy lunched with the Putnams at a restaurant near the Place de l'Opéra. Eddie Ryan in "Innocents in Paris" sees Sam at this time as "tall, thin, sallow; in fact he looked somewhat cadaverous. He wore a small mustache and there was a scar prominently slashed across his forehead."[19] Sam saw Dorothy as "a wholesome-appearing young woman with red hair," Jim as "a rather short young man with bushy hair and spectacles and an Irish face." Before long, he decided that Jim "was not in any sense a Montparnasse type. . . . We did not speak the same language. . . . [W]hat he brought with him was a new America that was coming up, one we did not know existed, an America that was shortly to find expression in the social-literary movement of the 1930's."[20] Riva already had told the Farrells of her and Sam's desire to live in Paris always, rather than return to America. Eddie Ryan recognizes that for him the pull of America ultimately will overcome his love for Paris. Fascinated with the beauty of the pre-Gothic Saint-Germain-des-Prés tower, he thinks: "This was an old world. Did I want to live here forever, for all of my life? I knew that I didn't. No matter what I might say, no matter what resentments from my past might boil up and pour out of my conversation in a kind of sizzling hot verbal steam, I would be going back."[21]

Although Jim wanted to learn more about why Sam favored Fascism, the two men did not discuss politics at this lunch. Personally, they got along well, as they always did in Paris. Later, at the Putnams' home, they discussed their different political values, but in a friendly way. At the lunch, Sam told the Farrells that he had broken with Titus because of the editor's opposition to his plan for the Italian number of *This Quarter*. He also told them that as foreigners they could not get *cartes de travail*, the French labor permit required for employment. Nor was there a ready Paris market for Jim's writing, and Putnam had no money to employ him on the *New Review*. All this was dismaying news. But Jim and Dorothy knew there was no return. Somehow, they would have to tough it out financially. Where else could Jim pursue his writing with such expectations? A hopeful note was Sam's assurance that Ezra Pound wanted to meet him.[22]

Dorothy and Riva hit it off immediately. Learning that Dorothy was pregnant, Riva took her to the distant American Hospital in Neuilly on the boulevard Victor Hugo. There, Dorothy arranged for a series of prenatal checkups. The two women began to exchange visits, and Riva became a reliable source of help and information for Dorothy.[23] Dorothy also liked Sam. "Sam was pleasant to me. Some people thought he was really hard to get along with, but I didn't think so, because . . . he wanted me to see Paris, and I was perhaps enthusiastic at everything he'd point out. Maybe more so than James, so it was an easier relationship. . . . But James liked him, and they got along very well."[24]

In "Innocents in Paris," Eddie Ryan and Marion Healy walk back to their hotel after lunching with the Putnams. Eddie remarks that he has seen enough of Paris "to know it's a beautiful city. For all I know, it might be the most beautiful city in the world." The beauty of Notre-Dame was

> solidly outlined in the distance . . . he noticed the green of the trees along the banks of the Seine, a fresh and light spring green reflecting the brightness of the sun.
>
> This, he thought, was the normal world of Parisians. . . .
>
> How different from Chicago! . . .
>
> Images from Chicago came to his mind, dusty streets lined with the flat fronts of brick and stone buildings, dull in color and growing in flatness with each passing year. The bridges over the Chicago River, swinging sidewise to allow boats to pass, the river flowing through a man-made jungle of industrial plants and buildings. And the Seine, the trees along its banks, magnificent and even imperial stone bridges, and it was dominated by Notre-Dame. He was oppressed by a sense of difference. He had crossed from one world into another. Yet in this world he was a stranger. But hadn't he also been a stranger in Chicago? (Text 2, pp. 63–64)

Putnam had been unable to offer immediate hope to Jim at their lunch. But he told him he was thinking of bringing out a booklet of Farrell stories or, if not that, helping him to find a publisher. He had already shown Ezra Pound others of Jim's manuscripts now in his hands. Also he had asked Robert McAlmon to read two of them, "Meet the Girls" and "Looking 'Em Over." But McAlmon did not care for Farrell's fiction, an opinion Pound seems to have known when he wrote to Harriet Monroe a month before Jim and Dorothy arrived in Paris: "When it comes to the yearn after vanishing Kulchuh I suspect Mr. McAlmon's feelings toward Mr. Farrell (who writes of American *low* life) are almost as H. J.'s [Henry James's] might have been toward Mr. McAlmon-/-/."[25]

On or about 6 May, at Pound's suggestion, McAlmon paid the Farrells a courtesy call. He gave them a copy of his *Distinguished Air (Grim Fairy Tales)*, a book Jim liked. McAlmon told him he had returned the two short-story manuscripts to Putnam. Pound and Putnam agreed that those two tales, along with "The Scarecrow" and "Honey, We'll Be Brave," should be published—by someone—in a booklet limited to those four stories. In the meantime, Pound, still in Paris and then staying at 42, rue Cambon, suggested to Farrell that they meet. Jim and Dorothy met him for lunch in an Italian restaurant on the rue Caumartin, probably on 8 May.[26]

Dorothy remembered Pound as friendly and jolly at the lunch—up to a point. He and Jim "talked about literature at the time and what was being published. . . . I didn't talk. They ignored me, they ignored me. . . . I was just there, a pretty little girl. Look at you once in a while and smile, that's it. . . . They didn't talk about politics at all at that time that I remember. They talked about literature."[27] During their conversation, Pound asked to see Farrell's other stories being held by Putnam. He also offered to help him find a publisher in England for the proposed book of four tales. He suggested that Desmond Harmsworth, a wealthy young Englishman and the nephew of Alfred Harmsworth, Lord Northcliffe, of Northcliffe Publications, might be interested. Desmond Harmsworth was one year younger than Farrell and had been educated at Eton and Oxford.[28] Recently, he had started a London publishing house, the Desmond Harmsworth Press of Bloomsbury. His Paris home was on the Ile Saint-Louis, and Pound believed that Harmsworth wanted to show his uncle, publisher of the *Daily Mail*, that he, too, could successfully put the English language into print.[29]

That day or the next, Pound gave Harmsworth's Paris address to Jim. "Please take the *four* stories to Desmond Harmsworth, 15 quai de Bourbon as soon as you can collect them."[30] By this time, Farrell had retrieved the other ten stories Sam held. He then delivered the four stories to Harmsworth, who received him cordially. Later in the day, he took the additional ten stories to Pound.[31] "I'm anxious to get your opinion on what ones you think should go into a book, if Mr. Harmsworth decides to do one," he wrote to Pound. In a postscript, he stated that he had now seen Desmond Harmsworth, who "expressed gratification at receiving the mss etc.," and that Harmsworth planned to send the stories to his partner in southern France for a second opinion. Harmsworth, Farrell later informed Pound, "was a pleasant, polite, civilized, and noncommittal young Englishman," but one who, he sensed, was inclined to publish his tales.[32]

Pound did not mention to Farrell during their lunch that he already had praised Jim's writing to Harmsworth and to Wyn Henderson, Harmsworth's partner and, before that, Nancy Cunard's associate in the Hours Press.[33] Later, Farrell would read in a letter from the London small-press owner Jacob Schwartz (who had been briefed by Wyn Henderson), that Pound, Harmsworth, Henderson, James Joyce, and the Patrick Colums had gathered in the spring at a Paris dinner party during which "Ezra talked away like cracked on your abilities; and even Joyce (who I *think* read some of your stories in typescript thru the kind and enthusiastic offices of Ezra) said 'Yes—Jimmy Farrell is a good man; he's got real talent'.[34] This is very unusual of Joyce—and Ezra asked Harmsworth, who was then only considering becoming Publisher—'Why don't you publish

Jamey Farrell—he's a big guy'—and Harmsworth said he never read your stuff so can't tell."[35] In his letter Schwartz then commented that "Harmsworth and his 'business' partner Mme. Henderson" obtained some of Farrell's typescripts "dug up . . . from somewhere . . . and were highly interested in them"—possibly the four stories Farrell delivered to Harmsworth in May.

Ezra Pound read the ten stories and in a two-page letter gave Jim his mostly favorable opinion of each one. Some stories, he felt, should be excluded because they were too similar in subject matter to the four tales already selected. He concluded: "Think vol prob *best* with 4 stories only. Those which cd be added are 1. Sunday 2. Casual Inc[ident]. . . . Can discuss further after next Thursday."[36]

Farrell rose early and wrote every morning at the small table in the hotel room. Dorothy accommodated. In the afternoons, he read or went outside—either with Dorothy or to do what was necessary to win acceptance for his writing.[37] They began going to the Louvre on Sundays, when admission was free. On fine May mornings, while Jim worked, Dorothy, like any good tourist, strolled in the Luxembourg Gardens or discovered favorite spots like the place des Vosges. Evenings were free for visiting or recreation, often followed by café-sitting. Farrell had learned that trying to write after dinner, unless he were especially driven, was a waste of time. The results would be poor, or his mind would go blank. Late in the evenings, he read.

Many afternoons he and Dorothy explored Paris. Once, in search of a cheap meal, they took a bus to the Fondation des États-Unis in the Cité Universitaire, where they slipped knives, forks, and spoons into pockets and purse to use with their Sterno stove. And once they paid homage at the grave of Balzac in the Cimetière du Père-Lachaise. Dorothy was free from Jim's anxieties about money. She was more willing than he to spend money when they had it—just for fun, or on a whim, or for self-indulgence. Although she wanted them to be on their own financially, she knew that despite her errant ways her mother would not let her down in an emergency. She won over Jim's reluctance to buy Amer Picons at the Sélect one evening. She persuaded him to have a drink in the famous Café de la Paix, which he thought too swanky, too crowded with the upper classes. Dorothy had heard of Larue's restaurant on the place de la Madeleine and wanted to eat there. Too expensive, Jim thought, but he gave in; then stuffed himself to make it worthwhile.

Dorothy shopped at Félix Potin and Au Bon Marché. Jim explored the bookstalls along the Seine quays, and he discovered Louis Tschann's bookstore on the boulevard du Montparnasse, and the American Library, just off the place de la Concorde at 10, rue de l'Elysée, where for fifteen francs a month he could borrow books.[38] Robert, the Jim-character in Farrell's unpublished manuscript "Paris Novel," "liked walking the streets, riding in the autobuses and tram cars, and, also, the Métro. . . . I liked the sense of harmony which you felt not only in the buildings, but also in the patterns of life of the people. . . . And it was easy to feel a depth of time and history in Paris. The past acquired more awe, more wonder for me."[39] Dorothy liked the excitement, the people, the unfailing novelty, and always the sense of adventure.

Robert McAlmon returned to show them some of his Paris. "Oh yes, Robert!" Dorothy recalled. "I knew Robert, surely. He took us to a wonderful jazz place. Robert McAlmon liked to drink. And there was a place up through Saint-Germain-des-Prés—or was it up through Montparnasse? —where they had very good jazz musicians. And he used to go there. It fascinated me. It was a small jazz club. He liked places like that." On the rue de Lappe in the Bastille district was another jazz club that Jim liked because the French black boxer Battling Siki went there. "James was fascinated by this Battling Siki," Dorothy remembered. "James always said: 'There's Siki. There's Siki!' He'd point him out."[40] There, too, the Farrells enjoyed the *danse des Apaches.*

During their first heady days on the Left Bank, the spring weather was inviting, and the open-air cafés drew the Farrells like a magnet. The cafés were near the Académie. An after-dinner walk for coffee to one of them became a habit. Although Farrell's aspirations as a writer were at first unknown to the Montparnasse literary crowd, one introduction made at the tables had a way of leading to a second—and Dorothy's attractiveness helped. One of their new friends was the ebullient and gregarious Abraham Lincoln (Linc) Gillespie, from Germantown, Pennsylvania. Constitutionally cheerful and a born storyteller, he was known in the Montparnasse cafés for his uninhibited manner and his neo-Joycean writings published in *transition.* Jim had read several of these while in Chicago. He disliked their obscurity and discounted their importance.[41] But like many others, he immediately took to Linc and the two men continued to meet in the cafés whenever Linc visited Paris from his home in Cagnes-sur-Mer.[42]

The Farrells also met Wambly Bald, the talented columnist for the *Paris Tribune* and a former University of Chicago student. Jim noted, without comment, the ribald name—Wobbly Balls—bestowed on Bald by some café-goers.[43] Probably during these early café-going days the Farrells had their first encounters with others in the literary and journalistic world they were acquainted with: Waverly Root, Walter Lowenfels, Ludwig Lewisohn, Samuel Beckett and his friend the poet Thomas MacGreevy, George Seldes, Harold Stearns, the red-bearded Irish poet George Reavey, Charles Henri Ford, David Karnow, who became a reporter for the *Chicago Sun.* They also enjoyed the companionable young journalist and future novelist Ira Morris, grandson of a Chicago stockyards magnate and a product of the Chicago Latin School, the Milton Academy, and Harvard University. The two men matched horror stories of their different schoolings, the one parochial, the other elite, and traded humorously extravagant scenarios of the damning books about Chicago they would write some day, Farrell dredging up reminiscences of Studs Lonigan and his Fifty-eighth Street cronies, Morris revelations of Chicago society's upper echelons.[44] More and more, the Farrells felt at home in Paris with its endless variety of people. Here, Jim exulted, writers and writing mattered; he had emerged from a dark tunnel into the sunlight.

Every day, he scanned the newspapers. After a mailboat had arrived from the United States, he went to the American Express office on the rue Scribe, his forwarding address. Sometimes, if impatient, he would take a bus. Mostly, as Robert of "Paris Novel" reports, "I'd walk to the quai, along the quai, over the bridge to pass the Louvre and walk through the Tuileries, past the statue of Joan of Arc at the rue de Rivoli and, then, on to the avenue de l'Opéra. I'd always stop to look at the books in the window of Brentano's. . . . I always glanced at the people seated at the tables of the Café de la Paix. . . . I'd turn the corner, go on by the side of the Opéra to the American Express. Afterward, I'd go to the Café Béaud and have coffee and, sometimes, also, hard-boiled eggs. I'd read my mail and the Paris editions of the American newspapers."[45]

Jim, who regularly read the Paris edition of the *Chicago Tribune*, would also, about once a week, drop by the *Tribune* reading room at 5, rue Scribe to look over the Chicago edition of the same paper. This allowed him to read the box scores and to keep up with the baseball pennant race at home.[46] He noticed that Red Faber, the only spitballer left in the major leagues, was still winning games for the White Sox. Faber had pitched in Chicago for seventeen years and was a long-time favorite. Jim read about Fred Lindstrom, a mainstay of the New York Giants, who broke his ankle while sliding into third base. Like Jim, Fred had learned his baseball in Washington Park. Farrell also followed the triumphs of two of his Chicago acquaintances who were making sports headlines in Europe that summer: George Lott, the world's premier doubles tennis player, starred at Wimbledon and in the French Open and represented the United States in Davis Cup matches on the Continent; Eugene Goodwillie, then a Rhodes Scholar, won the 100-yard and 220-yard dashes in a match pitting Oxford and Cambridge against Harvard and Yale.[47]

While waiting for word from Desmond Harmsworth, Farrell wanted most of all to hear from Walt Carmon that James Henle of Vanguard Press had accepted "Young Lonigan." Possibly, too, Carmon had sold some of his short stories. He did not know that Carmon had waited until 2 May, five days after the Farrells sailed for Paris, before submitting the

"Young Lonigan" manuscript to Henle. With it went a letter describing Farrell as "a young literary hopeful" with "lots of talent." Nor did Jim know that on 12 May, a few days after he and Dorothy had moved to the Académie, Henle had signaled his acceptance of Farrell's novel to Carmon: "*Young Lonigan* is a moving study. Of course, it is intensely brutal and I am not sure that it gains by forcing this feature; if you read it you will note that the passages where he relies on implication rather than explicitness are infinitely more effective." The next day, Carmon mailed a copy of Henle's letter to Farrell, and Henle also wrote to him. The letters arrived in Paris in eight days. He accepted the novel enthusiastically, but as yet offered no contract. He suggested a new opening chapter to bring out Studs's character more rapidly.[48]

By mid-May, the Farrells were running out of money. Jim had good reason to believe that Edward Titus was at best lukewarm to his work. Nevertheless, he jumped at the chance to make some money from the publisher's current project announced in the *Paris Tribune* on 15 May. Titus was soliciting "hitherto unpublished stories, poems, essays and plays by American and British writers" for a massive anthology to be christened *Contemporaries 1931*. He especially wanted manuscripts from "unknown writers of ability." His terms were generous: "definite advance payments" of five dollars per printed page and a percentage of the money earned in sales. Farrell took his story "The Merry Clouters" to Titus. If accepted, he figured it would bring him eighty-five dollars in advance payment—that was more than two thousand francs. Then he waited. He had given up hope when, five months later, in October, Titus took the story. Farrell wondered if the favorable opinion of his work held by Ezra Pound, Lawrence Drake, and Sam Putnam had anything to do with the editor's change of mind. But even if it did, Titus refused to advance more than three hundred francs (about twelve dollars). Eventually, he paid for "The Merry Clouters" when it was scheduled for publication, not in the abandoned *Contemporaries 1931* but in the October–December 1932 number of *This Quarter*.[49]

The Farrells owed the hotel and saw no way of getting money immediately from anyone in Paris. Dorothy took matters into her own hands. She cabled her uncle Art Althouse for help. She knew he was fond of her and that he liked Jim. Her uncle was her mother's only surviving brother and superintendent of a Kroger warehouse. Without mentioning it to his wife Hazel or to anyone in the family, he cabled a hundred dollars to Dorothy.[50] Jim wrote in his Paris notebooks that the gift was their salvation.[51]

A few days later they heard from Ted Marvel, the best man at their wedding. Ted had kept in touch with Maggie Butler in Chicago to discover what she believed about Dorothy's life in Paris. He reported that their fiction of Jim being in New York City was about to collapse. Knowledge of their marriage was still the secret of a few, but others were hinting broadly or speaking freely about Jim being in Paris. Only Dorothy's mother was still in the dark. Marvel advised Farrell to let it be known that he had crossed the ocean and gone to southern France to finish his book. Jim and Dorothy had already decided that when the marriage could no longer be kept secret, they would say that he had come to Paris to work on his book and that he had married Dorothy there. But whatever they said, they knew Maggie would disapprove of their union. Toward the end of May, Jim saw what he must do: he wrote to the Dalys that he was in Paris, but said nothing about Dorothy. Neither he nor Dorothy gave the news to Maggie or other members of Dorothy's family.[52]

At this time they began to meet other Parisian expatriates, some of whom also were trying to make their way by writing. The Farrells first visited the Putnams' home in Fontenay-aux-Roses on a Sunday afternoon early in May. Riva and Sam's curly-haired son Hilary, then almost five, immediately charmed them. Somewhat familiar with German and English speech, Hilary spoke French fluently. His face lit up when he greeted Dorothy by name—always with his rhyming joke: "Comment tu t'appelles, Dorothy Farrell?"[53] Dorothy knew that Hilary was special, but could hardly envision his distinguished career as a Harvard philosopher.

During this visit, Farrell learned that Sam recently had completed translations of Pirandello's play *As You Desire Me* and his *Horse in the Moon: Twelve Short Stories*. Currently Putnam was translating Pirandello's play *"Questa sera si recita a soggetto" (Tonight We Improvise)*, which he believed was the author's masterpiece. His admiration for Pirandello knew no bounds, but Jim's was qualified. This visit also began the Farrells' friendship with Riva's four other guests, Peter and Anna (Frankeul) Neagoe, Christina Stead, and Stead's companion William Blake.[54]

To Jim and Dorothy, the Neagoes' Parisian life had the degree of stability they sought. Anna, called Annie, was a respected painter, particularly adept at still lifes. She exhibited in Paris. Peter was a Romanian-born naturalized U.S. citizen. He was wealthy. His family owned a textile factory in Romania, where Peter had designed textiles. Having moved to the United States in 1901, he worked as an illustrator and translator until he launched his writing career in 1920. He and Annie lived at 10, rue de Douanier near the parc Montsouris. They rented a large studio-apartment in the Appartement Souris, where Annie painted and Peter wrote short stories and novels, chiefly about Romanian peasant life. When the weather warmed up, they returned to their second home in southern France at the Mirmande artists colony. Virtually alone among the expatriates whom the Farrells knew, the Neagoes owned an automobile. In December, Peter bought a one-half interest in Sam Putnam's *New Review* and became its coeditor and copublisher, starting with the fourth number (winter 1931–32). He and Putnam hoped to publish a series of paperbacks by American authors.[55] Noted for his rigorous work habits, in 1931 Peter was writing a book of short stories entitled *Storm* (1932) and compiling *Americans Abroad: An Anthology* (1932), a collection of short postwar (1919 to 1929) American fiction, which included Farrell's "Soap."[56]

Christina Stead, the Australian novelist, was as yet relatively unknown. A few days before the Farrells arrived in Paris, she had signed a contract for her first novel, *Seven Poor Men of Sydney*, and her book of short stories *The Salzburg Tales*, both published in 1934. She was secretary to

William Blake (Wilhelm Blech), her boss at the Traveler's Bank, her lover, and a prominent Marxist. They lived in an apartment near the Jardin du Luxembourg on the rue Jean-Bart, where Jim and Dorothy later visited her.[57] They both grew fond of Christina Stead, and William Blake impressed Dorothy as an outgoing, intellectually impressive man.[58]

One evening, while at the Sélect with the Neagoes, the Farrells were introduced to Gabriel Javsicas, an ebullient Latvian American, and his young Mormon wife Irma, an attractive blonde. They had just arrived from the United States—although in the past Javsicas had lived in Paris —and were staying at the Hôtel Delambre. Gabby, as Farrell came to call him, was outgoing and informal in his ways. Dorothy felt that he and Irma were lots of fun and she liked the Parisian flair of Gabby's beret: "He was much more French than the other people."[59] Politically, Gabby was an anarchist, a close companion-in-arms with Emma Goldman and Alexander Berkman. He was an economist who had studied at the London School of Economics with Harold Laski and, later in the 1920s, at Columbia University. While there, he had worked part-time at Vanguard Press. He knew James Henle and Evelyn Shrifte, Vanguard's editor in charge of book production.[60]

That night at the Sélect, he arranged to borrow Farrell's carbon copy of the "Young Lonigan" typescript. He soon informed Jim that he had written to Henle praising the book and urging its acceptance, and the day after this Jim went to the Javsicas's hotel room to retrieve his manuscript. Farrell's second Paris notebook picks up the story: "Gabby was not there. Irma was lying on the bed reading, and she was dressed only in a kimono. The kimono was on her loosely, and her breasts were exposed. She continued lying on the bed, and made no effort to cover her breasts, but she put down the book which she had been reading, and talked with me. I stayed only a few minutes, and left with my manuscript. I believe that I would rather have stayed, but I didn't." A few weeks later, when Evelyn Shrifte arrived in Paris, Javsicas met with her and again became Farrell's advocate.

During the final weeks of May, Jim and Dorothy continued their Sunday afternoon visits to the Putnams. They shared one of these afternoons with the painter Leopold Survage, the subject of Sam's book *The Glistening Bridge*.[61] They also often had dinner with the Neagoes, usually at the restaurant Corbeille on the rue Delambre, and afterwards coffee at the Sélect.

There one evening, they saw Maxwell Bodenheim, who recently had arrived from the United States, where his novel *Naked on Roller-Skates* had made a stir. His "Aesthetics, Criticism, and Life," heralded by Sam Putnam as Bodenheim's "extremely important . . . first extended foray into the field of criticism," had just appeared in the *New Review*, which Bodenheim served as associate editor.[62] Yet many Parnassians regarded him as hopelessly passé and a target for personal ridicule.

The Farrells noticed that this slender, light-haired poet with the rigid shoulders and a corncob pipe between his teeth was unusually well dressed.[63] He greeted them effusively as former companions from the Cube in Chicago. Jim and his friends had once helped him sober up there after he had fallen off the stage while reciting his poetry. In Farrell's manuscript "Paris Novel," Robert (Jim) tells of Kathleen's (Dorothy's) account of her first visit to the Cube, when she met Bodenheim: "'I was dying to see the Bohemians and to learn what they were like.'" She delivers her tale with spirit in the Sélect to the Chevanescus (the Neagoes). "As she spoke," Robert says in a rush of affection, "I remembered her then, almost three years before, a girl of seventeen, a strawberry blonde with lovely reddish hair, her long face plump and rosy, her blue eyes full of wonder and bewilderment. And she had a wide straw hat and wore a long, light summer dress, delicate pink in color with red flowers in the pattern. She still had that dress and I loved her in it, perhaps especially."[64] An evening or two later, the Farrells saw Bodenheim in the Sélect with a woman, identified by Putnam as "a Daring Young Woman on the High Divingboard, a performer in one of the outlying Parisian amusement parks."[65] Then, as suddenly as he had come, he disappeared—went to

Capri on his "honeymoon," the café gossips joked. By mid-June, he was back at the Sélect for a brief time before returning to the United States.[66]

The final week in May was an eventful one for the Farrells. On Thursday, 21 May, at the American Express office, Jim picked up the good news that Vanguard Press had accepted "Young Lonigan." In Farrell's "Paris Novel," Robert (Jim) reads Henle's letter while sitting in a café looking out on the place de l'Opéra. That afternoon, to celebrate, he and Kathleen (Dorothy) first stop off at the Deux Magots for coffee. Looking across the square at the abbey's tower, Robert thinks: "That old tower stood like a triumph over time. . . . That was one reason why I wanted to be an artist—to win out, to triumph over time." Kathleen looks more to this world. She senses royalties in the offing and wants to find an apartment. Robert agrees that an apartment would be better for both of them. It would mean less close confinement and more privacy for each. Feeling that her belief in her husband's future as a writer is vindicated, Kathleen plans to begin her search. That afternoon, to celebrate further, they revisit the Louvre.[67]

The next day, on the boulevard du Montparnasse near the Sélect, Jim and Dorothy were hailed by their Chicago acquaintances Reuben (Rue) and Ginny Menken, who had preceded them to Paris by two months.[68] Dinner at a Chinese restaurant followed, with the Menkens and six of their friends: two young German Communist architects, Heinz Mullender and his companion Rudy, the S. Henry Kahns, and Meyer Handler and his wife. Kahn was the Paris correspondent on economic matters for an English wool-and-hemp trade journal and other publications.[69] Meyer Handler was an aspiring young journalist from Chicago's northwest side. His wife had obtained a well-paying job with a U.S. corporation in Paris, and Meyer came with her as a writer on business and economic matters for a U.S. trade journal. At the restaurant that evening, Farrell, Kahn, and Handler quickly discovered their common interest in international relations and politics.[70]

The Menkens had a room in a hotel on the rue de Vaugirard and, like the Farrells, were hard-pressed to make ends meet; they lived on sixty dollars a month remitted by Ginny's parents. Rue lost little time in suggesting that the two couples find and share a place to live, perhaps an apartment in a Paris suburb. Jim feared that living with the Menkens would not work out, but reluctantly he agreed to try it. The search was on.[71]

Jim and Dorothy enlisted the aid of the Putnams at their home on Sunday, 24 May.[72] The Putnams suggested a place in their suburb, Fontenay-aux-Roses. But Rue had heard of a vacancy in Sceaux, a pavillon that, as he reported, Marie Curie had occupied for a few years, beginning in 1907. It was closer than Fontenay was to Paris and it rented at six hundred francs a month, about twelve dollars per couple. It seemed perfect to everybody, including the Putnams, who coincidentally also had lived there shortly before its last tenant, their friend the writer Pierre Loving, had moved in. Aided by the Putnams' recommendation to their new landlord, on 26 May the Farrells and Menkens packed up and hired taxicabs to take them to their new home at 6 bis, rue du Chemin de fer in Sceaux.[73] They moved in without delay.

# 3

# Sceaux

THE FARRELLS LIVED in Sceaux for seven months. Altogether, it was the happiest, and for Jim the most productive, period of their Paris year. Sceaux was a quiet, semirural suburb, south of Paris. They discovered that with care they could live there—just barely making it—on fifty to seventy-five dollars a month. In their new home, they were able to entertain friends during long, companionable evenings in comfortable quarters. There, Jim revised the "Young Lonigan" manuscript for publication. There, too, he completed the first draft of his second novel *Gas-House McGinty*, planned and wrote partial first drafts of two sequels to that novel, and tried to market many short stories, some of them newly composed. Also in Sceaux, Dorothy's pregnancy advanced almost to term. From Sceaux, it was easy to get to Paris. A short walk took them either to the Sceaux station of the *chemin de fer* or to the local stop of the slower and less expensive *autobus 128*. The lines passed through many suburbs—all of them, Farrell later wrote, "place names in my life"—including Bourg-la-Reine, Châtillon, Gentilly, Montrouge, and Malakoff—and connected with the Denfert-Rochereau métro exchange in Paris north of the Porte d'Orléans.[1]

Before moving to the "small pavillon in Sceaux," Farrell continued, "I had, except for a couple of odd weeks, lived my entire life in large cities. The noise and movement of big cities was an integral part of my experience. The hushlike quiet of this French suburban village was something very new, almost shockingly [new]. . . . At times, it was as though I could hear the silence and as though I could feel the tranquility as if that were a sensible object. . . . Sceaux, so quiet, so tranquil, is sharply different from a large, noisy industrial city like Chicago. But they are inextricably associated, linked up in my memories."[2]

In some respects, Chicago now seemed to the Farrells like a bad dream they had escaped. As they settled into their new home, they read a series of letters from Isabel Simpson, Dorothy's cousin in Hyde Park. She spoke of runs on Chicago banks, bank closings, and festering gang wars. The *Paris Tribune* reported that Anton J. Cermak, Chicago's new mayor, vowed so fervently to clean up gangs that Al Capone was constrained to "ponder deeply." Isabel told them, and the *Tribune* reported, that Al Capone had been arrested and sent to prison for five years for income-tax evasion. Later, he was convicted for bootlegging. Chicago teachers were going without pay. Thousands of unemployed were on the streets. By midsummer, Isabel wrote, banks were not making loans, the building trades had shut down, and evictions in the "black belt" were followed by riots. Prices were dirt cheap to lure customers: Isabel bought two "cute" dresses for $3.95 and $4.90. Michigan peaches, picked by the buyer, were twenty-five cents a bushel. She could not understand why the federal government did not initiate "big engineering projects, . . .

build new roads, . . . and make work. . . . I am afraid Hoover is an old lady after all."[3] For Jim, now comfortably located in Sceaux, even Paris had lost some of its appeal, or so he professed. "I shall not miss Paris or the cafés where everyone talks, and little is said," he wrote to Walt Carmon.[4] In Sceaux, he could concentrate on his work; but in fact, neither he nor Dorothy could consistently do without the unique pleasures of Paris.

Dorothy found Sceaux to be delightfully new and beautiful. She was enchanted with the flowers climbing on many of the houses and over the gray stone walls lining the streets. Each house had its meticulously cultivated garden. She believed she could peek over the walls or through the gates and see scenes like French paintings she knew—Monet or Renoir—and America seemed a world away. "It was a darling little town. And you know the storekeepers even gave me credit. . . . I could never say the French were mean to Americans, because they certainly weren't mean to me. . . . Oh, yes, I liked living there. I did. We enjoyed it. I never felt bored. We had a good time there."[5]

The Farrells could hardly believe their luck in getting the pavillon. Jim wrote to Riva Putnam that it was "an unbelievable place."[6] Their landlady was the wealthy, tart-tongued but kindly Madame Prévost, a widow living with her grown son Henri, a bachelor who worked for a Paris pharmaceutical company. Mother and son lived in a mansion on a tract covering almost a city block. They employed a maid, a gardener, and a chauffeur to drive their stylish French car. Surrounding their house was a spacious, inviting lawn and a large garden, from which Madame Prévost sold produce to the public but often left vegetables at the Farrells' door. The two-storied pavillon, built of rough-hewn stone, lay to the rear and a little to one side of the house. It had its own entrance at 6 bis, rue du Chemin de fer.[7]

Inside the pavillon was a spacious living-dining room area and a long, well-equipped kitchen with a stone floor. It was there, Dorothy said, that she really learned to cook. The Menkens ate most of their dinners in Paris. Fortunately, the two couples cooked and ate very few meals in common, because although Dorothy kept her peace with the Menkens, tension quickly developed between Jim and Reuben. Jim, Dorothy recalled, was the one who fought with the Menkens. "The only thing I didn't get along with, with her, she would take my dish towels . . . and I didn't like that."[8]

Next to the stairs leading to the second floor was an anteroom that Jim used as a study. It had "a darling desk with a very fancy kind of rolltop, all engraved," Dorothy fondly remembered. "He used to enjoy that place. He liked it. It had a door that went out into the garden, with a glass panel in it. . . . I think probably it was the first time in his life that he had a little office of his own, where he could sit and write."[9] Upstairs was an old-fashioned bathroom and two bedrooms in series, the Menkens' room to the front and the Farrells' to the rear. Because there was no hallway, the Menkens had to go through the Farrells' room to get downstairs. It was an arrangement that became increasingly disconcerting to both couples.[10]

Farrell's arrival in Sceaux was noted by Mathews Eliot in the *Paris Tribune* on 14 June 1931: "James T. Farrell, whose short stories have already been observed in intellectual circles of the Home Country, is among the newer arrivals in the colony here. Farrell has taken up residence in Sceaux, the place to which the put-put goes which sends its smoke up through holes in the pavement of the rue Denfert-Rochereau. He specializes in the language of the Chicago stockyards, and one of the local American publications plans to publish some of his stuff unexpurgated in the hope of getting it suppressed in the United States."[11] This plug possibly may have been written and planted by Sam Putnam, even though he had sailed for the United States on 9 June. He had been readying Farrell's "Jewboy" for the next number of the *New Review*, and in order to outflank U.S. censors he and Ezra Pound had discussed the advantages of the "blank page" option for handling Farrell's fiction in copies of their magazine sold in the United States.[12]

Jim and Dorothy often took short afternoon walks down their street to the Sceaux town square and the rue Houdan, the main street. There Jim would buy a newspaper and Dorothy would shop for groceries. Sometimes they ate their dinner at a restaurant near the carefully cultivated Jardin de Sceaux. Occasionally Jim would go to the quiet garden to read. They also enjoyed walking in the Parc de Sceaux, following the maze of paths through the spacious lawn and gardens of the seventeenth-century Château de Colbert. Once, at a fête in the park, Jim employed his pitching skill to win a bottle of champagne by knocking over three padded dummies.

One Sunday summer afternoon, Jim and Dorothy wandered into the neighboring suburb of Robinson, a popular resort. For the first time, they saw the famous "restaurant in the tree," ten or twelve tables with chairs attractively platformed and anchored on the massive limbs of several trees, approached by a sturdy stairway. They were hungry, and the scene was too inviting to resist. Shaded by leaves, cooled by a breeze, and anticipating the best, in their elevated position they savored, with lingering enjoyment, every morsel of food in their high-priced meal.[13]

Sometimes in the evening they walked to the railroad station and gazed "at the houses, the greenness, the hilly landscape towards Bourg-la-Reine. The sun would shine and polish the trees, the roofs would glitter. Or it would be twilight, and the scene would be soft, and wrapped in a gray veil of the fading day. We would gaze off, silent, moody, relaxed. Then, slowly we would walk back. Sometimes, bats would be flying in the streets. . . . We would go inside. We would eat, talk, and read, or else I would do more work."[14]

During the final weekend in May, the Farrells and the Menkens jointly entertained their first guests in their new home — the Putnams and four of the Menkens' friends, Heinz Mullender, Rudy, and the economist S. Henry Kahn and his wife. The Prévosts' yard and lawn furniture outside the pavillon added greatly to the fun of having guests.[15] The party brought together true believers in clashing social and political worldviews: Sam Putnam, then leaning toward Mussolini's Fascism; the young Communist architects Heinz and Rudy, fleeing from the flattened German economy; Rue and Ginny, the trendy American radicals; Kahn, the knowledgeable academician trained at the London School of Economics; and finally Jim, influenced heavily by the liberal thought of his university professors and the pragmatism of John Dewey and George H. Mead.

Their conversation turned to the coming world crisis. Jim spoke up combatively for democratic socialism and against the multiple evils of unrestrained capitalism. Heinz, in his broken English, lamented the poverty of his family and the suffering of German workers. He was expecting a Communist outbreak in Germany to establish a new, fair social order, but he saw the rising Adolf Hitler as a menace. Heinz was a reckless drinker; the more he consumed, the more despairing he became about his "poor faderland."[16] Rue, when slyly baited by Kahn or bested in argument, championed Bolshevism and envisioned the Red Army marching to take care of all reactionaries. Sam believed that Italian Fascism, a new, twentieth-century current, would save European culture. It was the hope of the world, whereas Marxism was going backwards to a nineteenth-century current. He believed a rich and daring new literature had developed in Mussolini's ordered and tightly run state and that the major Italian writers supported *il duce*.[17]

Within days, Sam loaned Jim his copy of Curzio Malaparte's latest book, *Coup d'État, the Technique of Revolution,* and recommended that Jim read it if he wished to understand Mussolini's brilliant statesmanship. Malaparte, Putnam said, was "Signor Mussolini's right-hand man . . . on the literary side" and "the poet of the black-shirt regime."[18] Sam believed Malaparte had shown how a revolution could virtually be reduced to the careful execution of a coup d'état by a strongman. As he read, Jim scoffed. He was sure Malaparte's analysis was superficial and that it ignored deeper causes of revolution.

On 1 June, a few days after their first party, Dorothy began having cramps. She feared a miscarriage. In the late 1920s, two miscarriages had taught her to know the symptoms. Madame Prévost recommended a local physician, who prescribed absolute bed rest, but Jim decided Dorothy should go to the American Hospital in Neuilly. That night, accompanied by Rue and Ginny, he rushed her there by taxicab. It was Dorothy's third visit to the hospital, following two regular prenatal checkups. She was under the care of Dr. Boeffe de Saint-Blaise, the head of obstetrics. He treated her gently and with great care. "I loved him," Dorothy said. "Indeed I did."[19] She remained there a week.

Farrell's Paris journal speaks of the all-night return to Sceaux he and the Menkens made. From the hospital, they walked to the nearby Victor Hugo métro station and took the train to the porte d'Orléans, only to find there that trains and buses to the suburbs were no longer running. Deciding to walk back, they followed the car tracks and arrived in Sceaux shortly before dawn. Along the way, Jim and Rue had a bitter argument over their political convictions. The next day, in his 1931–32 notebook, Jim entered a long passage unmistakably revealing his deeply felt love for Dorothy, his loneliness, and his fear of loss.[20]

In the hospital, Dorothy met Fanny Klein, who was expecting her baby in October and who became Dorothy's best Paris friend. Fanny and her husband Nathan, a New York City commercial artist, had come to Paris in February after several months in the Balearic Islands, where Nathan painted landscapes. They had saved their money so that Nathan could test his powers abroad as a painter. They lived in Montrouge at 40, place de Jules-Ferry, in a spacious studio-apartment in a new building owned by Edward Titus. The two couples began exchanging visits, and before long Dorothy was sitting for a portrait Nathan never finished.[21] Farrell particularly enjoyed Klein as a Paris walking companion because of the painter's sensitivity to color and form.

The Kleins soon had Jim and Dorothy over to meet a number of their friends: the well-known American painter Joseph Stella; the painter Lee Hersch and his wife Virginia, the novelist; and the Danish sculptor and painter Adam Fischer and his wife Ellen, a writer. Stella was enjoying his recent success in Paris. Twenty-three of his canvases had been exhibited in the Galerie Jeune Peinture on the rue Jacques Callot—"one of the most important expositions of American art ever held in Paris," according to Don Brown, the *Paris Tribune* art critic. Hersch was preparing canvases for an exhibit of American artists that opened in mid-January in the Galerie de la Renaissance on the rue Royale. Jim knew that Nathan Klein wished to equal their success, but he believed that Klein's talent was not up to it.[22]

The Farrells quickly grew fond of Virginia Hersch. A lawyer turned writer, she was known in Paris as the author of *Bird of God: The Romance of El Greco* and *Woman under Glass, Saint Teresa of Avila.* She and her husband Lee had only recently returned to Paris from a lengthy stay in Charleston, South Carolina. Jim and Dorothy liked the sharp precision of her thinking, her witty, uninhibited conversation, her spirited accounts of past experiences and writings. Jim, who knew that someday he would write about his family, and nursed the hope of returning to Ireland to research the story of his forebears and their migration to America, was fascinated to hear from Virginia that she had done just that for her ancestors. They were aristocratic Portuguese Jews who had gone to Charleston in the late eighteenth century after fleeing Santo Domingo following the island's slave revolt. Now she was writing their story in her new novel *The Carvalhos*,[23] centering on the Portuguese Jewish community in pre–Civil War Charleston. Jim found similarities between the problems and destinies of Jewish and Irish immigrants in America. The Hersches and Farrells exchanged visits in Paris and continued to see each other later on in New York.[24]

Like the Kleins, the Fischers lived in Montrouge. They, the Kleins, and the Farrells quickly came to enjoy each other's company. "Fischer," Jim wrote, "was a solid and sensitive sculptor, and he had known many of the French post-Impressionist painters. He had known Diego Rivera, too."[25] At the Fischers' home, Jim and Dorothy met Diego Rivera's first wife, Angeline Belloff. On the walls hung a number of Rivera's paintings that, Jim wrote, "bore the stamp of French influence." Jim admired Adam's sculptures, describing them as "simple, full of graceful little curves and informed by a feeling of love."[26]

Both Jim and Dorothy were attracted to the Fischers' daughter, Tora, an imaginative little girl with sparkling eyes and a love of stories. One evening, she showed them a book her parents had made for her, a "family venture" written by Ellen, illustrated with eye-catching photographs taken by Adam, and titled *The Dolls' Journey*. The Farrells found it to be charming. In the story, when Tora leaves her Danish home for Paris, the dolls "get mad" at her, and led by the most beautiful doll, Binkie, they run away. During their adventurous journey, they meet all kinds of animals never seen on land or sea, but they are eventually rescued by Tora. To illustrate the adventures, Adam Fischer took pictures of "landscape" scenes and their wondrous animals, ingeniously contrived by Ellen from common objects and materials—cloth, mounds of earth, clay, little flowers and weeds, pieces of sponge, a sheet that "served as a rough sea," a button hook, safety pins, sticks. To the Farrells, it seemed that the Fischers had created "a world of pure fancy, where illusion rides queenly over all plausibility. The conception is poetic, and touched with a gentle, sensitive humor."[27] Through Jim's efforts, the authors were able, in 1932, to get their book, a classic of children's literature, published in England by Desmond Harmsworth; this was followed by a U.S. edition the next year.

By the end of June, Dorothy had regained her strength. She noticed in the newspapers that an international dance marathon, the first ever in France, had opened in the Cirque Médrano. It was staged by Harold Ross, an American promoter who had assembled dancing partners from the United States, Italy, Poland, France, and Switzerland. This new "sport" caught on in Paris. Packed houses showered the dancers with one-franc and two-franc pieces. Wagers were made on which team would outlast the others. Dorothy considered herself "more hep" to dance marathons than Jim was. Remembering the fun they had at Chicago marathons, Dorothy persuaded Jim to go. The Paris marathon they saw was in the arrondissement "where all the ladies of joy were." But it did not come up to her expectations. It lacked the special features and drama of the American originals. "They were just catching on there with the

dance marathon," she explained. And besides, in its Paris setting it somehow seemed grotesquely American. Possibly Dorothy would have agreed
with Wambly Bald that it all came to little more than an exhibition of
"resolute masochists." After four weeks and four nights, the winning teams
received their prizes at the Moulin Rouge, and the marathon moved on
to Spain.[28]

The Menkens soon took Jim and Dorothy to the United States Students and Artists Club, established since 1927 at 107, boulevard Raspail.
The club became a favorite place for the Farrells to visit in the afternoons: there was tea and croissants, and dancing to the tunes of an old
Victrola, all for one franc. The club's director was the Reverend Harold
Belshaw—Dorothy called him "the big shah"—who was the Episcopal
minister at Saint Luke's Chapel on the rue de la Grande Chaumière.
Farrell described him as young, quiet-spoken, prematurely bald, and
friendly.[29] The student directors of the club, who were paid token salaries,
were Donald Sewarts and a young, pretty woman whom Farrell called
Catherine. They and two other "regulars," Tom Squires and the Ameri-
can pianist Maurice Rausch, became four of the Farrells' Paris friends.
They were often guests at Sceaux.[30] All the clubgoers could see that
Maurice and Catherine were in love.[31] In Farrell's "Paris Was Another
Time," Eddie Ryan (Jim Farrell) is immediately attracted to Catherine
(named Frances, then Marcella, Frost). She is always friendly to him,
and he desires her.[32]

The club had a small lending library made up of books donated by
members. On his first visit, Jim took out Upton Sinclair's *Boston* and *Oil*.
In following weeks, he signed out Wolfe's *Look Homeward Angel*,
Faulkner's *Sanctuary* and *The Sound and the Fury*, Henry James's *The
Bostonians*, D. H. Lawrence's *Lady Chatterley's Lover*, Sinclair's *The
Goose Step*, and Leon Trotsky's *Literature and Revolution*. He read ex-
tensively in Proust and dipped into Spinoza.[33]

Among the friends Jim and Dorothy made at the club were Kenneth
and Adaline Knoblock from New Orleans. Kenneth was a journalist on

the *Item-Tribune* and a friend of William Faulkner. Adaline's wealthy family owned a coffee company—the forerunner of Folger's. They had come to Paris for Kenneth to work on mystery novels he was preparing for the Sealed Mystery Series put out by Harper & Brothers.[34] Soon the Farrells and the Knoblocks, who lived at 6, rue Huysmans, were exchanging visits. Adaline liked to entertain, and she and Kenneth enjoyed the company of artists and writers. The New Orleans couple were soon taken into the Farrells' growing circle of friends. Early in 1932, Jim introduced Kenneth to a representative of the Gallimard's publishing house, and Kenneth sold them the rights to two of his novels.[35]

One afternoon, Rue Menken took Jim to the apartment of Roger Walter Ginsburg in the rue d'Assas. Ginsburg, whom Rue admired, was an Alsatian architect, a man of influence who had given jobs to his protégés Heinz Mullender and Rudy without first obtaining *cartes d'identité* for them. The visit gave Farrell further cause to dislike Rue Menken. John Dewey was a hero of Jim's, and to have Rue and Ginsburg slightingly compare him to the nineteenth-century German philosopher Rudolph Euken, who avowed an a priori religious epistemology, was, Jim felt, indefensible. Farrell was familiar with Euken's thinking, having reviewed W. Tudor Jones's *Contemporary Thought of Germany* for Sam Putnam's *New Review*. He later discovered that Ginsburg was the GPU (Soviet secret state police) general agent and central contact man for Russian Communists sent to Paris by the Third International.[36]

The day the Farrells moved to Sceaux, a note had come from Desmond Harmsworth returning the four stories Ezra Pound had recommended for the proposed booklet. The stories were unacceptable to Harmsworth because he and his partner, Wyn Henderson, agreed they stood no chance of getting by the censor.[37] All hope for a cash advance from Harmsworth was gone. Increasingly, Jim experienced what he characterized in "Sceaux Re-Visited" as a time of alternating hope and depression. He was not consoled by Ezra Pound, back in Rapallo since early June, who suggested that Harmsworth might reconsider if Vanguard

Press would bear half the cost of the edition: "In case of H[armsworth] you might consider just how much work a young man who does not HAVE to work for a living is capable of getting through."[38]

Farrell already had written Walt Carmon and James Henle appealing for help. He was in a tough spot, he explained to his agent, and would need money soon while he revised "Young Lonigan." Take your 10 percent, he urged Carmon, and get whatever advance you can as soon as you can from Henle. He was ready to work, free from the distractions of Paris.[39] He pounded away on his dilapidated typewriter, which had lost the typeface for numeral 2 and the "—the double quotation mark. Because of this defect, it turned out, dialogue in the first edition of *Young Lonigan* was not enclosed in quotation marks; evidently, editor Henle liked that effect.

Farrell's approach to Henle was more circumspect. He agreed with his editor's suggestions that he write a new opening chapter, handle the gang-shag episode—or gang-bang, to use the contemporary term—at Iris's indirectly, delete a masturbation scene, and "make the piece as a whole more lyrical and sensitive" in order "to assist the park scene with Lucy" in its service as "ballast" for the more brutal features of the narrative. Deleting the scene directly portraying the gang-shag was the most difficult concession to make. Also, he hated eliminating single phrases like Nate's "He schlipt it to her." But as he explained later, "it was my view that it would be better to save the whole, that is the book, and sacrifice this one chapter, rather than to lose the whole, that is to have my novel banned."[40]

Jim also agreed to lengthen the novel to fifty thousand words. To that end, he suggested that he add scenes of Studs trying to enlist in the army, Studs watching the punks lobbing tin cans in a vacant lot "war," and the Chicago Loop Armistice Day celebration—three scenes that he eventually placed near the opening of *The Young Manhood of Studs Lonigan*. But he insisted on keeping a full plate of brutal, nonsexual episodes, especially the scene of the gang beating up two Jews. "I consider this scene to be a summary, enforcing the criticisms made in the book as a whole. . . . I have had the feeling that a writer should hammer out his effect precisely and uncompromisingly . . . and have felt that I was getting my point over best by hitting fiercely and continuously."[41]

His main order of business now was revising "Young Lonigan." He wanted to keep financially afloat now that he and Dorothy were so favorably located in Sceaux. But funds were low. As he looked ahead, he knew he needed money from sources other than Vanguard Press. He plunged into the first of several frenzied efforts while in Sceaux and Paris to earn some cash by selling short stories and reviews. Out went a blizzard of submissions to magazines, among them the *American Mercury*, *Nativity*, the *New Republic*, *Pagany*, and *Story*, recently established in Vienna by Whit Burnett and Martha Foley. Mencken, Burnett, and other editors were not ready to buy his tales, but wanted to see more.

Jim asked Amy Loveman to make him the Paris correspondent for the *Saturday Review of Literature*. He tried to get book-review assignments from her and from his agent Walt Carmon, to whom he also sent manuscripts for distribution to other magazines. He informed Henle he had sent the "Young Lonigan" chapter of Studs and Lucy in Washington Park to an (unnamed) English agent. He wrote to Slater Brown at the *New Republic* asking that story manuscripts in Slater's hands be sent on to Mencken.[42] Sam Putnam had left for the United States on 9 June to see his New York publisher and to arrange for a Schubert production of a Pirandello play. He also planned to promote his forthcoming anthology *The European Caravan* through lectures in New York, Chicago, and elsewhere.[43] Farrell suggested to Henle that after Sam arrived, portions of the "Young Lonigan" manuscript be given to him to place in American magazines, if possible. He asked Sam to sound out Mencken on how he felt about his stories sent to the *Mercury*. Jim's thrashing about among editors was futile.[44]

During this frenzy, Farrell heard from Robert Carlton ("Bob") Brown, at Le Manoir, Cagnes-sur-mer.[45] Brown had been given his address by

Laurence Vail (Farrell may have forwarded Malcolm Cowley's letter of introduction to Vail, then in southern France.) He invited Jim to contribute to the unique anthology he was then preparing, *Readies for Bob Brown's Machine*—a collection of short fiction and poetry intended for use on Brown's visionary reading machine, designed, he maintained, to create four-dimensional writing. His machine, Brown wrote, enabled him to face-lift the art of reading. He wanted to take writing out of books, where for too long it had been bottled up. He believed he could recover the earlier naiveté and art-quality of writing. By doing this, "our reading vocabulary will be hygienically circumcised and circumscissiled."[46]

Farrell immediately readified his story "Jeff" and mailed it to Brown, along with Rue Menken's "Arles Paintings." "Jeff" begins: "Jeff the fat jewboy . . . Jeff the fatass of Fifty Eighth Street . . . Jeff was always easy to laugh at . . . Big Fat Jeff waved his fanny thru life." It ends with Jeff putting a gun to his head, and the poolroom guys from Fifty-eighth Street responding: "He was no good anyway . . . he was one big load uh garbage . . . they mustah had uh crate for uh coffin." *Readies*, replete with mild erotica, was a deliberate and joyful challenge to contemporary censors; yet Brown feared the action of U.S. censors against copies sold overseas and he deleted a few lines in "Jeff." Sometimes he substituted "tomato" for "ass." He thought "Jeff" was "wonderful." Jim, who tended to dismiss his readified story, agreed to the changes.[47]

Brown had lived in Chicago until he was twenty-one, and through their correspondence, the two men quickly found common ground in their Chicago backgrounds, as well as their opposition to censorship. The exuberant Brown wanted more of Farrell's work. He wrote: "Are you the Farrell Ezra Pound picked as good? If so, he's a good picker, and not for the first time. . . . I'm sick, and drunk and am writing on the typewriter with my toes. . . . If there were any more like you I would write too to them, drunk or sober, fingers or not [*sic*] toes."[48]

Farrell responded by submitting his tale "Sylvester McGullick" and two other stories he "adapted" for *Readies*. One of these was by his younger brother Jack, the other by Lloyd Stern, a friend since boyhood, whose novel *Star's Road* Jim edited for Vanguard Press in 1932. Brown accepted all these stories, as well as Rue Menken's, which he liked. He wrote to Jim: "I consider you and Kay [Boyle] and Laurence [Vail] the best in the book"—a compliment possibly intended to offset his inability to pay his contributors.[49] Jim explained to Henle: "I wrote the stories I gave by taking out 'the's,' 'and's' etc. and putting dots in the middle of sentences and was told that's swell, just the style for the Readies." Brown's book, he continued, was an extraordinary experiment that contained some freakish and senseless things like the piece by Linc Gillespie and Robert McAlmon's "Triplexicated Illustratification of Go-Getters."[50] He agreed with Arthur Moss that many stories in *Readies* "were written on the tripe-writer."[51]

That summer and fall, Farrell also wrote to Peter Neagoe, then with Annie in their Mirmande home. He wanted to place a story in Peter's *Americans Abroad: An Anthology*.[52] Neagoe wanted him to write a sketch of Montparnasse, but Farrell countered with a favorite story, "The Scarecrow," the first of many submissions Neagoe rejected. When the Neagoes came to Paris in September, they and the Farrells met at Riva Putnam's house. There, Peter agreed to accept Jim's Paris tale "Soap." Through Jim's efforts, Peter also accepted a story by Farrell's Chicago friend Ruth Jameson. The anthology went to the publisher in November.[53]

To Farrell's bemusement, Peter customarily expressed confidence in Jim's future and tried to encourage him. Peter was a student of numerology and astrology. He believed that the number of letters in Jim's name augured his future success as a writer. Sometimes he advised him not to submit stories for publication on certain days. He and Annie favored "positive" thinking verging on Coué-ism: every day in every way I am getting better and better.[54]

Before Sam Putnam left for the United States, he let Farrell know that "Jewboy" would be in the next number of the *New Review*. But Jim knew Sam could pay nothing for it. Even that small success almost collapsed. Before Sam sailed, he asked Henry Miller and Alfred Perles to bring the number out. But according to Putnam, they held "a deep grudge against a number of persons whose work I was publishing . . . and against Pound and Farrell in particular." They "began plotting to steal the forthcoming issue (no. 3) and fill it with obscenities composed by themselves." Riva Putnam, on the verge of leaving for Mirmande with Hilary while Sam was in America, "discovered the mess just as it was about to go to the printer, and salvaging what she could, managed to get out some kind of number," which included "Jewboy."[55] The *New Review* with Farrell's story came out in August.

Jim, ever uneasy, also tried to place his writing in French publications. A few days into June, the Menkens took the Farrells to the studio of the painter André Lhôte. There they met the Swiss novelist Ramuz and the French writer Henry Poulaille. Poulaille worked for Chez Bernard Grasset in Paris. He was a contributor of short stories to *transition*, a prominent historian and supporter of the French labor movement, a film and literary critic, and the author of many books including *Our Daily Bread*, a novel Farrell admired.[56] Poulaille edited the journal *Le Nouvel Age*, located at 7, rue du Panthéon. Jim met with him there while submitting a short story for translation and possible publication. Probably it was Poulaille who asked Farrell to translate into English an article on Henri Poincaré, the mathematician. It was an effort Jim gave up as a bad job because of other work and his limited knowledge of French and mathematics. The two men remained friends until Poulaille's death in the 1940s.[57] Farrell also approached Henri Barbusse, author of the war novel *Le Feu* (*Under Fire*) and publisher of the influential weekly *Le Monde*, in which Jim hoped to place a short story. Neither of these efforts succeeded.[58]

The summer was passing, and Dorothy was getting restless. Sceaux was pleasant, but Jim was nearly always preoccupied with work, nearly always at his typewriter, the best way to hold his anxiety at bay. She wanted to see more of France, even if only for one day, and traveling was becoming difficult. She suggested they go to Fontainebleau, and Jim agreed to take a day off. Leaving on an early train from the Gare de Lyon, they found time to hike into the vast forest after visiting the chateau. Ed Bastian observed that this was virtually the only part of France beyond the suburbs of Paris that they visited.[59]

Back in Sceaux, Jim expected daily to hear from Vanguard Press about "Young Lonigan." But while he waited, he failed to meet two of Vanguard's editors, Jacob Baker, the firm's founder and vice president, and Evelyn Shrifte. Returning from the Soviet Union, the two had stopped in Paris for a few days. Unknown to Farrell at the time, they were in the Sélect one evening when he and Dorothy were there. He had missed his best opportunity for a direct personal approach to Vanguard.[60]

In June, James Henle informed Jim that he had sent the contract for *Young Lonigan* to Walt Carmon. "With it," he told Farrell, "I am sure we shall introduce to the book-reading public an author who is going to go a long way." Publication would be in the fall, for a book of fifty thousand words. The author would receive an immediate advance of $100, with $150 on delivery of the manuscript, as well as 10 percent on each trade copy sold, up to five thousand, then 15 percent. Vanguard was to share in all subsidiary rights, getting 50 percent of reprint and foreign rights and 25 percent of movie rights. It also would have first choice on Farrell's next two books.[61]

To Jim, the contract with the advance meant recognition as an artist, justification of his choice of profession, and desperately needed money. Now, for the first time in his life, he informed Henle, he could write with a "sense of security and safety, and without immediate worries."[62] He confided to Bob Brown that he thought "the Vanguard people are about the best American publishers one could get." Henle, he said, has "given me a fair contract, with no hitches in it, and his letters have been decent, and he gave me a good advance, and right when I needed it like I never needed money before."[63]

Jim lost no time in writing to his grandmother, uncle, and aunt about the contract. On the following Sunday, to celebrate, Jim and Dorothy took dinner at the Restaurant Saint-Cécile on the boulevard du Montparnasse, then visited Notre-Dame. Jim had already decided that he would dedicate *Young Lonigan* to his Grandmother Julia, Julia Brown Daly. She was wheelchair-bound and seriously ill. He and Dorothy climbed to the top of the cathedral tower and he lightly scratched her initials JBD on an inconspicuous surface.[64] As related in *The Dunne Family*,[65] Eddie Ryan's (Jim Farrell's) grandmother, Grace Hogan Dunne (Julia Brown Daly), who can neither read nor write, reacts to the news about Eddie's book:

> "So he's written a book, has he?"
> "And he's dedicating it to you, Mother."
> "What's that you say, Jen? Say that part to me again."
> "He is dedicating his book to you."
> "What's that mean, Jen?"
> "He's putting your name in the book. On one of the front pages it will say, 'This book is dedicated to my grandmother, Grace Hogan Dunne.'"
> "Well now, isn't that nice, Jen. I think I'll put on me red blouse."
> "Mother!" Jen laughed affectionately.
> "Well, why shouldn't I wear me red blouse if I want to."

He also wrote to his Chicago friends Tom Freeman and Ted Marvel, who spread the word about his success. Ted visited Maggie Butler to tell her. He discovered she still knew nothing of Dorothy's marriage but feared the two would now marry in Paris. Don't worry about it, Ted advised Jim. "When you return to these parts, just put on a clean shirt, get a haircut, and shine your shoes, and she'll welcome her son-in-law with open arms, and even weep for joy on your shoulder."[66] Maggie also heard from Dorothy about Jim's book. Dorothy knew that this news of his success would make her mother think better of him. She hoped it would help control Maggie's inevitable outburst when she learned of their marriage.

Dorothy wanted to dispel her family's fears about her well-being. In her letters home, she began to build on the fiction of her teaching responsibilities. One of Jim's Paris friends—just who, is unknown—had suggested that Jim might pick up some money if he could arrange to give a talk at the University of Grenoble—an unlikely possibility. That would not happen, but Dorothy let it be known in her letters home and to her cousin Isabel Simpson that she had taken some of her students to Grenoble, and that she hoped to go to Ireland around Christmastime—a time when, in reality, she expected to be busy with her baby. The Grenoble ruse worked. Isabel congratulated her on being a "chappy" (chaperone) to the students.[67]

Henle was convinced that Farrell could achieve his best effects in *Young Lonigan* by "indirection" and that he should "keep to straight Anglo-Saxon and make people feel that the four-letter words are there, though actually they will be missing."[68] Jim smelled censorship in this advice. He felt a lurking dread that censorship would weaken his book. At Henle's request, he not only had deleted the masturbation scene and the gang-shag scene in Iris's apartment, but also had substituted *gang-shag* for *gang-fuck*, and had deleted *ass, krap, jazz, jack-off, tocus,* and *yentz*. Dorothy observed that when he softened language or deleted scenes in deference to possible censorship, he would frown and, referring to his uncensored version, say: "But this is the way it is."[69]

Farrell knew his editor was trying to protect him and his book, but he grew alarmed when Henle tentatively suggested the possible desirability of publishing a limited edition for psychiatrists, sociologists, and social workers. He was sick of censorship, he emphatically told Henle. "Pound tried to swing a book of short stories for me over here (in England) just after I arrived, and before I heard from you . . . it looked nice, and then the thing went flat because of fear of the British censors. I wrote a story for Brown's reading machine experiment, he liked it, and again the censors." Peter Neagoe, he recalled, had rejected "The Scarecrow" for his anthology for fear of the censors.[70] In a moment of passing depression, he wrote Bob Brown: "The snoopers are going to raise hell with my novel, and I'm having difficulty revising it to the extent that it won't be a direct invitation to the censors."[71]

Especially galling was Henle's reference to sociologists. Ever since his university days, Farrell had ridiculed sociologists, their methods, and their writing. To Henle, he was unequivocal in his response: he didn't like sociologists; he was thinking of writing a book on them. Their writing in the *Journal of Sociology* was atrocious. He ridiculed Frederic Thrasher's book on gangs: one of the author's solutions for gang violence was to form Boy Scout troops. He did not want his novel confused or associated with a sociological study.[72] Six months later, when imminent censorship threatened to do just that, he vented his anger to Henle:

> "I don't like to let "Young Lonigan" go as merely a case history, because it isn't. . . . The more I think of sociologists, the more I feel most of them to be stupid and unimaginative hams. Their current notions about case histories and personal documents is all a stupid bore and a farce. They go out and ask prostitutes—Why are you a prostitute?—and they get a sob story in return, and they put this in a book, and take its commonplaces, and add to them fake profundities. Hence they collect a lot of hokum and obvious facts, and tag them with polysyllables which look big and important. And I don't like to give them another case history which they can straitjacket with their goddamn jargon about adjustment and maladjustment, and behavior patterns and total situations and the rest of that rubbish." (JTF to JH, 17 December 1931)

After Riva and Hilary Putnam left for Mirmande on 28 June, Farrell occasionally sought out—away from the sights and sounds of his co-tenants the Menkens—the peace and quiet of the Putnams' empty apartment in Fontenay. Dorothy brought over some ham and eggs, and Jim later apologized to Riva for getting into her jam and coffee. The work went well for a few days, without interruptions.[73]

Jim's revision of the *Young Lonigan* manuscript was nearly complete when the *fête* marking Bastille Day began. This year, because 14 July fell on a Tuesday, Parisians began their celebration Saturday afternoon and continued for the full three and a half days. Under clear, sunny skies, the Farrells took off for Paris on Saturday. He welcomed the change of pace from his marathon performance at the typewriter. They found the general gaiety so inviting they stayed late and returned every day. In the Latin Quarter, they found crowds of revelers and overflowing cafés. Small bands—pianos, fiddles, accordions—were set up on corners under brightly colored kiosks in the neighborhoods and in front of the bistros and *bals musettes*. Japanese lanterns were strung between the trees lining the sidewalks, and medallions were on the buildings. The Tricolor was everywhere. Dorothy especially liked the "pretty little orchestras on the corners on Bastille Day—the whole three days. . . . We danced down the street with all the French people, because they danced out there. . . . And then they used to make circles, and . . . the musicians would come, maybe two or three musicians, and they'd hand out song cards, and you'd pay a sou for a song card and then you'd stand in the circle and sing with the little orchestra there. That was great fun. We did that often."[74] As the skies darkened, the city's great public buildings were brilliantly illuminated. Jim and Dorothy followed the crowds to see the torchlight procession winding from the Bastille down the boulevards. Atop Montmartre on Bastille Day, they watched fireworks bursting over the city and searchlights playing on the Eiffel Tower.[75]

Jim was impressed. He wrote to Herbert Rosengren, the editor of *Katharsis:* "Were you ever in Paris on July 14th . . . when they stop all the trolley cars and dance all night in the street? It's quite nice."[76] He also wrote to Riva Putnam in Mirmande that they had seen Christina Stead and her friend Eric Townsend "Sunday night [July 12] at the *fête* and spent a pleasant hour or so with them." Later in the month, the Farrells visited Christina and Eric in Christina's new apartment near the Panthéon.[77]

The Farrells missed the grand parade down the Champs-Elysées early on Bastille Day, featuring military detachments uniformed to represent the national and colonial armies from earliest days to the present.[78] After their late night, the parade came too early in the morning for them. But that afternoon, they watched the *danse des Apaches* at a club on the rue de Lappe. They spotted two Chicago friends in the crowd and were unable to reach them. Their friends were Paul and Jessie Rudnick, first met in Chicago in 1930 at a party in the home of political science Professor Fred Schuman and his wife Lily. Jim obtained their address at the American Express and they all had dinner together in Sceaux ten days later. Both Paul and Jessie were amused at the bedroom arrangement giving the Menkens access to their bedroom only by going through the Farrells', and this at a time when the two couples were barely speaking to each other. In September, the Rudnicks visited the Farrells again after returning to Paris from Innsbruck.[79]

On 16 July, Jim put the final touches to his "Young Lonigan" manuscript and sent it to Henle by registered mail on the boat train leaving for the steamer *De Grasse*. He wrote his sister Mary a bit about his life at this time: he was broke but was getting credit; beer cost three to six cents a glass; he and Dorothy had seen a dance marathon as goofy as those in the United States; and he was enclosing his letter with one to their brother Jack in order to save six cents postage.[80]

Dorothy's near miscarriage in early June, related hospital expenses, and mounting debts deepened Jim's depression about their lack of income. The future looked bleak financially and, worse still, professionally, unless the income from his writing picked up. While in Chicago, he had written most of the sequel to *Young Lonigan* but if he should prepare it for his next publication, could it get by the censors and would it sell? It had more sex and violence in it than *Young Lonigan* did. Much more.

He remembered his April conversation in New York with Walt Carmon and Mike Gold about the coming flood of proletarian novels. In his next letter to Henle, he casually stated: "Walt might have mentioned that I told him I planned to do a novel on the American Express that might be almost proletarian in nature." That novel, he told Henle, would draw on his experience working for the American Railway Express Company (as it was then called) in the 1920s. He was considering writing it in the fall. Henle promptly asked for more information.[81]

Farrell wondered: Should his writing take a new direction? He remembered a 1927 short story he had written for Professor Linn, "Harry and Barney," a story of two Railway Express Company workers. He wrote to his brothers Earl and Jack requesting a wide range of information about the company. Earl was an old-timer there and knew it from the inside out. He replied immediately with a summary of the company's history, its successive downtown locations, and its organization. He recalled with pleasure the raucous "barbering" (insult-trading) of the closely confined clerks in the Wagon Call Department (where Jim had worked), the practical jokes the men played on each other, and the nerve-wracking pressure that never let up. He described in detail the outstanding "characters" in the workforce. These included the chief dispatcher, Raymond J. J. (Gas-House) McManus, the original of Farrell's subsequent title character, Ambrose J. (Gas-House) McGinty. He explained the kinds of shipments the men handled and their working conditions during the depression years. Jack sent Jim the names of Chicago politicians and a songbook from which he could quote. Farrell's memory came alive. The Express Company novel was just the thing. He decided to call it "The Madhouse." The story began to take shape.[82]

Jim recognized that "the proletarian," the worker, was looming as the underdog hero in revolutionary and literary circles. It was so in the journal the *New Masses*, where the greedy capitalist fed off the exploited but nobly endowed worker. That weekly was booming, and Jim soon helped Walt Carmon and the business manager, Frances Strauss, find Paris vendors for it. Evidence of worldwide hard times piled up in the months ahead. His friend Heinz Mullender assured him in person, and later in letters from Germany, that unemployed German workers were near the breaking point. Jim's brother Earl wrote of layoffs in Chicago—even as many as four hundred being made by the essential American Railway

Express. Things in Chicago were so bad, Jack Sullivan affirmed, that "bum gin" — the liquor that the old gang was still drinking — "has dropped to one dollar a pint . . . on account of the depression." Farrell's Chicago friend Ruth Jameson informed him that "all your old friends are preparing to mount the ramparts in defense of the starving masses. . . . The day of individualism is past." She invited him to join them — to put his talent to work for the cause of the workingman.[83] Other Chicagoans he knew were helping unemployed laborers and defending evicted families. Vlad Janowicz was representing them in court. Jim would soon learn that Vlad, Jim's brother Jack, and other friends at home were members of the International Labor Defense, and that Vlad was rising higher in the Communist Party hierarchy.[84]

Farrell had read in Marx's works, and he knew that contemporary writers were producing proletarian novels, plays, and poems. A few years later in *A Note on Literary Criticism,* he demonstrated his awareness of the various definitions of "proletarian" and "proletarian literature." But at this time, he was simply confident that his personal, searing experience as a lowly clerk in the Wagon Call Department of the American Railway Express Company had given him unerring insights into the lives and thinking of U.S. laborers — those in the office and the wagonmen on the streets. His two years of work in the company had internalized, in a deeply personal way, his understanding of what it meant to be a "proletarian." "The Express Company had a strong effect on me," he wrote. "I began to feel that I was a nobody."[85] Farrell felt he could give fictional life to workers as they really were, not merely as flag-bearers of a revolutionary ideology, reeking with a too obvious "social significance."[86] Why shouldn't "The Madhouse" cash in on the popular demand for proletarian literature by giving a true picture of the daily experience of ordinary men on the job, while at the same time telling a good story reflecting a pivotal segment of his own youthful experience — his relationship to corporate America?

This change in literary direction spurred Jim to crystallize what he hoped to achieve the next few years. His thoughts at first turned to the history of his family. It was a subject—an enormous one—he had wanted to develop since he began writing. He foresaw the need for free time to do the research for it. To Henle, he confided that he would apply for a Guggenheim Fellowship to support him for six months or a year in Ireland in order "to gather material for the first half-volume of a . . . trilogy which will deal with two immigrants who come to America, in the sixties, and whose sons and daughters raise the family status to that of lower middle class, only to be rather severely crushed in the tightening circumstances of capitalistic America." He estimated that the entire job —research and writing—would take ten years. Obviously, he decided, it was a project for the future, to be written after he had completed his fiction on the mangled lives of American Railway Express workers, and on Studs Lonigan. The logistics of his long-range work plan dictated that he postpone his Guggenheim application for at least a year.[87]

He informed Henle he would turn at once to his American Express novel, the "almost proletarian" work. By 1 August, he was actively working on "The Madhouse." It seemed both to him and Dorothy that while he was writing it he remained chained to his desk, except at mealtimes. "He used to go there," Dorothy said, "down the stairs in the early morning to that wonderful desk, in the private little study that he had, and he'd stay there all day." She observed his habit of softly mouthing his writing to himself as he composed, presumably to test the phrasing and rhythms in a text heavily laden with dialogue.[88] So intense was his work, while he worked, that both of them came to believe he wrote the novel in about two weeks, with virtually no interruptions from the outside world. To Ted Marvel, he wrote: "I work like hell. I went ahead on my new book fiercely, and did 329 pages in a week and sent it off, praying to Jesus I could collect."[89] In fact, the writing took about one and a half months— he mailed all 329 pages of the first draft of "The Madhouse" to Henle on 13 September—but even so, he wrote the novel in an unusually brief time. His memories came easily. The humiliations he had suffered on the job still stung, and his detailed knowledge of the company's operations served him well. For many years, his father had worked at the company, at first as a wagonman, then a scripper, and finally a supervisor. Two of his brothers were still there, and he had been an employee during the summer of 1920, for a month or more in 1921, and from the end of May 1923 until March 1925.[90]

His new novel monopolized his imagination and fed his enthusiasm. "After coffee, I sat down at my typewriter and banged away. The book came. I was excited and really caught up in it."[91] The distinctive features of each of his fellow workers in the company came more clearly into focus. It was his hope, he recorded, "that the reader will see with them, feel with them, and out of such an experience, come to gain some added sense of what one part of the story of work and of striving means in our country."[92] "I was full of my material, and my mind was crowded with memories of Chicago. . . . I wrote with growing confidence and enthusiasm."[93]

To Henle, he dispatched an impassioned account of what he hoped to accomplish in "The Madhouse." His focus, he asserted, would be on the Wagon Call Department, the book's real protagonist. He explained the department's function, its organization, and workforce, from the superintendent down to the lowliest clerk. He briefly characterized some of the major characters he had in mind, including "Mushmouth McManus," later named "Gas-House McGinty." "The book," he wrote, "will be a composite picture of these people, who will be treated mainly as a function of a large corporation." It would reveal their personal lives, their hates, loves, frustrations, jealousies, and sorrows, and how they did their job, stayed in a rut, and faced old age. Most of all, he said, it would reveal the effect of occupation on character. "It will be a radical book, not in the sense that it will have a radical ideology. None of the characters will have any traffic with socialism. . . . However, it will show in their grumblings, their blind almost unconscious protests against the institution that is mangling them. It will be social criticism, not by much overt statement, but by implication."[94] As he got further into his work, he tried to individualize his characters, to make them "stand out more clearly as separate personalities" rather than as mere "functions" of the corporate body.[95] He could give Henle no precise outline of the novel's organization. He simply had to hammer it out.

> I'll work on my first draft the same as I did on the other [Young Lonigan]. That is, set myself to a minimum of a thousand words a day (it generally is from one to five thousand a day) and write until the book is organized. Then I'll dog it until I feel I can't do any more without destroying whatever value the book might have. . . . It cannot be written as a straight novel, but must have its own structure worked out; and I do not favor having that a simple series of stories, as, say, Seaver did in his The Company.[96] Rather it should be something in which the characters are massed, and in which the sense of the composite picture is more developed, so that one gets a sense of them squirming inside this large institution." (JTF, "On the American Express Novel to be titled 'The Madhouse'")

Henle suggested to Jim that John Howard Lawson's play *Processional*, produced by the Theatre Guild in 1925, "is the kind of thing you are attempting, if I understand your purpose correctly, with the scene limited to an express company unit rather than a mining town." Writing of his play, Lawson had indicated that he had attempted to catch "the colorful exaggeration" of native American idiom, "the grotesque of the American environment," and a sense of the crowded, violent, staccato rhythm of American life. Farrell responded to Henle that his American Railway Express novel would "be radically different from 'Processional.' Particularly I hope to make the characterization full and solid, and the atmosphere complete, and to depend on these things rather than plot, excitement, what is called dramatic action."[97]

Jim bent to his work every day he could, and he was encouraged to stick to it by Henle's promise of an advance when he had completed one-third to one-half of his manuscript.[98] But an annoying distraction sometimes took his mind from his work. Upon their arrival in France, the

Farrells had failed to obtain *cartes d'identité*, required of resident foreigners during their first six months in the country. Failure to comply mandated a heavy fine and possibly expulsion from France. In June, Jim and Dorothy had been stopped by the Sceaux police, who discovered they had no *cartes d'identité*.[99] To obtain them, they must pay a fine they could not afford—three hundred francs apiece for the three months (April–June) they had been in the country, and one hundred francs each for every month thereafter. Jim was required to obtain a date-of-residency statement from his landlord. But neither Riva Putnam, to whom Jim appealed, nor other friends could devise a scheme that would exempt them from the fines.[100]

For a time, Jim and Dorothy considered the option of briefly living in Belgium and then reentering France, making sure to obtain their *cartes* at that time. That would be cheaper, Jim wrote to his sister Mary, than paying the fines. But it would disrupt their lives, and Belgium was unknown to them. Bob Brown had invited them to Cagnes-sur-Mer. The possible Belgian interlude was one reason Farrell notified Bob that he and Dorothy could not "get down your way." The frustration, the worry, and the fines continued to mount through August and September as he pounded out "The Madhouse."[101]

Early in October at the Dôme, Linc Gillespie, now back in Paris from Cagnes, introduced Jim to Pierre-Jean Robert, a swarthy, well-built young man, twenty-nine years of age and an outspoken royalist in his politics. An editor at Gallimard, he was then translating a series of English-language detective novels. Robert was streetwise—knew all the angles. He urged Jim to register himself and Dorothy for study at the Sorbonne at a nominal fee. As students, they could then be issued *cartes d'identité* by the proper authority. And better yet, the accumulated fine would be reduced to twenty francs a month.

Pierre took Jim to the cabinet of the prefecture of police at the Hôtel de Ville, where a friend of his worked. The friend gave Jim a note that, he wrote later, with "a little dérangement" paid to a minor functionary, gained them admittance "into a small bare room" where they "met an authority who also received his little *dérangement,* and with the speed that is characteristic of the French in all such matters, we received our *cartes d'identité.*" They now were "legalized in France . . . and need no longer worry about being picked up by the *flics* for not having our papers in order. Jean-Paul [Pierre-Jean] . . . had helped us save over five hundred francs [apiece] in fines."[102] As part of the arrangement, their *cartes* were predated to show they had been students all along. For a brief period, Dorothy attended a French literature class. Jim concentrated on his writing.[103]

A second distraction also tore Jim from his desk. Bob Brown promised the Farrells top-drawer amusement with "our local Montparnasse"— Laurence Vail, Kay Boyle, and Linc Gillespie—if only Jim and Dorothy would come south. Jim refused the enticing invitation, explaining: "Entangled with a lease. Trying to get someone to break it, but haven't succeeded." The Farrells' cotenants, Rue and Ginny Menken, were laying plans to go to Russia. Ginny's relative, the Russian Commissar Mikhail Borodin, had sent Ginny two passes to the Soviet Union. And now, Jim wrote to Riva, the Menkens were trying to persuade Madame and Henri Prévost that the Farrells had plenty of money and should take over the entire lease at six hundred francs a month. The unsettling disagreement dragged on well into August. Fortunately, the Prévosts had come to dislike the Menkens and some of their friends. Dorothy recalled that Henri eventually said to Jim: "We understand you can't pay the whole of six hundred. You can pay your half. So we paid our half, the three hundred . . . for the rest of the six months. . . . Which was extremely kind of them." Jim wrote to his friend Sarajo Caron Krumgold about this. She replied: "The Menkens? You were half-witted to ever attempt living with them. They are slovenly, braying asses."[104]

Before the Menkens left for the Soviet Union, the ill feeling between Rue and Jim climaxed in a brief, inconclusive scuffle between the two men in the United States Students and Artists Club. It was sparked, Jim said, by Rue's slighting remark about Dorothy and an unpaid debt to Jim. The Reverend Harold Belshaw helped smooth things over between the two antagonists. Rue and Ginny left Paris for the Soviet Union in August, and the Farrells had the pavillon to themselves.[105] The Menkens had not returned to Paris by the time Jim and Dorothy left for home, eight months later.[106]

The Farrells were happy to see Ed Bastian—their University of Chicago friend—arrive in Paris. He had come to study history at the Sorbonne under Albert Mathiez, a specialist on Robespierre and the French Revolution.[107] Bastian was a superior student of wide interests and had graduated at age twenty-one from the university in June. On campus, he had helped edit the *Daily Maroon* and had cofounded the undergraduate magazine *The Circle*. At the time Farrell was campus reporter for the *Herald-Examiner*, Ed was a South Side correspondent of the *Tribune*.[108]

Ed knew no one in Paris, but quickly fit into the Farrells' circle of acquaintances. For Jim and Dorothy, he was a reliable friend and companion, a confidant always ready to lend small sums of money when needed. He was particularly sensitive to Dorothy's needs and inclinations. "He was a darling man," she remembered. "He really was. At that time he was still a boy. I loved Ed."[109] Being with this young Chicagoan helped reinforce Jim's growing certitude about where he belonged. He wrote to Tom Freeman: "I find I'm not in great sympathy with this expatriate attitude of running away to damn America from a Parisian café. It's all right to come to Europe etc. but the American writer's place is America. I know I won't be able to finish my next book until I return."[110]

The three friends had much catching-up to do. They met for dinner at the Cité Universitaire, Ed's temporary residence. At the Sélect that night, Jim introduced Ed to Heinz Mullender, who understood little English, and Ed, well trained in French and German, interpreted Farrell's tales of Chicago gangsters to him. Two nights later, Bastian and the Rudnicks bunked all night at the Farrells' place, and on the following Sunday Jim, Dorothy, and Ed explored the Louvre and Notre-Dame.

Then on Wednesday, they ate at the Russian restaurant Dominique's on the rue Bréa, followed by a long evening afterwards at the Sélect. They planned a picnic in the Bois de Boulogne for Thursday, but the sudden arrival at the Hôtel Ritz of Dorothy's wealthy Aunt Grace and Irene Cody, a family friend, changed their plans. Neither of the visitors knew that Dorothy was married and pregnant. Dorothy dressed appropriately to stay overnight at the Ritz and returned the next day—her secret, surprisingly, still hidden. She came bearing gifts of a pair of gloves and a beautiful Chanel suit that Grace and Irene Cody had given her.[111]

While Dorothy was away and Jim was at his desk, Ed, still in Sceaux, began reading Scott Moncrieff's translation of Proust's *Swann's Way*, a book Farrell had recently read. During his stay in Paris, Ed continued to read Proust. Before he left Sceaux that evening, Jim loaded him down with his copies of Joyce's *Ulysses* and *A Portrait of the Artist as a Young Man*, as well as Herbert Croly's *The Promise of American Life*. In return, Ed loaned Jim a copy of Albert Mathiez's book on the French Revolution. The historian's "special form of semi-Marxist handling of the French Revolution" appealed to Jim.[112]

Since mid-July, the Farrells had scrimped and lived on borrowed money. Then on 12 August, Jim received the final advance on *Young Lonigan* from Henle, a draft on the Banque Nationale for $135 ($150 less Walt Carmon's 10 percent). His editorial work on his manuscript was completed; now with more than three thousand francs in hand, he could pay off some debts. Since Ed Bastian's loan had helped tide the Farrells over until the check came, Jim arranged to meet Ed at the Dôme and reimburse him there. Two days later, Jim and Dorothy put on a "celebratory dinner" for him at Sceaux. Only a modest sum remained after many debts were paid.[113]

Seizing this rare moment of financial success, modest though it was, the Farrells informed their families they had married (supposedly in Paris).[114] Dorothy also wrote her cousin Isabel Simpson, telling her only that Jim was in Paris. Jim's Aunt Ella, his Uncle Tom, his brother Earl, and his Grandmother Julia, greeted the news with joy, although Julia expressed her feelings in typical fashion, promising to "whale his arse" when he returned. They all liked Dorothy. Aunt Ella, always a loser in love, was carried away.

> "You see James ever since you were a new born baby Aunt Ella was always there with your mother. And I loved you just like you were my very own child and still love you. I made mistakes for lack of experience and knowledge but that's what the rubber was put on the pencil for to errase the mistake. . . . Oh you have a bright future and with Dorothy at your side you will succeed and be on top. You are so rich in so many ways so fortunate that please count your blessings dear you have so many blessings. Life is Wonderful . . . God bless guide and protect my little fellow my baby. That's what you are to me my darling little blond curly-headed baby."[115]

But Maggie Butler let Dorothy know she was devastated. "You will never know until you will have a child of your own do the same things you have done, how badly I feel. I am just crushed to think you just a little girl getting married so soon. . . . I can never feel the same to Jimmie for going over there to marry you when you were so young. . . . Now you give up every thing your teaching study and all. . . . Yesterday . . . I was insane grief stricken and today I am worse . . . Jimmie cannot support you he is not ready yet he should of waited . . . I can not tell any one try and keep it a secret for a year or at least until your school ends in Spring. . . . I cry all the time and hide from every one."[116] Maggie did not know that Dorothy was neither teaching nor studying, and she did not want her wealthy sister Grace Roney and Grace's husband John to know of the marriage.

Within days of pocketing his advance, Farrell received his copy of the *New Review* that printed his "Jewboy." The *Paris Tribune* reviewed the issue favorably on 17 August. He was surprised and pleased that his name was mentioned as a contributor along with those of Ezra Pound, Samuel Beckett, Emanuel Carnevali, John Sherry Mangan, George Reavey, Richard Thoma, and Neagoe.[117] Two days later, he turned to Wambly

Bald's widely read column in the *Tribune*. Bald dismissed all the critical essays in this latest number of the *New Review* as "the weakest gibberish of this decade." The magazine was "carried by its fiction. The short stories and chapter extracts of novels have brought to the fore a number of brilliant young writers, each of whom shows astonishing fertility and inventiveness. Most interesting of all is the range. The gap between James Farrell's *Jewboy* and Richard Thoma's *Tragedy in Blue* is wide. The former is a slice of life by an artist whose work shows crudity at its best. The latter stands head over heels above the other contributors." Bald and Thoma were regular contributors to the *New Review*, and Thoma was an associate editor of the magazine. Bald admired Thoma's "bizarre and pulling metaphors" that smell of "musk and other content," and he praised Thoma's "ability to finger brocades of words and squirt perfumes" in his prose—accomplishments poles apart from the ways of re-creating objective reality and emotional intensity that Farrell valued in fiction.[118]

Also in the *New Review*, Jim read a notice by Nancy Cunard, whom he knew by reputation. She was seeking contributions for a massive anthology titled *Negro* that she had been putting together since May.[119] Jim mailed a letter to her Hours Press on the rue Guénégaud suggesting the poetry of his talented Chicago friend Donald Jeffrey Hayes. He offered to supply her with short stories by whites about blacks—about "the expansion of the Negroes to white sections of the South Side; mobbings, riots at bathing beaches, and things like that."[120] He may have had in mind some of his own tales and some by his brother Jack or his friend Bus Stern. A flurry of letters passed between the two. They met twice at the Café de Flore and got along well. After the first long meeting, Jim returned to Dorothy drunk on Pernods. Dorothy came to the second meeting. Nancy, she realized, "was not interested in me. She was interested in James. She liked the young boys, you know. That's what she liked. He thought she might help him, but that was not her intention at all. She just had a little yen for him, a little case for him. Well, I shouldn't be so cruel as to say that, but that was the case."[121]

By the end of August, Farrell had completed one hundred pages of "The Madhouse," and he was ready for a change of pace away from his desk. Ed Bastian, in a letter to Laura Bastian, his mother, described the weekend's highlights. On Saturday, 29 August, he, Jim, and Dorothy shared "a tasty Jewish supper" with Nathan and Fanny Klein in the Kleins' Montrouge studio-apartment. The three men then "philosophized on many things" for many hours while the women slept. At 4:00 A.M., they all took a streetcar to see Les Halles, the famous market, during its "dawn hours of business." Getting off at the place du Châtelet, they trudged through a drizzling rain to the rue des Halles, the rue Baltard, and others, and made their way through the swarms of shouting and dodging porters transporting loads of produce. They squeezed through congested alleys lined with pyramids of vegetables encumbering the sidewalks, squashed through a spinach-strewn lane, and lingered before the wicker baskets of flowers that perfumed the air. They went on to look in at Notre-Dame early Sunday morning, took the streetcar back to Montrouge, where the Kleins dropped off, and then on to Sceaux for a morning nap.[122]

That afternoon and evening, while Jim wrote letters, Ed read through *Young Lonigan*. "I recognized with great joy and satisfaction the atmosphere and the characters," he wrote to his mother. And to his Uncle Bert: "*Young Lonigan* . . . cries aloud its truths of Chicago street kids from every page; in fact, no other book I ever read is so particularly and concretely realistic about Chicago streets and their swearing, emotion-driven, blindly-acting adolescent inhabitants." And to a family friend and editor of the *Chicago Tribune*: "I rejoice to find a book which shows that kids are not what the Mark Twains and the Booth Tarkingtons make them out to be, entirely. It is a scrupulous, brutal, horrifying, and altogether charming book."[123] To his former Hyde Park High School teacher, Walter J. Hipple, once a student of Woodrow Wilson's at Princeton, Ed wrote: *Young Lonigan* is "so realistic that I laughed and winced at the memories it provoked. Not all of it is realistic; there are crudities (remember it is a first book), but the greater part of it is *truth*, and I am not at all being ironical when I advise you to buy it when it comes out just to see what your own son might experience at one time or another."[124] A few days later, Ed read through Farrell's still incomplete manuscript of "The Madhouse." He disliked it so intensely that when the completed manuscript was published as *Gas-House McGinty*, he gave away the inscribed copy the author sent him.[125]

Letters rejecting Jim's short stories continued to pile up while he labored on "The Madhouse." Leading editors like H. L. Mencken, Whit Burnett, Richard Johns, and Lincoln Kirstein (who wanted to see excerpts from *Young Lonigan*) were interested yet still reluctant to take his work, sometimes for fear of censorship.[126] Nevertheless, he was heartened in the days ahead by several bits of good news and a major opportunity. He learned that Horace Gregory wanted to review *Young Lonigan*; his tale "A Casual Incident" appeared in the September–October number of the newly founded magazine *Story*; and Ezra Pound agreed to read the first draft of his new novel when it was ready.[127]

Another boost in morale came in a letter from his friend Sarajo Caron Krumgold, still in Los Angeles. She let him know that his story "Jewboy" had created a small "sensation" among the Jewish community there. Wambly Bald had sent a copy of the *New Review*, with "Jewboy" in it, to a Los Angeles acquaintance, and Sarajo's Jewish friends insisted it was so authentic that only a Jew could have written it. Jim grinned while reading her letter. He remembered the passages from Emerson's essays he had copied into his University of Chicago notebooks and wondered if the gift of "Jewboy," by Wambly Bald, who had panned the story in his column, was a sinuous expression of Emerson's Great Law of Compensation.[128]

Farrell took time out from his work on "The Madhouse" to inform Bob Brown that the staccato, broken-sentence style he had used in his *Readies* stories proved to be "quite efficacious in the book I'm writing. Parts describing a busy time in the Wagon Department of an express office, when shippers are calling up for service, and there are all kinds of noise, seemed quite amenable to that type of treatment." To himself, he wryly observed that his mechanical, offhand creation of a jerky, chopped-up syntax in his "Readies" had laid bare an unexpected field for his talent.[129]

On 13 September, Farrell shipped 329 first-draft pages of "The Madhouse" to Henle with a lengthy cover letter. His second book would be dedicated "To my wife . . . Dorothy." He intended his typescript to make up the first one-third of a novel on the Railway Express Company; it would be section one of three sections.[130] "I took it into Paris," he later recalled, "to get it off on the boat train. I met George Seldes and he took me to lunch at a restaurant near the Left Bank. He talked about Mussolini, and about how he had been expelled from the Soviet Union, and also about Majorca. He was going there and planned to paint."[131] Seldes was writing his book *Sawdust Caesar*, a study of Fascism, and had just published his book *Can These Things Be?*, an attack on the inadequacy and corruption of the commercial press. He found in Jim an interested listener to his stories of how the press, through deceit or censorship or simply reportorial incompetence, obscured the truth and failed in its task of informing the public.

Farrell wrote to Henle that once he returned to Chicago he would "check up on details of location [and] revisit depots etc. to get the stuff more vivid." He realized he was sending "only a beginning," but sending it "with the frank hope of securing an advance. . . . I am in a hell of a hole. To be brief on the matter, my wife is having a child in November, and other plans of mine have so far fallen through." Two days later, he put it this way to Ted Marvel: "I'm down again, and almost as flat as a pancake. But not without some hopes." Once again, he and Dorothy were depending on loans from Ed Bastian and Tom Freeman. He did not know at this time that the manuscript he had submitted to Henle, when revised, would make up the bulk, and not merely the first one-third, of *Gas-House McGinty*. But he believed that an advance on his second novel, if coming at all, would be weeks away, and in the meantime, the old uncertainty and anxiety gripped him. So he asked Henle to cable his willingness to grant him an advance, based on the promise shown by his submitted manuscript.[132]

Farrell explained in his letter to Henle that the manuscript he had submitted dealt with the Wagon Call Department while it was managed by Chief Dispatcher "Mushmouth," or "Gas-House" McManus ("Gas-House McGinty" in the novel). Sections two and three, still to be written, would carry on the story of the department under the two dispatchers who succeeded Mushmouth. A brief epilogue would provide an appropriate conclusion. The main focus throughout would remain on "the little Wagon Department world that is built up," the "central stage" of the workers' life, the place where they bring their habits, worries, frustrations, jealousies, and biases and "dump" them. In that sense, "the department was to be the protagonist and the characters functions of it."

At the same time, he would lightly paint in, as background, a few scenes relevant to the workers' social life, such as one of them at a wake, or in a bowling tournament, or at a Knights of Columbus initiation ceremony, or "ushering in the Catholic church at Cicero." Also, rather than using the "news reel" and "camera's eye" techniques, as Dos Passos had done, he preferred to bring in the outer world by revealing "the impact which current events make on the consciousness of my characters"— events such as sensational crimes, sports results, racial strife, and political elections and scandals. In that way, he could reveal the quality of his characters' mentality and their ingrained values. He believed that "if the atmosphere is rendered faithfully, and the characters are put down honestly, they and it will be sufficient" without formal plot.[133]

His novel dealt with social themes, but once again he drew the vital distinction between sociology and what he was attempting. Sociologists

assume the human phenomenon is like so many atoms, electrons, etc. . . . And holy Jesus, they investigate. They investigate. They investigate. They keep on collecting facts, and clutter up the libraries. . . .

Personally I feel that Art, yes Art in capital letters, would do a hell of a lot of good for . . . the university sociology fact finders, for statistical economists and the rest of the boys who are rapidly getting a corner on the educational market. One thing the artist knows is that life has meanings, that there are values, and that for human beings these values are the most important thing.[134]

Farrell stopped off at Edward Titus's office on his way back to Sceaux after mailing his manuscript. He wanted to see Lawrence Drake, who had vaguely expressed an interest in publishing one or more of his tales. He spoke of Drake's proposal in a letter to Henle: Drake "asked me if I had . . . a book of short stories unprintable in America. I told him I didn't write stories either to be printable or unprintable in America, but that I had a book in mind that might be what he wanted, and that included . . . stories that would do more than invite censorship." Jim's idea was a volume to be called "Chamber of Horrors." "It would include a limited number of stories, all dealing with sex, and mainly with the sexual problems of middle class young people," problems exacerbated by parental attitudes. Jim outlined for Henle a handful of stories already written. He explained it was the kind of collection Ezra Pound favored. It was not a miscellaneous grouping, but a collection that explored different aspects of a central problem. Drake, he told Henle, believed he could publish such a book; priced at fifty francs, it would sell from three to five thousand copies. Jim, flat broke, implied to Henle that he was intrigued by this possibility, if Henle should not exercise his right of first choice for such a book.[135]

Two days after mailing his manuscript to Henle, Farrell resumed work on "The Madhouse." Within a week, he was well into section two, the proposed novel's most difficult part. He anticipated that section three would be less difficult to write because it would deal with the time when he was most familiar with his material.[136] He pressed on; his concentration on writing blocked out everything else. Seeing that it was making him tired and irritable, Dorothy arranged for an evening of relaxation and drinks with Ed Bastian and the Kleins. For a special treat, she bought "a pâtisserie, a little pastry, a little mocha cake." After their company had left, Dorothy said, Jim blew up. "He made such hell for me because I had spent a franc for a pâtisserie. . . . The only time he ever did, because we didn't fight." Ed Bastian remembered that Dorothy wanted "to eat better and drink better than they could afford at the time. And I remember," he said, "two or three occasions when Farrell had to caution her. But he cautioned her in good temper."[137]

After receiving the manuscript pages of "The Madhouse" and Farrell's accompanying letter, Henle was quick to respond. "I like them, I like your method of work and I like everything about you." The story was "marvelous material." To Walt Carmon, he wrote: "The boy is certainly good. We'll make them all sit up and take notice." With Carmon, he drew up the contract for Farrell's second novel and authorized Walt to advance $200 less agent's commission. Then, answering Jim's plea for financial help, he cabled him on 30 September that he was advancing the money.[138]

Farrell went at once to the office of Vanguard's Paris agency. This time he met Evelyn Shrifte, again briefly visiting Paris. Henle also had notified her about his decision to go ahead with "The Madhouse"—eventually to be retitled *Gas-House McGinty*. Jim learned that his advance would be available in about ten days (he got it—4,538 francs—on 9 October), and Evelyn Shrifte reassured him of his good standing with Vanguard. He told her about Lawrence Drake's interest in publishing a book of his tales, a proposal never realized. Then, carrying the good news to Dorothy, Jim returned to Sceaux. That afternoon, he wrote a letter to his Grandmother Julia informing her that his second book had been accepted. He wanted to send her a gift. He and Dorothy walked to town, where Dorothy selected a colorful scarf, which they mailed with a card. In a long letter to Henle, Jim profusely thanked his editor for the advance. He outlined his hopes for publishing the collection of his stories he called "Chamber of Horrors" and he assured Henle he was back at work on "The Madhouse."[139]

While at the Vanguard Press Paris agency, Jim met two of Evelyn

Shrifte's friends, Nat Turkel and his sister Pauline. The next afternoon, he and Dorothy had them to tea and began a lasting friendship with them. Nat ran a printshop on Twenty-fifth Street in the Bronx and had come to Paris planning to bicycle through France. Pauline, a woman of thirty-two, was then secretary to the U.S. ambassador in Rome. A confirmed anarchist by her late teens, in 1916 she became Emma Goldman's secretary in the *Mother Earth* office and soon developed close ties to Alexander Berkman and other anarchists. She also acted with the Provincetown Players in Eugene O'Neill's early plays and became a friend of O'Neill, Hart Crane, and Djuna Barnes.[140]

The Farrells continued to see Nat and Pauline in New York City in the 1930s. "I had, several times," Jim later wrote, "stopped in to see Nat at his print shop. I liked him. He was kind and a decent fellow. His sister, Pauline, was a woman of charm, dignity, and intelligence." Having been deeply affected by the execution of Sacco and Vanzetti a few years earlier, Farrell responded with a special interest to Pauline's anarchism. He appreciated the humanism and respect for the individual in the anarchist approach to social change, something lacking in communism. He characterized Pauline's later political views as those of a democratic socialist.[141]

Now that he was about to get some U.S. dollars, which would be converted immediately into francs, Jim was afraid the exchange rate would plummet before his advance from Vanguard arrived. News from the United States continued to be bleak. Newspaper headlines played up the futility of President Hoover's debt moratorium for Germany. Other European powers as well as the United States faced worsening social and economic conditions. There had been fifty murders so far in the explosive Harlan County, Kentucky, coal miners' strike; come winter, there would be four hundred thousand estimated unemployed in Chicago; there was another stock-market debacle on Wall Street, and there would be an estimated seven million unemployed before the winter was over. An ominous sign was England's abandonment of the gold standard, causing the value of the pound to nosedive.[142]

Fearing the worst would happen to his coming advance on "The Madhouse," Jim informed Ed Bastian that if "the dollar is going to take a tumble . . . I shall be in a hell of a fix." He asked Ed to keep him posted by *pneumatiques* from Paris about any anticipated drop in the dollar's exchange rate, then hovering around twenty-five francs, and Ed obliged.[143] Fortunately, the exchange rate was still favorable when his advance arrived on October 9. Yet as October wore on, economic forecasts remained gloomy. Newspaper headlines reported an excessive outflow of gold from the United States. Savants predicted the country would abandon the gold standard and that inflation would decimate the dollar's value. Thinking about his and Dorothy's future in Paris, Jim still felt financially vulnerable, tossed around on a sea of uncertainty. Fortunately again for holders of U.S. currency, over the next few months the dollar declined in value only slightly, but the *crise* intensified in France and was reflected in political turmoil.

Ed and Jim shared an interest in French politics. Ed was politically liberal, and in France he was particularly drawn to Léon Blum's Socialist Party. Farrell's politics, too, were consistently to the left, but critical of Communism, and he was apprehensive about the rise of Italian Fascism and of Hitler in Germany. He was interested in all political opinion and capable of friendship with persons with whom he disagreed; for example, with Pierre-Jean Robert, whom Farrell once described to Bastian as "the kind of man who, on Franco's side, would defend a position to the death." Farrell, as Ed observed, "had a sharp eye for pretenders of one sort or another, in literature and in politics."[144]

In Paris, street demonstrations by the Communist Party and the right-wing *L'Action Française* dominated the public's political attention at this time. Ed and Jim planned to observe a Communist gathering scheduled for 3 October on the rue Dupetit-Thouars in the working-class district of eastern Paris north of the Seine. But only Ed was able to go.[145] Later that month, Dorothy remembered, the Farrells went to a large Communist demonstration. The Communists "had a big showing outside the café [La Closerie] des Lilas, up at the end of Montparnasse which had become the boulevard [de Port-]Royal. . . . We went up to see it. . . . I enjoyed it . . . but James thought he was not part of it. He was a strange kind of socialist, you know. He was both toward the Left, but if it got too rau- cous— . . . . He didn't like Stalinism, but of course that became more prominent later on. . . . Communism still at that time was a little bit rosy in people's eyes."[146]

The morning of 3 October, the day of the Communist meeting on the rue Dupetit-Thouars, Jim received cables from his brother Jack and Uncle Tom that his Grandmother Julia Daly had died. Two weeks be- fore, Jim had ordered long-stemmed roses for her; they were delivered to her home the day after her death. Julia had been "Mother" to Jim since he was three years old. She replaced his birth mother, who became his ever more distant "Mama." His scarf to Julia had been mailed too late to reach her.[147] It hurt. "When I read the cablegram announcing my grand- mother's death, Chicago seemed both far away and near. . . . I thought of her death back there on the South Side. When I had left Chicago in April, she had cried. Now I cried. It was a muggy, gray October after- noon. I sat in a café, looking at the crowds. There was nothing for me even to tell myself . . . a few black words on a blue sheet of paper . . . snapped a link with the past, with that South Side of Chicago which had remained so much in my mind while I was in Paris."[148] Julia's death fol- lowed by three months that of Jim's close Chicago friend Paul Caron, who, like Jim, had desired to go to Paris and write, but never did.[149]

Both Jim and Dorothy wanted to send a cable and flowers to their fam- ilies. But they lacked the money and were already in debt to Ed Bastian. Jim decided to see Edward Titus, who still owed him money for his story "The Merry Clouters." To his surprise, as he wrote in a letter to Henle, Titus "was exceedingly gracious to me, and considerate, and asked me how much money I needed. I only needed two hundred francs [for the cables and flowers] but could have gotten more if I had asked for it."[150] He immediately sent two cables, one to his Uncle Tom and the other from Dorothy to her mother. He informed Henle that he wanted the dedication of *Young Lonigan* changed to read: "To the memory of my grandmother, Mrs. Julia Brown Daly."[151] Jim's family and his friends Lloyd Stern and Joe Cody wrote him the details of her death and funeral.[152]

With some of Jim Henle's advance payment on "The Madhouse" in her purse, Dorothy shopped three times at Au Bon Marché for towels, dishcloths, and diapers. Then she and Jim spent an evening with Ed Bastian at a Paris restaurant and the Sélect.[153] They visited Riva and Hilary Putnam in Fontenay-aux-Roses, and—Sam not being expected back from the United States for several weeks—Jim wrote to Putnam in New York about the visit. "We got Hilary and took him to the Parc de Sceaux one afternoon and he made me be his horse. When we entered the park he told me to stand outside by the gate because horses weren't admitted. And also he made me put hats on a pole and go around the park with him selling chapeaux at vingt-cinq sous a pound."[154] During an earlier Sunday visit with Riva, the Farrells had seen Hilary learning to ride a bicycle, which both Jim and Dorothy had done in Chicago. They went with him "while he took his bicycle all over Fontenay. . . . Every two minutes he'd look in back to see if anyone was pushing him, and if so, he'd sound off in a big way, and tell us to keep our hands off." The contrast between a kid playing in Fontenay and a kid playing in Chicago streets surely must have been in Farrell's thoughts at this time.[155]

The Farrells had cut down on their entertaining, but at this time their social life took a more active turn. When Jim had last seen Heinz Mullender, Heinz was greatly worried about his family in Frankfurt. He needed money to return home, and Jim loaned him the railroad fare. Ed Bastian, too, was planning to leave Paris, making a visit to family relatives living in Alsace. They had the two men over for a farewell dinner on 14 October, Ed then leaving for Alsace and, later, Heinz for Frankfurt. Ed was eagerly anticipating a new experience, but Heinz was filled with dread at what he would find. Front-page newspaper stories had reported Hitler-led Nazi riots in Brunswick that had injured 161 people. Ed returned after ten happy days, having been warmly entertained in Alsace. Dorothy, who needed a change from inactivity, arranged a dinner for him and Don Sewarts, Tom Squires, and Maurice Rausch. Heinz did not return to Paris, but for months he wrote the Farrells friendly, thoughtful letters tinged with despair about what seemed to him to be his country's plunge toward self-destruction. Jim never learned what happened to Heinz, who remained a haunting presence in his memory—one that he returned to in his tale "Fritz."[156]

Farrell suddenly was presented with the possibility of having *Young Lonigan* published in a French edition by Gallimard (the Nouvelle Revue Française, or NRF). The English-to-French translator at Gallimard, Pierre-Jean Robert, who had helped the Farrells get their *cartes d'identité*, asked Jim to let him read the manuscript.[157] Farrell gave him seven sections, and Pierre responded immediately. You are, he assured his friend, "a writer," and one who "deserves the title. Your little tough guies and their girls are now part of my life. They belong to the few thoughts that one cherishes in the most intimate cell of one's mind."[158] He promised to urge the firm's directors—the brothers Gaston and Raymond Gallimard, André Malraux, Louis Chevasson, and Ramon Fernandez—to give Farrell a contract. Jim at once forwarded Pierre's letter to Henle.[159] He and Dorothy had Pierre and Ed Bastian out for dinner.[160] Pierre let them know that Ramon Fernandez, the respected, much-published critic, was then reading the manuscript. A favorable decision from him would assure its French publication. "I'm once again praying for more luck, and it's liable to materialize," Farrell wrote to Peter Neagoe. "Got a very favorable report on my book from one reader of the Nouvelle Revue Française, and if it passes the second guy (Ramon Fernandez) they should be buying it for translation."[161] Jim waited for word from Fernandez, and Pierre remained confident the NRF would buy the novel.[162]

For Dorothy, the fall of the year stretching into November was a time of anticipation and waiting. Nathan Klein told the Farrells that Fanny had gone to the hospital on 28 October and given birth prematurely to their little girl, Judy. Dorothy wanted to see Judy, but did not make the trip to the hospital.[163] She and Jim let Ed Bastian, Bob Brown, the Neagoes, and Christina Stead know that they fully expected their baby in November, even early in the month. Jim went to the American Hospital to make arrangements. "We are waiting for things to happen," he informed Tom Freeman, "and they should this week. I got matters all fixed up at the hospital, and got the best obstetrician in Paris (or one of the best) all on a promissory note.... Dorothy is all right."[164] While Paris celebrated the anniversary of Armistice Day on 11 November, the Farrells remained in Sceaux.

Dorothy did not get to Paris very often and had little news to send home. So she wrote to her mother and to Isabel Simpson (who worked for a Chicago music company) about the growing demands made by her study and teaching of music. Isabel's letters to Dorothy are full of the subject. Izzy was glad Dorothy was making progress in music by studying diligently. Ed Bastian, in the know, felt a mixture of shock and admiration for Dorothy's dedicated deception.[165]

Jim's concern about Dorothy's condition was overlaid by a number of professional demands that made October and November the most frenetically hopeful yet frustrating months of his Paris year. Two books in their early stages, "The Madhouse" and "Chamber of Horrors," demanded his attention, and still to come were the galleys of *Young Lonigan*. French and English editions of "Young Lonigan" and an English edition of some of his stories also became distinct possibilities to be pursued. And for the present, as always, there were the nagging money worries and the pressing need for more time at his desk.

Jim was back at work on "The Madhouse" in October. Within two weeks, he completed more than one hundred rough-draft pages of section two. By month's end, he had five hundred pages of sections one and two. He explained to Henle that he wanted to provide more background to his portrayal of the office workdays. To do this, he planned to include "a movie scenario, depicting the daydreams of . . . McGillicuddy [Farrell's current name for McGinty] as he stands before the office at noon watching telephone operators pass." The work was going well. He told Henle that he was mailing parts of the book to several magazines, that Titus liked an excerpt shown to him, and that Ezra Pound had agreed to read the manuscript.[166]

Farrell informed Henle he was sending short stories to his new agent Maxim Lieber, hired in October to replace Walt Carmon, whose editorial duties on the *New Masses* had become overwhelming. Lieber represented many younger writers, including Josephine Herbst, John Hermann, Paul Peters, and Charles Yale Harrison.[167] Furthermore, Joe Krumgold, husband of Jim's friend Sarajo, wanted to consider *Young Lonigan* as film material for Paramount Studios. Jim doubted it was adaptable to the movies, but he asked Henle to send Krumgold a set of proofs, which Henle did, though decades would pass before Studs Lonigan made it onto the screen.[168]

Farrell's work on "The Madhouse" stopped abruptly with the arrival of the proofs of *Young Lonigan* during the final week of October. After a labor of five or six days, he returned them to Henle. Most of his changes, he explained, were for the sake of accuracy and correct pronunciation. He confided to Ed Bastian that he believed his author's changes in the proof had set him back three hundred dollars—a debtor's mountain of francs for one who only recently had to borrow three hundred francs from Ed as a contingency fund after paying backrent. But seeing and handling the proofs left him elated, as well as grateful for having a cooperative publisher.[169]

While working on his proofs, he reminded Henle that after "The Madhouse" was completed, he planned to do a sequel to *Young Lonigan*. In his letter, he made clear that the tug of Studs's story on his imagination was undiminished. He wanted to "portray the way the characters drank themselves to death, died of venereal disease and in saloon brawls, and the way the whole neighborhood disintegrated and with this disintegration, the way the older people realized that it had been their life, and they were losing it, and that with their children gone to pot they were in the position where they had nothing to wait for except death." He assured Henle that writing this book would go well. Already, while in Chicago, he had completed a first draft.[170]

Farrell decided to write several book reviews before returning to work on "The Madhouse." He also wrote to Henle and his brother Earl for more background material: copies of *Captain Billie's Whizbang* and the Express Company's inhouse letter, the "Express Messenger." He sent off a note to the letters column of the *Chicago Daily Tribune* asking the paper's readers to send him parodies of popular songs. He told himself he was putting on a literary juggling act, keeping half a dozen balls in the air at once. Still, by the final week of November, he had completed well over five hundred manuscript pages of "The Madhouse."[171]

The juggling act grew even more stressful. News came from Sam Putnam that Desmond Harmsworth's publishing house in London had acquired the rights to two English-language books recently brought out in Paris. Why not *Young Lonigan* for Harmsworth's list? Jim asked himself. Hurriedly, he asked Henle for permission to make preliminary negotiations, should Harmsworth be interested in obtaining the English rights for *Young Lonigan*. He explained to Henle that "when I first came over here, Pound introduced me to one of the Harmsworths who was trying to make up for the sins of his uncle or father, or grandfather or some such thing (Lord Northcliffe) by publishing 'literature,' and he thanked me all over the place for letting him see the stories I sent you, and was very intent on publishing them but then got cold feet. . . . If you want me to, I shall . . . see if he is interested . . . and what he will offer if anything." Even if Harmsworth was not interested, Jim added, "I might be able to get thanked all over the place again, and that is very satisfying to one's vanity."[172]

Without waiting for Henle's response, Farrell wrote Harmsworth in London, reminding him of the stories Harmsworth had considered and rejected in the spring. He assured him that "the book is different from some of the stories I showed you." He informed Harmsworth that a reader for Gallimard had recommended it for a French edition. Harmsworth's response was immediate and favorable. Jim forwarded Harmsworth's letter to Henle and asked for a set of proofs that he would personally deliver to the publisher in Paris.[173]

He also continued to press Henle for a favorable decision on publishing *Chamber of Horrors.* He informed him that his idea of the book was "expanding a little, to include a few other stories that could fit under a title such as *Chamber of Horrors,* taking in other aspects of American life, and other types of characters." His letters to Walt Carmon and Maxim Lieber asked them to retrieve his tales they had submitted to U.S. magazines and forward them to Henle. He sent his editor what he had on hand, some dozen tales, and also gave extra carbon copies to Lawrence Drake in Paris. Having recently sold "The Merry Clouters" to Titus, Jim was convinced that this editor, too, was flirting with the idea of including a volume of his tales in the series of books he was publishing. He brought Titus another story, a copy of "Saturday Night," and reported to Henle that Titus liked it.

With three publishers seemingly interested, he wrote to his sister Mary that he believed he was on the verge of selling a book of short stories. But he preferred Henle over the other two, whom he considered unreliable. He wanted Vanguard to do the job. He wanted most of his tales that were already written to be published together, and soon, because, as he explained to Henle, "most of this stuff belongs, or will (I believe) belong to a definite period in my writing, and hence I'd like it all sort of embalmed together. I think, and sort of hope, to change the style and material, and to try other things, particularly in that trilogy ["The Madhouse"]." Henle's response was encouraging. He was reading the tales and hoped Vanguard could publish a short-story collection.[174]

At this time of rising expectations, Farrell received infuriating news. One morning, he opened a letter from Henle and read that on the advice of Morris Ernst, Henle's lawyer, who had read the proof, *Young Lonigan* would have to be published in a limited edition for psychiatrists, doctors, social workers, and others with a professional interest in the psychology of adolescents. Morris Ernst was a prominent civil-rights advocate who had been in court battles on behalf of free speech. He knew that without the precautionary restriction, *Young Lonigan* would surely be censored. As Jim put it to Tom Freeman, Ernst had "marked my proof up like a Chinese laundry sign, and it is out of the question selling my novel openly." Henle urged him not to be discouraged. For a splendid book like *Young Lonigan,* this predicament was ridiculous but necessary, he insisted. He would not ask for further expurgations or wholesale revision, but publication would now be postponed until spring.[175]

Jim felt trapped. "I am so angry as I write," he exploded to Tom Freeman, "that I feel impotent with fury, but then what the hell can you do, when ignorant fools have the right to censor work they don't know anything about, and the censors make good money out of their racket. . . . Anyway, I'll make the rare book room at U. of C." To Peter Neagoe, he wrote: "It's quite discouraging. . . . I wish to Christ I took up bricklaying or some other goddamn thing." His bleak state of mind temporarily destabilized his political leanings: "I am getting more and more in sympathy with the radicals and communism," he proclaimed to Tom. "Doing anything in America seems to me hopeless. . . . This is an age that will be lots of fun for future historians . . . but it's hell living in it."[176]

The irony of what had happened did not escape him. For years, he had intensely disliked the methods, the writing, and the products of sociologists. Yet now he felt that the work he had tried to make a unique artistic creation with wide appeal was being tagged as merely a document suitable for reading by sociologists and their professional bedfellows. On further reflection, he told himself he might have known this would happen. H. L. Mencken recently had rejected seven of his tales, some of them for the reason he gave for returning "The Scarecrow": "This is an excellent story, but printing it in this great Christian country, at least in a magazine that goes through the mails, is impossible."[177]

After two days, he had cooled off enough to answer Henle: "I don't know what to say. Naturally it is very discouraging and also irritating; but I don't see that it does me any good, either to feel martyred, or to get angry and curse. This sort of thing has happened before . . . since American authorities [and] millions of our fellow citizens work on the assumption that everyone is a child. . . . I have met the same kind of stupidity, and have lost much time bumping into it among my relatives, in-laws, teachers, former employers and so on." He assured Henle he understood "the kind of stupidity a publisher is up against" and "wouldn't want you to take any serious financial risks with any of my books."[178] Henle responded by saying he was raising the price of *Young Lonigan* to $3.75 as additional protection from prosecution.[179] And Peter Neagoe tried to cheer him up: "If Henle is an enterprising guy he can make the book a huge success, just because of its supposed restriction." He cited the famous sex manual *Ideal Marriage*, supposedly "limited to the medical profession" but that "anybody can get."[180]

Maybe Peter was right, Farrell thought. More angry than discouraged, he lost no time writing to four University of Chicago professors asking for their aid. He, as well as Henle, asked Lovett to write the introduction. He asked Ernest Burgess, of Sociology, Harold Lasswell, of Political Science, and T. V. Smith, of Philosophy, to supply jacket comments. Robert Morss Lovett read the final proof and told Henle in New York that he liked the book. Although he turned down the request to write the introduction, he offered to get a sociologist who would. None of the men supplied a comment. Farrell also wrote Jane Addams and Carl Sandburg, both of whom he had interviewed for his article "Liberals in Chicago." Both replied, but the Addams letter is lost, and Sandburg regretted his inability to read the proof because of his work and his eye trouble. Jim looked up Jerry Nedwick, whom he formerly knew at Chicago's Dill Pickle Club and who was then in Paris. Nedwick was the owner of a well-known Clark Street bookstore specializing in rare books and limited editions. He agreed to write several book dealers, asking them to push the book. Maybe, Jim thought, these measures would partly offset the damage done to sales by the restriction.[181]

Although his schedule was swamped by the volume of his outgoing letters, Farrell still set aside time in the evenings to work on a bassinet for the baby.[182] Dorothy's movements about Sceaux and Paris were becoming more limited. She knew how to sew and had been making simple baby clothes for some time, as well as collecting what was needed to feed the baby. In mid-November, she and Jim were surprised to receive a box from Kay Boyle, a writer Jim admired but had not met. Bob Brown had mentioned to Kay, "rather urgently," that the Farrells were expecting a baby and needed baby clothes. Staying with Kay Boyle and Laurence Vail in Nice at that time was their friend Nina Conarain, who spent several evenings mending the baby clothes of Kay's children and "running ribbons in the knitted jackets." Kay got the box off to the Farrells.[183] Dorothy recalled that the clothes "were all beautifully mended and tidy and nice," and Jim was "touched and impressed because they were washed and knitted and sewn and sent in good condition."[184] Within days, more baby clothes arrived from Christina Stead, and a little later the Neagoes sent a baby blanket and a baby doll.[185]

Dorothy was keenly aware that her secrecy about her baby's coming birth deprived her of the support and comfort her family and Jim's surely would have provided had they known of the event. They began planning to move out of Sceaux to be nearer the American Hospital. She and Jim both believed the stone floor of their kitchen caused her feet to hurt and her ankles to swell, making walking more difficult. The pavillon lacked central heating. In Paris, Jim had noticed that the vendors selling *glaces* in the summer now had roasted chestnuts in their pushcarts—a sure sign winter was closing in. Despite his efforts to keep burning logs in the fireplaces of four rooms, the outside cold seeped indoors more and more as winter approached.[186]

Worry, intense work, late hours, and a jumble of unresolved problems plus a new and tantalizing possibility finally took their toll on Jim. In a mid-November letter to Ed Bastian, he complained: "I got a lousy cold, feel rotten, and my eyes are gone kerflooie, and I can scarcely work."[187] But despite the pain from eye strain, he had to work, if only in spurts. A week earlier, he had written Henle that a friend (unnamed) of his who also knew the rare-book dealer Jacob Schwartz, a well-paying small-book publisher located in the Ulysses Book Shop in London, had told him that Schwartz wanted to do a limited edition of one or more of his stories that had been recommended to him.[188] He wrote Schwartz and received a remarkable letter in return. Schwartz told of a dinner party at which Ezra Pound had extravagantly praised Farrell's tales to James Joyce, Padraic and Mary Colum, Harmsworth, and Mrs. Wyn Henderson, the latter's partner in the Desmond Harmsworth Press of Bloomsbury. Schwartz looked up Farrell's "Jewboy" in the New Review and liked it. In his letter to Farrell, he asked for a copy of "Meet the Girls" (incorrectly remembered by him as "Talking It Over"), the story Mrs. Henderson had liked best and had recommended to him. Schwartz painted a rosy picture. Prepublication in England would mean that the big guns in New York "will offer you God knows how much for a dozen lines of your stuff." He proposed a plan for getting a brief preface either by Joyce or Hemingway. Send several copies of "Meet the Girls," he asked, and he would distribute them to English critics for advance notices. He would pay well. "I'm not Tite-Ass [Titus] the rue Delambre puke—he stinks."[189]

Nearly broke, Jim turned again to Ed Bastian. He asked him to send two cablegrams to Jim Henle and Walt Carmon requesting that they return copies they were holding of "Meet the Girls." He typed out the cables, with addresses, for Ed to use. He already owed Ed three hundred francs. He knew the cablegrams would cost more than one hundred francs, but they would save valuable time, and "it is practically a certain sale." Ed obliged. Farrell immediately wrote to Schwartz, whose reply virtually assumed the plan would go through. Jim believed he would earn at least fifty dollars from the booklet. He also explained to Henle that a deal with Schwartz might help the sale of English rights to Young Lonigan.[190]

Farrell now paid a price: his eyes continued to hurt, reawakening an old fear that he would go blind at an early age. "My eyes still on the fritz," he wrote to Ed Bastian later in the month.[191] All of this, he gloomed, was coming just before Dorothy's baby was due, and when a small success was almost within his grasp. Dorothy observed him closely. She saw his frantic outpouring of letters and she worried about him, as well as the coming baby. She knew that her condition and Jim's prospects required that they stay in Paris at least a while longer. She walked into Sceaux, and much as she disliked giving in, sent a cable to her mother: "Need one hundred seventy-five immediately James eyes strained cable money American Express. Last resource. Please."[192]

Back came two letters from Maggie Butler, one to Jim and one to Dorothy. To Jim, she chidingly confessed: "I could not find it in my heart to forgive you for what you did in marrying Dorothy as you did with out telling me or with out any thing to provide for her. Now I get a cable from Dorothy saying you had to have one hundred and seventy five dollars for eye strain. What does it mean. Is it an operation on your eyes, or is it a hoax to get money for Dorothy." Maggie vowed she would send money only if it were for his eyes or for a ticket to send Dorothy home. Ending on a conciliatory note, she mentioned having had Jim's mother and his Aunt Ella over for tea and that she liked them a lot. Jim's brother Jack, too, was a fine boy.[193]

Maggie came down more severely on Dorothy: Dorothy, she said, was lying when she claimed James had sold his book, was working hard, and had strained his eyes. "I am sure I would not be so crazy for a man that I would have to keep him. What is more you had a good home. You got into a family that I would rather see you dead than mary into his mother is so ignorant well I put up with all because I loved you now you want me to keep him well I *wont* now you and your man have got to pay me back. . . . If you are starving to death over there you come home and let Jimie go home his aunt can take care of him and I can you. I cannot trust you I feel you have done such terrible dastardly things there is nothing I can believe you say."[194]

The Farrells got the $175. Jim wrote Ed Bastian: "Nothing to recount except some unexpected money came like a blessing from Jesus."[195] One week later, Dorothy wrote a promissory note to her mother: "I promise to pay Margaret F. Butler on or before October 5, 1932, one hundred and seventy-five dollars ($175) for value received." In a separate statement, Jim in effect cosigned the note, promising to pay the money to Maggie from "royalties accruing to me from the Vanguard Press . . . on my novel *Young Lonigan*, and on a novel yet unnamed which deals with scenes in an express office."[196]

Jim and Dorothy believed the birth of their baby could come any day. At first, they had planned to move into a warmer apartment near Sam and Riva Putnam in Fontenay-aux-Roses. Then they decided that they could get to the hospital more quickly from a Paris location. Peter Neagoe recommended the Hôtel de la Paix at 325, boulevard Raspail. It was near the rue Delambre and the juncture of the boulevard Raspail and the boulevard du Montparnasse. A taxicab would be easy to get. Jim went there and engaged a comfortable room on the second floor. They used some of Maggie's $175 to pay off debts to friends and to Sceaux merchants. Some went for long-overdue rent. But they arranged with Mme. Prévost to leave while still owing four months' rent—six hundred francs. She kept a few of their belongings and their trunks. They kept the remaining money to give them a running start in Paris.[197]

On 24 November, the day Dorothy wrote her promissory note, she and Jim moved from Sceaux into Paris. They piled their bags into the taxicab driven by Bazin, Pierre-Jean Robert's roommate, who took them to their new home. They were back in Montparnasse, awaiting the arrival of their child.[198]

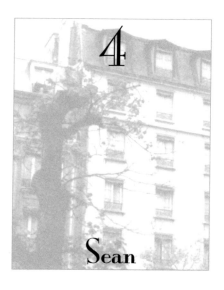

4

Sean

WITH THE BABY expected any day, Dorothy stayed close to the hotel. Jim got back to work on "The Madhouse" at the table in their room; when he went out, they tried to keep in touch. Perhaps laying the groundwork for getting more money from home, Dorothy wrote to her cousin Isabel Simpson that her meager teacher's salary had been cut.[1] Jim worried that Dorothy or the baby might die in childbirth. But if all went well, "how was he going to support a family? How could he do this and still write? . . . The uncertainty weighed upon him." He was moody and often brooded about the situation he and Dorothy were in. Yet he was glad to be in the city he had come to love. And beneath all his worries, there bubbled up a joyful pride in becoming a father. He hoped the baby would be a boy. Altogether "there was much joy, much sympathy, much fun, and . . . many good moments. And there was his work."[2]

In early December, Farrell's hope for the future rose. Maybe, after all, he could remain a writer while supporting a family. Pierre-Jean Robert had dropped by to see the Farrells. He reported that Ramon Fernandez liked *Young Lonigan,* and he believed the NRF would accept the book within a week. He estimated that Jim could expect to earn twelve thousand francs from the NRF edition of *Young Lonigan.* All of that was good news. Jim urged him to hurry up the brother Gallimards' decision. In addition, Jim was becoming more confident that Vanguard would publish his short stories.[3]

Best of all was the encouraging word from Jacob Schwartz in London. On 1 December, Schwartz offered to buy Farrell's story "A Casual Incident" for three pounds, which would pay Jim's fare to London and back; he would pay for Jim's room for a week and feed him dinner each night. "This all means that I really (no hot air) like your stuff . . . [and] I'll try to steer you amongst the *decent* literary agents and publishers." To top it off, Schwartz thought he might "take a flyer on your novel . . . and I think with Pound's and my help we'll land your first novel over the top and get the *best* English reviews—and if we do *that*—then *all* the American publishers will throw thousands of bucks to you for a mere scrap." Avoid that hot-air Harmsworth crowd, he warned Jim, and keep away from Titus, "the meanest punk in Paris."[4] Farrell swung into action. With the baby coming, he could not go to London, but for 128 francs, borrowed from Ed Bastian, he cabled Henle to send *Young Lonigan* galleys to Schwartz.[5]

Ed, who often felt lonely in Paris, was a regular visitor to the Farrells at the Hôtel de la Paix. In their late night talks, he and they drew sustenance from each other. Ed wrote to his mother, Laura Bastian: "I have always been thankful that he [Jim] is in Paris, for there are so many common interests between us and he has a certain hardboiled good sense that probably does me good." Jim's hard times did not diminish Ed's confidence in him. "I have faith in Jimmy Farrell; he will get out, he will get out," he assured his mother. Yet, realistically, Ed observed, "Jimmy's situation is always in potentialities; he told me the other day that there were forty-eight short stories of his in the hands of American, English, and French publishers."[6]

The potential for greater security opened up with a letter Farrell received in December from Riva Putnam. She had been talking with Maeve Sage, manager of transition's Paris office and the wife of Robert Sage, formerly an associate editor of transition. Jim agreed with Riva that a letter to Mrs. Sage offering whatever editorial assistance she might need at this time was worth a try. He asked Riva to forward his letter to Mrs. Sage: "It might lead to a job." So far as is known, Mrs. Sage did not make him an offer.[7]

Anticipating the coming birth, Jim wanted to be closer to the American Hospital while Dorothy was there. He arranged to move into the apartment shared by Don Sewarts, Tom Squires, and Maurice Rausch at 15, quai de Bourbon on the Ile Saint-Louis during her hospitalization.[8] A few days later, on 8 December, Jim took her to the hospital. She was attended by Dr. Boeffe de Saint-Blaise and Doctor Harrington, an American obstetrician. For twenty-two hours, Dorothy suffered severe contraction pains before Sean, weighing eight pounds, was born, by instrument, at 2:30 in the afternoon of the next day.[9] During Dorothy's labor, Jim stayed by her side until she ordered him out. He got a bite to eat in a café in Neuilly, then returned, pacing the hallway, hearing her screams and afraid she would die.

"I was screaming," Dorothy remembered, "and Harrington said, 'Stop screaming!' and Dr. Boeffe just came over and pinched my cheek and said—I'll never forget it—'That's all right. C'est toi, Bébé,'—he called me Bébé—'That's all right. You scream as much as you want.' He was very sweet." Sean, apparently healthy but weakened by the difficult birth, was taken to the nursery. Dorothy, greatly fatigued, was returned to her room, where Jim saw her briefly.[10]

After Sean's birth in the delivery room, Dr. Boeffe came to Jim in the hospital corridor to tell him he had a son. "He was a small, and slightly plump man with gray hair, a gray moustache, and twinkling, confident eyes. . . . I spluttered my thanks to him."[11] Jim returned to the apartment to get a few hours' sleep. Pierre looked him up and took him to a restaurant on the Boulevard du Montparnasse, where he treated Jim to dinner and a bottle of good wine.[12]

In his Paris notebooks, Farrell described his elation at becoming a father. The morning after the birth, he wrote Riva Putnam that "Dorothy had a rough time from 5 the afternoon before — was resting all right when I left the Hosp yesterday. Baby all right also."[13] The next three days, he spent most of his time in the hospital with Dorothy. But he made quick trips to Montparnasse "to see all of my friends whom I could find to announce the news."[14] He talked with Ed Bastian, dropped by the United States Students and Artists Club, and walked the streets and ate dinner with Pierre-Jean Robert. On the third day following Sean's birth, Dorothy was permitted to hold her baby for a few minutes. Jim saw him in the nursery: he was taking oxygen; his face was clear, his head well formed, his eyes blue.

Sean died at 5:45 on the morning of 13 December. Farrell was awakened at that time by a telephone call and went immediately to the hospital. That morning, it fell to him to break the news to Dorothy — to comfort her and answer questions. According to Ed Bastian, Dr. Boeffe assured them after Dorothy "had recovered somewhat from the birth, that he had had to choose between her and the baby; that if he had wanted to save the baby, he would have been obliged to cut her even more than he did — which would probably have meant her death." Dorothy confirmed Ed's account: "Thank God I lived. That's why they kept me so long. A matter of touch and go. The baby died, but I lived." Ed wrote his mother later that the Farrells told him Dr. Boeffe said Sean "had had convulsions and had died of internal hemorrhages. It," he wrote, referring to Sean, "seems to have been completely fatigued at its birth." In January, Jim wrote to Tom Freeman: "The basic cause of . . . [Sean's] death was the fact that the birth was very difficult, and also three weeks or so overdue."[15]

After being with Dorothy, Jim went to the morgue, where he saw Sean, well-formed and with dark hair, and, Farrell thought, looking like his father. On Sean's death certificate, Dr. Boeffe de Saint-Blaise certified the cause of death as bronchopneumonia. His body was cremated, and the burial was in the new cemetery at Neuilly-sur-Seine. Jim paid the *embaumeur* one hundred francs for funeral expenses. Dr. Boeffe, in Jim's eyes "a peppery and witty little man, but also very kind and sympathetic," billed Dorothy fifteen hundred francs, but forgave payment.[16]

Dorothy remained in the hospital fifteen days following Sean's death, Jim making daily visits to be with her. Other visitors included Ed Bastian, Pierre, and Sam and Riva Putnam. While Sam was there, he burst out that Sean's death and Dorothy's suffering cast doubt on God's loving providence. He offered to lend Jim money, an offer accepted in a few days.[17] "God only knows what went wrong at the birth," Ed wrote to his mother in Chicago. He noted Dorothy's need for special postnatal medical treatment. "It is natural that Dorothy herself should be broken up about the death, for she had been building her whole future life around the baby; the new unity to her thoughts and emotions which her expectations were creating suddenly melted, on that Sunday morning. . . . Jimmy himself was moved, but not so much as his wife."[18] More than sixty years after Sean died, Dorothy remembered that, broken up as she was, she tried not to show her grief to Jim, "because by that time he was kind of anxious to have the child. . . . We knew for some reason—we suspected—it was going to be a boy, and I think he kind of liked the idea, at that time."[19]

The day Sean died, Jim wrote to Riva Putnam and Kay Boyle. To Riva he noted that Dorothy "feels badly" but "is holding herself together." As for himself: "I was just shot to hell . . . I've got the blues over the way things turned out. . . . I felt rotten as hell."[20] He walked the Paris streets alone "in a sunken mood all day. . . . I realized with a sudden sense of loneliness that I was poor, a stranger in a foreign land, scarcely able to speak the language. . . . The streets of Paris which I had grown to love, suddenly became the streets of a foreign city, not my own. Frenchmen passed me on those streets, a shabbily dressed young man . . . as I walked around, absorbed, my thoughts turned inward, feeling a sense of humiliation."[21] Additional rejections of his short-story submissions to H. L. Mencken and Lincoln Kirstein of *Hound and Horn* did not improve his mood.

That evening, Pierre-Jean Robert tried to rescue Farrell from his funk. Jim wanted a drink but wished to avoid noisy places like the Sélect or the Dôme. Pierre steered Jim to the Sphinx, a new but already famous bordello on the boulevard Edgar-Quinet that Jim had not seen.[22] They would go there only for food and drink. The nightly trade had not yet begun. What Jim saw on the first floor was a large, dimly lit café, chromium-plated, almost deserted, and decorated in red, with a bar and tables. As he relates it in his story "The Girls at the Sphinx," the unnamed character representing Farrell and Sorel (Pierre) ordered beer for themselves and for the young, scantily clad girls, fresh from the country, who soon flock around. The two men refuse to go upstairs. When Sorel mischievously protests the eternal fidelity of the two to their wives, the girls—"so gay and spirited, so attractive"—stormily question their male potency and suggest that Sorel's companion (Farrell) is homosexual. They laugh at him, insult him, and wish he "were *ordure* floating on the Seine. . . . I listened and watched them and liked them," Farrell relates. "We sat there. I forgot myself, my troubles. . . . I had something to forget, a hurt feeling to let sink out of my consciousness. . . . I couldn't help but believe that the cynicism of these girls was merely skin deep. I even envied them this shallow cynicism."[23]

When the dark-eyed girl next to him places his hand on her thigh, he draws it away and pats her head, "as though she were a small girl." He takes out his cheap, shiny cigarette case, "bought for ten cents in New York," and sees her look at it "as a child would at a bright new toy." He hands it to her and assures her she can keep it. She looks with pride at the other girls and speaks out. Pierre translates:

> "'She's saying that she curses you and sings insulting songs about you, and then you give her a present. She doesn't understand you. She wants to know if all Americans are like you.'
>
> "Now the girls became friendlier. I talked about America. . . . They listened and no longer urged us to go upstairs with them. And when we left, they asked us to come back. The dark-eyed girl clutched the tawdry ten-cent cigarette case, looked at me with simplicity on her round and pretty face, and said:
>
> "'Merci, merci bien, m'sieu.'"[24]

Dorothy's memory of the episode remained with her sixty years later: "I remember James once went to a—well, what can I call it?—a whorehouse. He went to visit it. He later described it to me. I don't think he went to partake, but he went with some Frenchman to see this famous place. . . . He told me about it. Yes, I wasn't concerned. My God, when I think about it, he had a lenient sort of woman!"[25]

Two evenings later, as Farrell was passing the Sélect, he was hailed by Gabby and Irma Javsicas, huddling close to a charcoal brazier while sitting at a table with Emma Goldman and Alexander Berkman. Gabby introduced Goldman and Berkman to Jim and he joined the group. Farrell had known Emma's former Chicago lover Dr. Ben Reitman; he had read and admired some of her writings and understood the validity of her disillusionment with the Soviet political system. Gabby and Irma knew that Sean had died. Gabby told Jim that a writer on the *Paris Herald* had praised him as a promising Chicago writer.[26] But what Farrell remembered in their conversation was Gabby's remark, made "in all sympathy, that because Dorothy and I were so hard up financially, the baby's death had been for the better. His remark affected me forcefully. It was wounding. But I took no offense because of it. I thought Gabby just did not understand. . . . When Gabby made this remark, however, Emma Goldman turned quickly and reproved him."[27] When Jim left the table, he had a new appreciation of Emma Goldman as a warm and understanding woman who realized the complexity of his feelings about Sean's brief life and death.

As though echoing his despair at the loss of Sean, Farrell's prospects for publication took a turn for the worse. Within the next few days, he heard from H. L. Mencken, the magazine editor who above all others he hoped would like his writing. Mencken returned his story "Accident" for the second time. It still was too confused and ineffective. In the same envelope, he returned "McGinty King of Ireland," an excerpt from "The Madhouse." It was far too extravagant, he explained, for the *American Mercury*. Along with this letter came one from Henle, whose inclination to publish a collection of Farrell's tales had cooled. He believed it was best to wait and see how well *Young Lonigan* was received. Henle followed up this bad news by returning four tales that Maxim Lieber had given him: they lacked compression and "the almost rigid objectivity which prevails throughout *Young Lonigan*."[28] This dose of bad news was sweetened a little just before 25 December by modest presents of money to Dorothy and Jim from their families and by Titus's final payment for "The Merry Clouters."[29]

The sharpest, most unexpected blow came from Jacob Schwartz. The six critics and editors whom he had asked to read Farrell's manuscripts "all condemned them . . . one thought it [the batch] too coarse, another said it was too artless, but most of them considered it too tough for any consumption and all agreed that they couldn't possibly be printed in England." They all warned Schwartz that if he published Farrell, they would not give him "any more of their stuff to publish." He was "operating business on a shoestring" and had "to consider their tastes." If Jim would send him a tale "that wouldn't rile and discomfort the limeys," he would publish it in "a small edition." He enclosed two shillings and sixpence to cover Farrell's expenses. Schwartz vowed in a later letter to Farrell that personally he liked his writing. He said he had praised it to Kay Boyle and Laurence Vail during their recent visit to London.[30]

Jim later learned that the English writer John Collier, whose poems Schwartz had published in 1931, had violently objected to his tales. Also, one "Alf," of Long Wittenham, England, excoriated the stories. They were "entirely devoid of living quality, and as pornography are merely elementary and unpleasant. They might be printed on toilet paper *and* hung up in urinals—they seem to have no other office."[31] Softening the sting of Schwartz's about-face was a letter from Kay Boyle noting her distress at the news of Sean's death. She wanted to meet the Farrells when she and Laurence Vail came to Paris in a week. "Everything I have ever read of yours I have liked very much and it will make me very happy to talk to you and read more."[32]

Early in January, in a restrained letter to Schwartz, Jim wrote: "It's too bad we couldn't do any business together." He returned the two shillings and sixpence Schwartz had sent him for expenses and noted he had paid one hundred and twenty-eight francs for cablegrams to secure the galleys sent Schwartz. By return mail, Schwartz sent him one English pound and reiterated that personally he had "none but the highest opinion of your work." To Henle, Jim reported that Schwartz turned out to be a louse, as Henle had suspected.[33] He bundled up his Schwartz correspondence and sent it to Sam Putnam. Outraged, Sam forwarded it to Ezra Pound and urged him to write an exposé of Schwartz for the next number of the *New Review*.[34]

Pound replied to Putnam: "Re/Yakie, vott a pewteeful correspondence. How de Zoul scheins outd off hiss eyes!! . . . Do you vantd Jakey's ledders pack? or do I keep 'em and preserve 'em in aspic?? . . . So long as Farrel [sic] is gettin' pubd that seems to me to fill the bill." Jim urged Pound not to write a condemnation of Schwartz. Kay Boyle had told him, he said, that Schwartz "really wasn't a bad guy." He did not want to hurt the Englishman's business. Moreover, he added, the publicity would be bad for him personally.[35]

While Dorothy was in the hospital, Jim kept himself busy visiting her, revising short stories, writing letters, and seeing his friends. He also pored over copies of *Captain Billie's Whizzbang* and copies of old songs and their parodies sent to him by Henle, which he used to spice up the "barbering" and horseplay between the wagon-call clerks in "The Madhouse."[36] He had moved back to the Hôtel de la Paix after ten days on the Ile Saint-Louis. Kay Boyle wrote, and she and Jim arranged to meet for a late-afternoon drink at the Coupole on 23 December after she and Laurence Vail arrived in Paris. That same morning, Jim heard from Pierre-Jean Robert that the NRF had accepted *Young Lonigan* "on principle"; the Gallimards had agreed to publish a French translation.[37] He immediately went to Robert's apartment—the one he shared with Bazin, the taxidriver. Robert told him and Bazin that "on principle" meant that the actual contract and an advance would come but that he must wait. Farrell portrayed Robert's scorn of his bosses: "Ah, you should see the Dubisson [Gallimard] *frères* in their offices. They sit there like fat, sleek business men. Ah, I can't stand them. . . . Those megalomaniacs . . . must take their time. They must spit on art before they publish it."[38] The three men agreed to have dinner that evening at the Dôme.

That afternoon, after telling the good news to the Putnams and to Dorothy in the hospital, Farrell had drinks at the Coupole with Kay Boyle and Laurence Vail. They were joined by Djuna Barnes, Lillian Fiske, and Charles Henri Ford, who had published Farrell's tale "Slob." Responding to Kay Boyle's beauty and vivacity, Jim spoke of his and Dorothy's eight months in Paris and of his Chicago origins. Bob Brown had suggested that the Farrells should spend some time in southern France, where living was cheaper and the climate warmer than in Paris. Kay Boyle was quick to urge the same, especially for Dorothy's sake after the loss of Sean. Jim explained that he wanted to but doubted he could scrape up the money for the visit. Kay gave him a copy of her novel *Plagued by the Nightingale*, which he read and recommended to his sister Mary. Laurence Vail invited Farrell to an evening party to be given the day after Christmas in his studio on the avenue du Maine.[39]

After leaving Kay Boyle and Laurence Vail, Jim ate and drank at the

Dôme with Pierre-Jean Robert and Bazin, as planned. Pierre again assured him of Ramon Fernandez's interest in *Young Lonigan* and promised to arrange a meeting with him. Pierre wanted to translate the novel into French for the NRF edition personally, and the two plotted ways to speed up the go-ahead decision from the Gallimard brothers now that they had accepted *Young Lonigan* "on principle."

In the early morning hours, Bazin proposed that they go to Saint-Germain-en-Laye. It would be a fitting celebration for Jim's success with NRF, and he wanted his friends to see the moated Château Vieux there. The three piled into his taxicab and after a wild ride with many wrong turns they saw the Château at sunrise. Ed Bastian later commented (mistakenly placing the destination as Fontainebleau, which Jim and Dorothy already had visited) that this ride was Farrell's only trip out of Paris. "His year has been fruitful as far as literary production and friendships have been concerned, but he has done no travelling in France. . . . They will return from France without having seen France."[40]

The following day, Jim slept late and had a midday meal with Dorothy at the hospital. He and Ed Bastian had planned to *faire la bombe* (to go on a spree) on Christmas Eve. They joined Pierre-Jean Robert and his current mistress, the American tennis player Ruth Bailey, at a restaurant on the boulevard du Montparnasse. Then as Farrell has described at length in his Paris memoir, the four, joined by Don Sewarts and Tom Squires from the club, spent the evening at the apartment of Kenneth and Mrs. Knoblock on the rue Huysmans. To Farrell's surprise, Padraic and Mary Colum, the Knoblocks' other guests, soon joined the party from their apartment upstairs. Jim, who had read Colum's plays, was especially fond of *Thomas Muskery*, and he let the playwright know it. He mentioned his desire to some day do a book on Irish writers.[41] Colum's response was kindly and open. He questioned Farrell about his use of Chicago Irish in his fiction. As the two men talked, Farrell tried to reconcile in his thoughts this amiable, friendly person, whom he would later describe as "a sweet man, and a gifted one," with the angry, riotous youth who in 1907 resigned from the Abbey Theatre in Dublin after the opening of Synge's *Playboy of the Western World*.[42]

The party broke up at 1:00 A.M. and Jim and Ed then went to Robert's apartment for drinks and food on their way home, stopping off at the Lipp brasserie for coffee.[43]

Jim spent most of Christmas Day with Dorothy in the hospital. He showed her an invitation from the Putnams and Neagoes for a New Year's Eve party. The co-editors of the *New Review* and their wives had invited "the present-day writers and the modern artists of the Left Bank" who were most closely associated with their journal to join them at the Galerie Jeune Peinture on the rue Jacques-Callot and—for drinks—at the requisitioned café across the street. "'We simply had to do it,'" Sam Putnam was quoted as saying. "'It is all part of our offensive against aesthetic boredom.'" Dorothy knew she would not be up to it. She and Jim had to be content with reading about the party in the *Paris Herald* for 2 January. Among the participating artists who exhibited their work were their acquaintances Joseph Stella (whose portrait of Sam Putnam was displayed), George Seldes, Lee Hersch, and Lillian Fiske. Ludwig Lewisohn, Emma Goldman, Thomas MacGreevy, and several dozen others packed the small gallery "to suffocation" and remained in the café to hear the New Year rung in.[44]

Jim and Dorothy also tried to figure out a way to finance a trip to southern France on money Ed Bastian had loaned them for that purpose. But they decided against the trip and kept the money. Jim wrote to Ed: "I've got to straighten up with the hotel and have money to continue existing on . . . we're down to about two hundred francs and need it now." Perhaps they could go "if the Nouvelle Revue deal goes through"—but Farrell knew that was unlikely. He hoped that Henle might advance more money. A week earlier, without making a specific request for another advance, he had written Henle about Sean's death and the toll it was taking on Dorothy. He did not know that Henle received his letter on 28 December, the day Dorothy was released from the hospital, and immediately mailed him one hundred dollars. Jim received the money on 11 January.[45]

Losing no time, he wrote Bob Brown: "I'll know if I'm coming down your way soon. Here's the kind of guy Henle is. He heard I had a lot of trouble, and without my having asked, sent me an additional hundred bucks advance on my first book. After I pay my debts, I'll take stock and see if I can afford to go away." Even with Henle's generous aid, the longer-term future still looked bleak — so bleak that Jim and Dorothy determined not to go south and decided to seek a less-expensive hotel. Jim notified Brown, who replied: "Sorry you're not coming down here. We might be good for each other."[46]

On the day after Christmas, Jim went to the party at Laurence Vail's studio on the avenue du Maine, carrying the box of baby clothes Kay had sent to Dorothy. In 1976, having forgotten that she and Farrell already had met at the Coupole, Boyle recalled in a letter to the author that Jim, as a total stranger, came late to the party:

> A lot of people were in the studio, and most of them were drunk by the time Jim arrived. . . . I can still see him so clearly, with a long shabby overcoat, a wool scarf around his neck, some kind of shapeless hat on his head, and a large cardboard package under his arm. . . .
>
> He stood hesitant, and probably a little drunk in the dark of the doorway, and I couldn't get to him at once because of the people milling around with their glasses in between us, but I called out: "Come in! Who are you?" And he answered: "I'm Jim Farrell, I'm bringing you the baby clothes." The entire roomful of people burst into laughter, shrieks of laughter. It was a ghastly moment. No one there knew that Sean had died, or what the bringing of the clothes meant. I know that neither Laurence nor I laughed, for the figure standing there in the door way was as memorable and as moving as Charlie Chaplin at his most moving moments. (Boyle to the author, 10 April 1976)

Kay Boyle then recalled the conversation she and Laurence Vail had with Jim before he left the party: "By that time, Jim was quite drunk, and we probably were too. . . . I remember so clearly how he said he wanted to be my bodyguard, he wanted to protect me from danger forever, and he told us how strong he was because he had worked in the stockyards in Chicago. I remember that indelibly." Boyle insisted that "that night when he came to the studio is as clear and terrible to me as if it had happened just this evening. . . . It somehow was metaphor for all man's misunderstanding of man, and it remains that metaphor for me. Love and tragedy stood in the doorway, and out of ignorance, men and women laughed like maniacs."[47]

Farrell's brief and muted contemporary record of the party is in a letter to his sister Mary: "Kay's a swell gal, I got drunk at a party at her place the day after Christmas and so did everybody else—No, Dorothy wasn't well and wasn't there."[48]

Farrell read Kay Boyle's 1976 account of what happened at the party a week after she wrote it: "There was no incident of my handing the baby clothes back in such a way that everybody laughed. . . . The party was a party. I got drunk at it, and left, as did others. I talked of books with Donald Friede [of Covici-Friede Publishing Company]. I didn't talk much with Laurence Vail. . . . [He] stripped, but he merely posed and was not belligerent, although I thought he was crazy. . . . The reference to the stockyards gives away the mistaken memory. It is merely dragging in a Chicago cliché. . . . I did not come from back-of-the-yards. . . . It was not my custom to brag that I could fight. I could fight, but somebody had to start the fight with me."[49] "I liked Kay but not most of those at the party. . . . My account is correct. Kay's isn't."[50]

Jim picked up Dorothy at the American Hospital on 28 December and took her to the Hôtel de la Paix. She was weak, and unsteady when walking. She could not reconcile her feelings with the reality of what had happened, and over the next few weeks Jim bore the brunt of her emotional outbursts. While she regained strength at the hotel, Jim worked on his long tale "Their Little Moments of Glory." When it was completed, he sent it off as an entry in a *Scribner's Magazine* contest. Not having

James T. Farrell, early fall
1932 [From *Americans Abroad:
An Anthology*]

Dorothy Farrell, early 1930s
[Courtesy Dorothy Farrell]

The South Shore homes of the Dalys and Farrell, and of Studs Cunningham (*Studs Lonigan*)

Farrell's apartment, 7136 East End Avenue, June 1928–September 1929

Farrell's apartment, 7046 Euclid Avenue, October 1929–November 1930

Farrell's apartment, 2023
East 72 St., November
1930–April 1931

The Cunninghams' apart-
ment at 7822 Luella Avenue,
where Studs died

Rue des Deux Gares, location of Hôtel de l'Ouest, the Farrells' first Paris hotel

Hôtel Victoria-Palace, rue Blaise-Desgoffe, the Farrells' second Paris hotel

Café du Dôme, boulevard du Montparnasse

Samuel Putnam
[Courtesy Morris Library, Southern
Illinois University]

Ezra Pound, 1933 [Arnold
Genthe Collection, Library of
Congress; New Directions
Publishing Company]

Hôtel de l'Académie, rue
des Saints-Pères, the Farrells'
third hotel

Café Sélect, boulevard du Montparnasse

Café aux Deux Magots, place Saint-Germain-des-Prés and boulevard Saint-Germain

Saint-Germain-des-Prés tower, place Saint-Germain-des-Prés

Dominique's restaurant, rue Bréa, where
the Farrell's occasionally ate

Gallimard Publishers (*NRF*), rue
Sébastien-Bottin

Wambly Bald [From
*Americans Abroad: An
Anthology*]

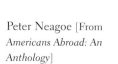

Peter Neagoe [From
*Americans Abroad: An
Anthology*]

Entrance to the Farrells' Sceaux pavillon and, on either side, the rue Chemin-de-fer, now the rue Jean Mascré

Sceaux railroad station

Rue Houdan, Sceaux, where the Farrells shopped

A central square in Sceaux

Jardin de Sceaux

Château de Colbert in the Parc de Sceaux

Virginia Hersch [From *Americans Abroad: An Anthology*]

Bob Brown [From *Americans Abroad: An Anthology*]

Hôtel de la Paix, boulevard Raspail, the Farrells' hotel following their return to Paris from Sceaux

Kay Boyle
[Courtesy Morris Library,
Southern Illinois University]

written home during her hospital confinement, Dorothy now sent letters explaining her silence. To her mother and her cousin Isabel, she explained that she had been hospitalized for a tonsillectomy. Isabel responded that the removal of tonsils was always a shock. Dorothy, she advised, should not work so hard during the current semester.[51]

During the afternoon of New Year's Eve, Dorothy was well enough to receive Kay Boyle and Laurence Vail for a short visit. They brought with them a copy of Bob Brown's *Readies*, fresh from the printer, for Jim to see. Vail laughingly told them about his surrealistic burlesque crime novel, the newly published *Murder! Murder!*, in which the hero, according to Arthur Moss in the *Paris Herald*, "tries to track himself down as the possible murderer."[52] Kay Boyle mistakenly remembered that during this visit "Jim showed me how he painted his sneakers with black liquid—maybe just plain paint—to make them look like leather shoes."[53] That evening, during the first, light snowfall of the season, all of Paris celebrated its gayest night of the year, the traditional Réveillon celebration on New Year's Eve. While their friends partied at the Galerie Jeune Peinture, Jim and Dorothy managed to get to the Sélect, where they sat for an hour feeling lonely and sad. They were in bed and asleep before the New Year came in.[54]

# 5

## Final Days

A S 1932 BEGAN, Jim and Dorothy wanted to hold on in Paris until the spring. Dorothy needed time to regain her strength. Jim hoped that still another advance from Henle, and his first from Gallimard, would help to keep them in Paris. He wanted to be there while the French edition of *Young Lonigan* took shape. Still, he knew that in the United States he would have more opportunities to publish and that he could collect information useful for "The Madhouse." A more basic reason also argued his return. In March, it would be vehemently stated by his Chicago friend George Brodsky: "When are you going from Paris? It's a no-good place for a guy like you. You're someday going to write the 'novel of the city' and you've got to be near it, and in it. Come back home."[1] Jim agreed. Ahead lay the task of completing Studs Lonigan's story and writing his own and his family's stories. He knew that he was an American realist who would be dealing with the American scene and American characters as far into the future as he could see; he felt he belonged at home.

Moreover, he was increasingly sensitive to the difference between his literary intentions and those of other Americans then in Paris, especially the *"transition* maniacs." He read his copy of Bob Brown's *Readies* and gave his reaction to Bob: "Honestly can't go most of the writing. . . . I can't see this Stein, *transition* writing for dust." Bob's strong defense of Stein did not override Farrell's desire to write an article titled "Paris — the Psychopathic Ward of America." And to George Brodsky, he insisted that "most American Parisian writing is sterile or else plain nuts. The city is charming and poetic."[2]

But he had to have money for immediate needs, and he put out feelers in all directions. Sam Putnam let him know that William Targ, an antiquarian bookseller on Chicago's Near North Side, had written expressing his admiration of the tale "Jewboy." Early in January, Farrell wrote two letters to Targ, one proposing a small booklet of his Chicago stories and the other a limited edition of his fifteen-thousand-word tale "Their Little Moments of Glory" (later printed as "Saturday Night").[3] He persuaded Pierre-Jean Robert to translate his tale "Meet the Girls" so that he could submit it to the *Nouvelle Revue Française*.[4] He began negotiating with an editor at the Paris newspaper *Le Figaro* to publish his *Young Lonigan* in serial form.[5] He submitted an article "Observations of American Life and American Literature" to Edward Titus, who rejected it as too fragmentary and inchoate.[6] He asked his friend Lloyd Stern in New York to interest the *New York Times* in employing him as its Parisian book reviewer.[7] And at Ezra Pound's request, transmitted through Sam Putnam, he sent Pound "Jewboy" and "The Scarecrow" because Pound wanted to have one of them translated and published in Italy.[8] These efforts came to nothing.

Ed Bastian wanted to help Jim find work. Through his visits to the American University Union he recently had come to know its director, Horatio S. Krans. Krans moved easily among well-to-do Parisian Americans. He was widely known throughout the city for his generous support of worthy causes and persons. Shepherded by Ed, Jim spoke with Krans in the union's Paris office at 173, boulevard Saint-Germain and explained his need. Krans promised to do his best to find a suitable job for him, in view of Jim's "urgent need of remunerative work." As a goodwill gesture, he sent Jim and Dorothy tickets to the Odéon for Racine's "Béjazet" and Franc-Nohain's "La Belle Eveillée." A week later, he loaned them some money. But the *crise* in France was taking hold. Krans found no job for Farrell.[9]

Bob Brown tried to help Jim make a little money. He was selling *Readies* for fifty francs and offered to give him a 50 percent discount on copies that he could sell personally and a 10 percent discount for copies he could persuade bookstores to order. Not wanting to become a book agent, Jim turned Brown down, but did ask several bookstores in Paris and the United States to stock *Readies*. He sent Bob Brown the names of various Paris bookstores to contact and offered to try to get Eve Adams to sell the book.[10]

Farrell put in what time he could on his longer fiction. He turned again to section three of "The Madhouse." By one week into the new year, he had four hundred pages beyond those already sent to Henle. Bothered by a random quality in his story, he began trying to make it more coherent by giving either McGinty or Willie Collins, a successor to McGinty as chief dispatcher, more of a unifying role throughout. But soon he admitted that he was "coming along rottenly."[11] Each section opened up its own lines of interaction between the workers and the boss then in control.

With the arrival of Vanguard's catalog listing *Young Lonigan*, his attention was diverted to that novel, now in proofs. He racked his brains for potential American buyers of his book and gave Henle sixty-three names of persons in the United States to send the catalog to. Word came from Henle's assistant, Alexander Schlosser, that Frederic M. Thrasher, formerly of the University of Chicago Sociology Department and presently associate professor of education at the Washington Square branch of New York University, had agreed to write the introduction to *Young Lonigan* and needed biographical information from Farrell. Jim put together a brief vita and sent it on to Schlosser. Now that *Young Lonigan* would soon be out, he wryly remarked to his sister Mary: "I only got to sell 1742 copies before I start making money which I haven't drawn advances on, or borrowed on." The first edition sold less than one-third of that number.[12]

Jim Henle's unsolicited check for one hundred dollars, sent in sympathy after learning of Sean's death, was soon eaten up by payments on debts. Within one week, Jim was explaining to Tom Freeman: "Gone busted again and trying to figure out a way to get back to NY."[13] His friend Bus Stern assured him from New York that the American consul in Paris could arrange to send the Farrells home.[14] Bob Brown, head of a family of five, had a plan for returning home that he shared with Jim. He would set sail "as soon as I run through the remnants of seventy thousand dollars I had this time last year. My God how it has dwindled . . . you can appeal to the American Society in Paris and they'll put you and your wife on a freighter, pay the fare and send somebody down to make sure you get off."[15]

Ed Bastian noted the Farrells' "precarious" situation and Jim's concern: "The Farrells are living on what the American publishers send them from time to time on the future royalties of the book. . . . The Farrells' situation . . . is sorry and uncertain. For they are thinking seriously of returning to America in the next couple months, sooner if Jimmy can gather in no money. . . . Besides, Farrell is not content with the literary connections he has made in Paris."[16]

Although not content, Farrell was still trying to cement those connections. Ezra Pound had agreed to read the *Young Lonigan* proofs. On

6 January, Jim wrote to him that he had just recently asked his publisher Henle to send a copy of the proofs to Pound. He hoped Pound might write a blurb for the book. That same day, after a telephone call from Pierre-Jean Robert, he made an appointment to see Ramon Fernandez and Pierre two days later. They were to discuss the terms of Farrell's contract for a French edition of *Young Lonigan*. Farrell described the meeting in "My Friend, Jean Paul." He waited a long time in an outer office while the members of the firm conferred. Instead of feeling joy and triumph, he felt anxious, nervous, depressed — like a helpless stranger. Eventually, Ramon Fermandez appeared. He was gracious and praised the book.[17]

They agreed on a contract calling for an advance of fifteen hundred francs when the book was translated and the same amount upon publication. Farrell's royalties were 10 percent on the first ten thousand copies sold, 12 percent thereafter. Gallimard retained the rights of preemption on his next four books. At the urging of Pierre but against his better judgment, Jim agreed to personally hire Pierre as the translator by paying him two-fifths of his royalties for the translation. To his sister Mary, he wrote: "I'm giving a hog's share of my royalties to the translator to get a decent job done," and, he hoped, to expedite publication — which would not come until 1934. Walking home from his interview, he felt despondent. He had sold *Young Lonigan* to Gallimard but had received no advance, and he would not get one even when the contract was finalized. Ed Bastian dropped in to see them that night, but found no sign of celebration — a contract that carried no hard cash with it would not pay the bills.[18]

Word from Kay Boyle, back from England, picked up Jim's spirit. She reported that Desmond Harmsworth now wanted to see the proofs of *Young Lonigan* with a view to possible publication in London. Also Harmsworth and Wyn Henderson had been visiting her in Cagnes. Both she and Bob Brown had praised his writing to them. But the one set of proofs within Jim's reach was with the NRF, and Pierre convinced Jim not to mail them off. He needed them for his ongoing translation.

Ezra Pound read the *Young Lonigan* proofs sent him by Henle. In a letter to Farrell, he ruled that the beginning needed to be tightened and that its effect was "a bit too much Joyce of the *Portrait.*" Joyce's and Farrell's characters, he granted, "were all oirish, and the ijum [idiom] the same. Only escape there is to keep the langwudg but change the rhythm or movement of the printed page. . . . Thought yr/ stuff in Readies damn good," he added.[19] At Jim's request, Pound then sent the proofs to Harmsworth, who already had written Farrell that he wanted them. Jim's hopes rose.[20]

Farrell learned of Caresse Crosby's new publishing venture, Crosby Continental Editions. She planned a series of inexpensive reprints of avant-garde writing and began it in December with Hemingway's *The Torrents of Spring.* After talking with New York publishers, she had returned to Paris on 22 January and made known her intention to produce "popular priced, readable books of good quality" for Europeans and Americans. "I am on the lookout for works which might interest them." She announced her plan to publish books by Dorothy Parker, John Dos Passos, and Maurice Hindus. Copies would cost approximately nineteen francs. Here, Farrell believed, was an opportunity for a combined European and American edition of *Young Lonigan.* "I am going to try the proofs out on the Crosby outfit also," he wrote to Pound, "because after all one has to live." This plan, too, fell through.[21]

Dorothy's recovery continued to be slow. "Dorothy is all right," Jim wrote Tom Freeman, "but not as well as she might be."[22] He was becoming convinced that the hospital had botched the birth. Ed Bastian, trying to be encouraging, nevertheless picked up their worries and uncertainties. He wrote his mother: "Dorothy may have to undergo an operation in a month or so; God only knows what went wrong at the birth, but if she does not attend now to the trouble, it will get worse, her doctor says, and show itself more viciously if she ever has another child. I do not know whether it is the shortcoming of somebody at the American Hospital or not which is responsible for this, and neither do the Farrells."[23]

Worried about Dorothy and finances, in mid-January Jim began looking for a less expensive yet comfortable place to live. He asked Rev. Harold Belshaw at the United States Students and Artists Club for help. He already had asked Belshaw if he knew of any wealthy American who might loan him money on the strength of his NRF contract. Belshaw did not, but he did find them a place to live at Le Home Joli, which advertised itself as a *Hôtel recommandé aux familles*. It was a fairly modern structure located at 7, square Grangé, a small square, with buildings on three sides, opening onto the rue Glacière just north of the boulevard Arago. For three hundred francs a month, they rented a furnished, one-room kitchenette apartment on the sixth floor, with an electric burner to cook on. The furnishings were drab and the brownish carpet was worn. They soon found out that the advertised "chauffrage central" was no match for the piercing cold they had to endure that winter. When not active inside, it was best to be under a blanket or wrapped with one. The Farrells moved into their final home in Paris on Saturday, 20 January, and the next evening had Ed Bastian to dinner.[24]

Ed, carrying a bottle of burgundy wine, was back with them a few days later on his twenty-second birthday. He reported to his mother that "Dorothy had baked a white cake for me which was eatable for an experiment on her part (inasmuch as she never did any cooking, at home, nor even touched housework, I believe); and we accompanied the cake with great square crackers smeared with Roquefort cheese, and, too, coffee [and] cherry brandy."[25] Since Dorothy had offered to darn his socks, he brought eleven tattered pairs with him and in return gave Jim, who needed handkerchiefs, six of his own.[26]

Having company dispelled some of Dorothy's loneliness and cheered her up. Lawrence Drake dropped by Le Home Joli. So did Pierre's roommate Bazin, the hearty, pleasure-loving Basque taxicab driver, who was making a habit of it. He liked the Farrells and sometimes generously lent them money. Dorothy, especially, was diverted by his melodramatic tales about his loves and adventures abroad, the fortunes he had won and lost. She grew fond of this "jolly fat little old Frenchman."[27] She and Jim entertained the Knoblocks, the Putnams, and Ed Bastian on 1 February. Jim had been reading some Faulkner novels and had begun to reread *Ulysses*. The talk that evening went from Faulkner, whom Kenneth Knoblock had known in New Orleans, to Joyce, and then to Proust, whom Ed was still avidly reading. Jim observed how Dorothy's spirits perked up when she was with friends—no matter what was being discussed.

Ironically, Dorothy as well as Jim tried to avoid their nearest neighbors. Larry and Jane Cohen lived above them at Le Home Joli. The Farrells and Cohens had met at the United States Students and Artists Club, where the Cohens were known as "the mystery couple" who loved to play bridge. Jim discovered that Larry was a Harvard graduate and a rich man's son. He "was supposed to be on some kind of . . . fellowship to study something about French workers. I never got it clearly. He seemed to be a bit mysterious." Jim and Dorothy did not like to play bridge. Furthermore, they sensed in the Cohens some of the qualities they had disliked in the Menkens. They kept their unavoidable meetings with their neighbors as brief as possible.[28]

One night, as related in "Paris Was Another Time," Eddie Ryan (Farrell) is lying on the sofa-bed in their room at Le Home Joli while Marion (Dorothy) is washing the dishes. He is so absorbed in reading Faulkner's *The Sound and the Fury* that he fails to notice Marion watching him closely. She feels ignored, jealous of the book, "dead to the world as far as he was concerned." When he becomes aware of her serious expression while watching him, he smiles apologetically. "It was a matter of Marion's life, as well as . . . his own life. He could give her so little of life. He feared this . . . he was also fearfully jealous. What he couldn't give her, maybe somebody else would. . . . But his work. His work came first. It had to. And reading was as much . . . a part of his work as writing was." Eddie feels "self-reprobation and . . . guilt." Then Marion smiles brightly at him. They both break into laughter when she says "I'm going to darn your socks."[29]

Dorothy's dark moods, in evidence since the loss of Sean, were unpredictable. When severe, they climaxed in a tumultuous venting of unfocused anger and a sense of hopelessness. Her loneliness, their poverty, her feeling that life in the Paris she loved was passing her by, all helped to sink her into temporary spells of depression. More than once, while Jim was busy at work, she unexpectedly burst into sobs, saying "I want my baby."[30] Jim, half-way understanding her feelings, felt guilty and a little resentful of the turmoil. But her moods passed swiftly.

Seeking a change and some recreation, they spent an afternoon at the United States Students and Artists Club, where Farrell hoped he could find someone to lend him money. They had walked there in bitterly cold weather, and Jim's feet hurt. His only shoes were falling apart. He liked to dance, but for the most part he watched Dorothy dancing with others. The rough wooden floor was splintered in spots. Jim was afraid that a sliver might enter his foot through the holes in his shoes. Already in debt and—as Ed Bastian observed—"scraping poverty," he wondered how he could get not only a new pair of shoes but food to eat. He mentioned his plight to Don Sewarts and Tom Squires.[31]

The Farrells were soon down to their last franc. They were hungry, with no food in the house, and no soap. Nothing had "happened," no help had come through. Which should they buy—bread or soap? They chose bread. Farrell has told the story in his tale "Soap." Dorothy remembered: "That was a real story! We were so poor at that one time. That was the poorest we ever were. . . . We didn't have anything. Nothing."[32] When the bread was devoured, they decided to raise cash by pawning Jim's portable typewriter; he could use his pen. As they crossed the rue Delambre, Jim limping while lugging the typewriter, Dorothy picked up a twenty-franc note—unbelievably good luck. The pawnshop owner refused to take the typewriter without a bill of sale, long since discarded. They remembered the friendly owner of the Hôtel de l'Académie on the rue des Saints-Pères, where they had stayed in the spring. Would he exchange some cash for the typewriter? At the hotel, the proprietor gravely considered the request from the writer who had spent hours at his typewriter in his hotel room. No, he would not take the typewriter, but he would let Jim pawn his inexpensive fountain pen. "Can you imagine such a thing?" Dorothy recalled. "His *fountain* pen! He wouldn't take the typewriter, but he said: 'You can pawn your fountain pen.'" The Farrells left, twenty francs richer, with forty francs they had gained that day.[33]

The Gallimard contract for *Young Lonigan* arrived in the mail the very next day. With it came Ramon Fernandez's undated two-page type-script, headed with vernacular formality as "Mr. Fernandez Looks at 'Young Lonigan.'" As Farrell read, he could not believe his good fortune. Jubilant, he savored such passages as these:

> These boys and girls . . . have learned all that the street so quickly teaches; yet all the while, they remain naive, for the reason that the majority of them do not as yet know what it means to live. . . . These young ones are waiting for the thing for which they long to come to them . . . as in that exquisite scene of the pair in the tree, one of the most telling, and one of the most touching, which I have read in a long time.
>
> It is this feeling for youth and for what lies "ahead" that gives Mr. Farrell's work a psychological aura, so to speak, that is altogether delightful. At the same time, it permits a wholly realistic vision, which is none the less poetic for all that. . . . Nothing could be more "pure" than this novel, if by purity one means, at once freshness and a clear-seeing eye. The author's stroke has to be heavy at moments, in order to show how delicate it is.

Ramon Fernandez, Farrell felt, was someone who understood what he had tried to do.

Jim lost no time showing Fernandez's statement to Sam Putnam. In "Paris Was Another Time," Eddie (Farrell) relates his friend's reaction: "'You can't hope for anything better than this, Eddie . . . there's no need to fear; you ought to get off to a flying start here in Paris once your book's translated and put into circulation. You don't need a bigger name than Ferdinand Reyes [Ramon Fernandez] behind you. His support counts all over Europe; and even back in New York too.'"[34]

How, Farrell asked himself, could Gallimard refuse him an advance now? He decided first to seek Ramon Fernandez's active intercession, while thanking him for his report on *Young Lonigan*. The two men met at the critic's apartment on the Ile Saint-Louis. Fernandez spoke English fluently, and Farrell was impressed with his wide-ranging, discursive mind. Each had recently read Robert and Helen Lynd's *Middletown*, and their discussion turned to social conditions and literary trends in the United States. After an hour, Farrell left, feeling he had a friend in his corner.

With Ed Bastian to act as his translator, Farrell then arranged for an interview with Gallimard officials on 8 February. The two friends met at the Sélect for coffee, then trudged to Chez Gallimard. The winter's "big freeze" for 1932 had begun, and Jim's feet were miserably cold, wet, and sore by the time they arrived.[35] They were permitted to speak only with Bruce Parrain, NRF's financial director. His answer was brief and decisive. An advance was impossible. The company's expenses were heavy, *la crise* was hurting business, and Farrell was an unknown author in France. Ed Bastian's account to his mother concluded: "So Jimmy will have to wait for his advances till the translated manuscript is handed over to the company (1,500 francs then)."[36]

Walking back to Le Home Joli in the stinging wind, Jim felt deeply depressed. If only he had twenty-five dollars a week to live on; he knew that Ed Bastian saved money from the monthly remittance of 150 dollars from his family. In his frayed and spotted suit, his thin shabby overcoat, and his disintegrating shoes, he felt helplessly different from his Parisian friends and acquaintances, both French and American. He felt impotent and isolated. With no *carte de travail*, he was cut off from remunerative employment of any kind, and his writing offered merely token support. He had no money to buy a new pair of shoes. He felt shame, humiliation, and surges of anger.

The next afternoon, Farrell walked to Pierre-Jean Robert's apartment on the rue Guilleminot and found both Pierre and Bazin at home. Pierre noticed Jim's shoes, flapping on the sides. "'Man, you can't wear those on your feet,'" he said, and Jim answered: "'I know I can't. But I've got to.'"[37] Pierre's shoe size was smaller than Jim's. He went to his closet and returned with a pair of white sneakers and a can of brown shoe polish. The sneakers were tight but wearable. Pierre smeared the brown polish on the sneakers to make them look like "winter" shoes, admired his handiwork, and said "It's not too bad."[38] Before Jim left, Bazin pushed a few francs into his pocket.

The cobblestones hurt his feet as he walked home on his thin crepe-rubber soles, but he admitted to himself that the sneakers were much better than his worn-out shoes. When he entered his apartment that evening, Dorothy noticed him limping and saw the tennis shoes. As Farrell tells the story in "Paris Was Another Time," Marion (Dorothy) bursts out:

> "But these are only tennis shoes. You'll catch your death of cold wearing them this time of the year."
> "It's all I have to wear, Marion."
> At first what Eddie said did not sink in on Marion. . . . Then she started to cry. Her face crumbled and fell apart, much the way a child's face does.

Dorothy decided it was time to act. She and Jim laid plans for the morning. Before Dorothy went to bed, she sewed a red flannel remnant into his overcoat as a lining to keep him warm.[39]

The next day, Jim sent a *pneumatique* to Ed Bastian, asking for another loan, this time to buy shoes. Then he walked to the American University Union headquarters and borrowed seventy-five francs from Horatio Krans to cover the amount Dorothy needed to send a cablegram to her mother: "Will be destitute today money absolutely necessary please cable American Express."[40] Ed Bastian came through. He went with Jim to buy shoes. New and stiff, they hurt the blisters on Jim's feet.

Maggie cabled one hundred dollars. In a letter to Jim, she asked if his eyes were the problem. She said she had heard that Dorothy was not teaching, that she had not graduated from the university, that Jim had known it, and that "she went away because she expected to become a mother . . . now James is it true please for my sake tell me the truth. . . . I cannot believe everything Dorothy tells me. Now James dear I am so sorry. . . . You know my dear when you love my Dorothy I can love you just like one of my own children, but I do not know you much." Come back home, she pleaded, "if you cannot make a go of it."[41]

Jim's new shoes hurt his blistered feet. He remained indoors in his stocking feet for two days and used the opportunity to write letters to editors and friends. He typed a copy of his NRF contract for Henle, who later assured him that he could keep all the royalties from the sale of the Gallimard edition.[42]

The Putnams had not seen the Farrells for some time. Now that Jim had failed to receive an advance from Gallimard, they were even more concerned about the younger couple's poverty and isolation. Sam had been working steadily translating Pirandello's latest play, *Questa sera si recita a soggello (Tonight We Improvise)*. He advertised it in his *New Review* as "a new Pirandello play, possibly the greatest; probably one of the world's great dramas."[43] Pirandello recently had come to Paris and the two men were consulting frequently. His play *L'Homme, la bête, et la vertu* had enjoyed a successful November run at the Saint-Georges Theatre, and his *As You Desire Me* was scheduled for a future performance.[44] Sam arranged for a public reading of his translation of the new play on 9 February, with Pirandello present to greet the guests. It was held at the apartment of Willard and Mary Widney, a young, independently wealthy American couple whom Sam had befriended and who were interested in avant-garde art and jazz. "The Widneys," he wrote, "were popular and intelligent hosts and they and their cocktail parties were popular."[45]

Farrell had mentioned his unpublished 1928 article on Pirandello to Sam. Sam knew of Jim's youthful interest in the dramatist, dating from his viewing in the 1920s of *Six Characters in Search of an Author* at the Cube and at the Goodman Theater in Chicago. He and Riva decided to take the Farrells with them to the reading. But the play and the reading did not reignite Farrell's interest in Pirandello's writing.[46] Pirandello was a likable, simple old man, but the play was average. The party, Dorothy said, "was in one of those old big French apartments. . . . And I remember we had wonderful hors d'oeuvres and champagne. . . . Oh that was a very fancy party, yes."[47] For Dorothy, it provided a welcome break. To Jim, it gave a brief glimpse of the unpretentious, grandfatherly writer, and an unsettling sense of the life, so different from his own, led by wealthy Left Bank residents.

"Paris Was Another Time" reveals his depressed state of mind: "He didn't know what they were going to do. His hopes that *Young Jed Jennings* [the equivalent in the tale to *Young Lonigan*] might have brought some money and security had gone down the drain. He had believed in taking his chances; he had quoted Nietzsche about 'living dangerously.' . . . Their days in Paris were numbered. . . . As the danger of their having to return to America increased, Eddie [Jim] loved Paris all the more. He wanted to be able to remain in the city."[48] At such gloomy times, Farrell wryly had to agree with Mike Gold. A recent letter from his friend Lloyd Stern, who had spoken with Mike in New York, reported: "Gold says you will lose your ass in Paris."[49]

Having seen Jim's disintegrating shoes, Don Sewarts and Tom Squires spoke to their friend Kathleen Coyle, the Irish novelist, about the Farrells' poverty. Coyle was then living in Paris with her two children. She offered to ask her friend Gabriel Marcel, the Roman Catholic philosopher, to urge his close friend Ramon Fernandez to persuade the Gallimard brothers to give Jim an advance. She invited the Farrells, along with Don and Tom, to her one-room pension at 85, boulevard de Port-Royal. Jim knew of her novels but had not read them. That evening, both he and Dorothy found this frail, crippled woman completely captivating — simple, warm, sensitive, courageous. She had just submitted the manuscript of *The French Husband*, her most recent novel, to her publisher, Dutton, in New York. Like Farrell, she was trying to support her family by her writing.[50] Jim quickly realized that Kathleen Coyle "understood poverty as well as suffering. . . . This was why he had liked her so readily on this first meeting; she seemed a genuine friend."[51]

Before the evening ended, it was arranged that Coyle would speak to Gabriel Marcel about the Farrells and thus pave the way for a visit from Jim. Within a few days, Farrell made his way to Marcel's home at 23, rue Émile-Dubois. The philosopher received him cordially and agreed to write to Fernandez and the NRF.[52] Assured of this support, Jim visited Fernandez again to restate his need for an advance. But he soon learned from Pierre that the critic's intervention had not prevailed. The Farrells continued to exchange visits with Coyle while they remained in Paris, and they introduced her to Ed Bastian and other friends. With characteristic generosity, Kathleen Coyle tried, but failed, to secure Ed a summer teaching appointment in Switzerland.[53]

Don Sewarts and Tom Squires also spoke with Reverend Belshaw. They told him the Farrells planned to leave Paris within two months, but in the meantime were in danger of eviction. Reverend Belshaw asked Don to tell Jim that he would lend him two hundred francs a week for the next eight weeks; not much, but enough to help see them through. They received the first installment in February.[54]

As Jim approached his twenty-eighth birthday, he took stock of what he had accomplished in Paris. He thought of his Chicago friend George Brodsky, a classmate in Professor Linn's advanced creative writing class English 210. Together in Chicago, they had mapped out their separate paths to literary fame. "Since being over here," he confided to George, "I rewrote, revised, proofread 4 times my 1st novel, and have done almost 1,000 pages of work on the second one. Besides, I've written a number of new and revised and retyped a number of old stories, have written hundreds of letters, done some reading, tried in odd moments to read a French grammar, and have had a number of mundane problems, some of them very serious."[55]

He admitted to George that in Chicago he had written even more. But in Paris he had had to contend not only with the editorial tasks of seeing *Young Lonigan* through, but also the challenging nature of "The Madhouse," which was "something of an experiment. . . . My pen," he continued, "is not run dry by a damn sight. I am, however, taking more time and trying to learn more about writing. . . . What little success I've had so far has been gained by sticking to my own blundering methods and not taking his [Teddy Linn's] expert advice, not picking my audience and writing to it, not bothering about plot, not worrying about being tasteless enough to offend nostrils as Victorian as his are, in brief, not writing to get an A in English 210." He promised George he would smuggle a copy of *Lady Chatterley's Lover* (banned in the United States) into the country for Brodsky's wife Bella Rubinson Brodsky, an instructor of English at the University of Chicago.[56]

Jim and Dorothy tried to put aside all anxieties on the evening of 27 February, his twenty-eighth birthday. Ed Bastian, Don and Tom, the pianist Maurice Rausch and his girlfriend Catherine, the Knoblocks, and the Kleins joined them for champagne and refreshments (Pierre could not come). With mixed anger and mirth, Fanny Klein told the gathering of a middle-aged American woman, a heavily powdered, expensively dressed platinum blonde, seated in the Café du Dôme on a moderately warm February day feeding scrambled eggs and toast on the table to her fluffy poodle, a *serviette* tied around his neck. With pointed annoyance, the woman refused the plea of two beggarly street musicians, and haughtily stalked out when the *garçon* scornfully bounced her one-franc tip on the table.[57] Don remarked that times were now noticeably more hard, even in Paris; more beggars were on the streets. Everyone agreed.

Ed Bastian injected a more somber note into the conversation. Albert Mathiez, his professor at the Sorbonne, had died of a stroke the day before while lecturing to his class. The discussion turned to the uncertain status of painters, writers, musicians, and educators during a time of economic depression and political dangers. Only when Jim opened his champagne, the first he had purchased in Paris, was the gloom dispersed.

As he liked to say, a party is a party; and for a time the Farrells forgot their personal troubles.[58]

Jim's birthday was followed a week later, on 6 March, by Dorothy's—her twenty-second. They observed it, again with Ed Bastian and their friends from the United States Students and Artists Club. With Albert Mathiez in mind, they all walked to the Musée Carnavalet to see the famous exhibits on the French Revolution. They found the museum closed. Walking back to the Deux Magots, they heard a report that Aristide Briand had just died. At the café, the tables were abuzz with the news.

France went into a period of national mourning for Briand. The day of the funeral was clear and cold. Jim, Dorothy, and Ed Bastian plowed their way to the Place de la Concorde through more than an estimated million onlookers lining the streets in triple rows. The jostling crowd, waiting for the cortege to pass, laughed and jeered at the police who tried to control them. Dorothy marveled at the street periscopes sold by vendors. "People who could not get up close to the curb had these funny little things—tubes, with a mirror on the top and a mirror on the bottom. And they'd stand there looking through those things, and then they could see the procession going by," a black hearse followed by a long, double line of dignified men in dark suits. Afterwards, the three friends ate an early dinner—and warmed up—at the Café Alsacien on the boulevard Saint-Germain.[59]

One week into March, Jim believed that the break he was hoping for had come. Sam Putnam excitedly told him that a letter from Albert M. Newman, a rich American businessman then in Paris, had asked him to recommend a literary man to rewrite his book. Newman had written that he wanted "an American writer living in Europe, preferably with interest in ideas and social questions," someone who could transform Newman's "academic style" into "scintillating and pungent English, who could give me half or full time during the next three or four months."[60] Newman and Farrell met at the Dôme. Jim learned that Newman was a naturalized U.S. citizen born in Russia. His bulky typescript, almost four

hundred pages in length, was titled *Enough for Everybody*.[61] The introduction stated that the author's purpose was to help "England and America avoid the distresses which revolution brought to my native land by
laying out the reasons to create an intelligently planned economy which
will advance (guarantee?) both communal and individual values by non-
violent, constitutional means."[62] Newman offered Farrell five hundred
dollars for a complete revision. He offered him five hundred francs to in-
spect and rewrite chapter one. He wanted the rewriting completed as
quickly as possible. Jim left the Dôme with chapter one under his arm,
fully expecting a temporary solution to his money problems. On five
hundred dollars, he could take Dorothy to the Riviera and pay for their
passage home.[63]

In "Paris Was Another Time," Farrell portrayed Eddie Ryan's (Farrell's)
state of mind as he walks back to Le Home Joli with the good news.
Eddie feels that a great burden has been lifted. But as he goes down the
boulevard Saint-Michel, he begins to have doubts. He had not liked
David Benjamin (Albert Newman). He suspects Benjamin's ideas are
cockeyed. He fears Benjamin will be demanding. Will Benjamin really
give him a free hand in the revision, or will he want him to write untruths
to buttress his theories? And can he reasonably expect to put his own
writing aside for two or three months—even for five hundred dollars?

Hiding his mood from Marion (Dorothy), he takes her to the Restaurant Sainte-Cécile on the boulevard Saint-Germain to celebrate. They
order ten-franc dinners and chateaubriands. But Eddie is reticent and
unenthusiastic, and Marion senses his hidden feelings. She thinks:
"Edward was telling her that he did not want to take this work . . . and
that he was doing it because they needed money, and that maybe it was
her fault." Each reads the other's mind, and each knows that their "celebration" will be spoiled by a quarrel or recriminations.[64]

They decide to go to the Sélect for coffee. There, sitting next to a hot
brazier, they are joined by Richard Metz (Maurice Rausch) and Frances
Frost (Catherine), and Hank and Ida Minton (Mr. and Mrs. Meyer

Handler). They talk about Chicago's financial crisis (like Eddie, Handler was a Chicagoan), the march of Cox's army of unemployed on Washington, D.C., and the danger of war breaking out. Marion and Eddie submerge their differences in the warmth of good companionship.[65] And once again, Eddie wants to sleep with Frances.[66]

Back at Le Home Joli, Jim tested his ability to concentrate on his fiction while he rewrote Newman's chapter one. But the progress on his own writing suffered. He felt revulsion and guilt. He found it difficult to sustain his effort to revise a sloppily reasoned text. Sitting at the cluttered table, he turned compulsively to his short stories and "The Madhouse," which he had decided to call "Gas-House McGinty."[67] Dorothy was not surprised at his worried intensity. She knew that his calling was to write out of his own feelings and ideas, and she had faith in his future. She also knew that without money they could not continue living in Paris. Reluctant to appeal again to her mother, she wrote to her cousin Isabel Simpson, asking for funds to get them home. Unable to help, Izzy informed Maggie Butler, who cabled Dorothy one hundred dollars.[68]

After a week, Farrell returned the revised chapter one to Newman. Although the author angrily disagreed with many of the changes in his text, he finally agreed to pay the five hundred francs. Jim was ready to call off the entire deal, but gave in to Newman's appeal and left the Dôme with chapter two. But it was impossible for him to go ahead. At the Dôme on Saturday, 26 March, Farrell told Newman he was not interested in the job, and he returned chapter two. Surprised and believing he had been treated unfairly, Newman spoke angrily of "temperamental literati." On Sunday, someone — it is not known who — told Farrell that Newman had a poor "Parisian reputation for intellectual honesty, sincerity, and common decency." On Tuesday, Jim received Newman's written complaint coupled with an appeal for him to change his mind. He answered that day in a harsh letter: Newman, he spit out, could not write or think clearly; Newman belonged "in the junk business, and the second-hand clothes racket, rather than in writing."[69] To Ezra Pound, Jim swore that

Newman was "a crook," and to Henle he stated his intention of referring the biggest louse he knew in Paris to Newman to apply for the job he had given up.[70]

Newman was rejected, and so was the five hundred dollars. The Farrells knew that Paris would soon be a memory. They decided to give one more party. Their guests were the Kleins, who were preparing to leave for the States, the Knoblocks, Ed Bastian, Don Sewarts, Tom Squires, and Pierre-Jean Robert. The party was given on the eve of a rumored public execution at dawn at the nearby Prison de la Santé. In "Guillotine Party,"[71] Farrell's fictional account of the gathering, the partygoers enthusiastically plan to climax their evening by attending the execution. "I know that actually happened," Dorothy said emphatically sixty years later. "All these people were avid to see this guillotining. . . . We were both kind of appalled about it. But we entered into it, I'm sure, just as much as everybody else did. You know the way people do . . . when they're sitting down [and] they're going to go out and rob a bank, and everybody's going to do it."[72] In Farrell's tale, while the partygoers await the dawn, their talk flits superficially over a range of topics, such as the causes of war and violence, the Japanese attack on China, and social injustice under capitalistic means of production. No character representing Dorothy is present, but the host speaks up frequently and aggressively. The guests are mildly crestfallen but actually relieved when they learn the guillotining will not occur.[73]

Ed Bastian's firsthand memories of Jim and Dorothy in this and similar social gatherings is more vivid and telling than the portrayal in "Guillotine Party." Jim, he recalled, was not "a calculating man. He was an exuberant man. . . . He seemed to be a very tenacious fellow — reading and writing and loving to talk. . . . I think he was very sociable. . . . He loved society. He loved gossip. I remember him telling me . . . that novelists love gossip. At times he was voluble, at times he was aggressive. I think he was rational, he certainly tried to be. . . . And I think his very sociability carried him along in part. If you were not *quite* certain about yourself, about your associating with people and enjoying their company and discussing ideas, by being sociable you could get over some rough ground."[74]

Ed remembered Dorothy as an "unimpeachable" hostess. He and she were both twenty-two, and "there were times when I thought she was very enticing," with "good hair" and "a good figure." She was rather quiet with others; but with Jim, she was "candid" and open, just as he was candid and cautionary with her. "She supported him, she encouraged him, she never spoke slightingly of his work." So far as Ed could tell, she truly believed in Jim's future as a writer. He noticed the "fondness" she and Jim had for each other. They "cared."[75]

Throughout March, as Jim battled another stubborn cold, he struggled to find time for his writing. Editors were still rejecting his tales, and Henle was lukewarm toward "Chamber of Horrors," the story collection intended to center on the sexual problems of young people. Farrell rethought his plan. He decided to bring together a dozen stories "diverse in material, writing, or treatment," but all of them laid in Chicago. The title of the collection would be *These Chicagoans*. "Among other things," he wrote, this plan would better "permit me to do what I've long wanted to — slander my native city." A letter from Milton Abernethy, editor of *Contempo* magazine in Chapel Hill, North Carolina, egged him on. "Do us something hot along the line of giving somebody or something hell," Abernethy wrote. "You can't get too strong for us. We'll print it."[76] Jim was bucked up by receiving a copy of *Story* magazine containing his "Spring Evening." The publication earned him no money, but the tale was praised in the *Paris Tribune* for being "written in the spiciest of American vernacular."[77]

Farrell also turned to his second draft of *Gas-House McGinty* with renewed vitality. From his brother Earl he received a helpful packet of the bulletins issued to employees along with the Railway Express Company's in-house newspaper the *Express Messenger*.[78] To Henle, he explained his reasons for inventing additional characters and his method of introducing the social background into the novel through the use of interchapters, or "interludes." Italicized passages preceding some chapters were designed to take the reader out of the wagon-call office onto the streets with the wagonmen. Most of all, he was proud of a new dream-sequence that he attributed to his recent rereading of *Ulysses*.[79] "Chapter five is an innovation, depicting the dream life of McGinty, and I hope to get out of this depiction something of a sense of heavy, troubled, painful, frustrated sleep. I think the idea is well worth flirting around with. . . . Also, I'll love to beat the *transition* maniacs at their own game, and write of dreams and hallucinations in very realistic accurate terms, and yet make all the tattered insanity of dreams perfectly legible to the reader."[80]

McGinty's dream became chapter four of his published book. Farrell's effort, he said, was to probe below McGinty's surface consciousness and "to bring forth elements of his nature of which he is not fully aware. When he sleeps, we can perceive his restless vanity stirring. . . . Then, ambition, guilt, fear, apprehension have a free play. . . . The images of his dreams flow out of his waking life." McGinty spends a restless night and returns to another nerve-racking day at the office.[81]

Writing about kids, Jim told Henle, was easier than writing about expressmen. But still, his enthusiasm for his new book was growing by the day. During late March and into April, the composition flowed more easily. He completed hundreds of pages, bringing the total for sections two and three to fifteen hundred. These, like section one, often portrayed men massed and "squirming" within a confining office. Section two shaped up as a novelette on Omar James, a new character he invented to be the chief dispatcher, in succession to McGinty. Section three centered on Willie Collins, the next chief dispatcher. His book, he saw, was becoming either a massive single volume or a trilogy going far beyond the first section on Ambrose J. McGinty.[82] No matter how his manuscript was packaged, he believed, it would be a hard-hitting revelation of the miserable, regimented lives of American workers.[83]

While he was working on his Express Company novel, Jim received from Henle the proof of Frederic Thrasher's introduction to *Young Lonigan*. It was highly complimentary of Farrell's accomplishment. The tale, Thrasher wrote, "captures the inner life of adolescence . . . better than Studs himself could have told it." It displays an "introspective insight coupled with realism which makes this story a classic in the literature of boyhood." This "social world . . . of sex, race, religion, and life as they are really met and experienced by young people . . . is portrayed with a consummate artistry of verisimilitude. . . . As a picture of adolescent struggles and attitudes in such a *milieu* this book is unequalled. It possesses what Christopher Morley calls the 'fine vulgarity of plain truth.'"[84]

Thrasher had taught in the University of Chicago Sociology Department and Jim was familiar with his study of Chicago gangs in a book titled *The Gang*, but he did not think highly of it. In his polite response to Thrasher, he praised the introduction for being succinct and for accurately focusing on the novel's subject and milieu rather than on the author.[85]

To Henle, he expressed some minor reservations about the introduction, but admitted Thrasher's sociological concepts applied accurately to the novel. When he was first composing it, he explained, sociological jargon like that Thrasher used got mixed into his writing and he had trouble getting rid of it. The characters

> had a time of it with accommodations to total situations, adjustments to their milieu, the acquisition of behaviour patterns, etc.
>
> When I revised Young Lonigan over here I worried the factor of background sick, wondering about putting in more, and putting up signposts to say, here, the character's background represented in a social agency, the playground, fails to produce adequate objects of gratification, which would enable the character successfully to form social rather than asocial habits, to direct and canalyze his impulses. You see that contains a lot of big words too. Thrasher's introduction makes me glad I dropped all the junk anyway. (JTF to JH, 16 March 1932)

Henle understood Jim's point. He replied he would have preferred to publish *Young Lonigan* as a novel rather than as a kind of sociological document. But he noted that Thrasher's introduction nullified the possibility of censorship by validating *Young Lonigan* as a study of adolescent psychology.[86]

Farrell admitted as much. He recognized that Thrasher's introduction "attested sociologically to what I had written in *Young Lonigan*." But as he eventually realized, Professor Thrasher's introduction unintentionally and ironically "contributed toward motivating a criticism of my fiction continuing in recurring repetition down to the present day. This is the general charge that my fiction is sociological or documentary, and that it is not art or literature."[87]

Desmond Harmsworth, having returned to Paris from England, informed Jim that he was reading the proofs of *Young Lonigan*. A few days later, he wrote that he was "strongly tempted" to accept the novel for his fall list but had decided it would "prove too local and too specialized in subject to be of wide interest in England." England, unlike France, had no "predilection . . . for the tough-guy schoolboy subject." He was worried about censorship. As a friendly gesture, Harmsworth showed the manuscript to Cape and other English publishers. Cape was interested, and Jim, acting on this last slim hope, had Sam Putnam send his copy of Fernandez's statement to Cape. *Young Lonigan*, however, did not appear in England until 1936, when it came out as volume one of an expurgated edition of the trilogy *Studs Lonigan*.[88]

Even before his break with Newman, Jim knew his days in Paris were numbered. One way or another, he and Dorothy would soon have to be on their way home, like Linc Gillespie and Harold Stearns, who had recently left for the States, and like Bob Brown, who, he knew, would follow.[89] The solution came when Jim talked again with the Reverend Belshaw at the United States Students and Artists Club. The minister promised he would try to work their return through the American Aid Society, which helped indigent American citizens in a variety of ways.[90]

Arrangements were made for the Farrells to sail on the steamer *Roosevelt* on 14 April.[91] Jim wrote to Tom Freeman: "Paris has licked us and we got to go back." He was "going nuts getting everything together." To Ezra Pound, he lamented: "Am throwing up the sponge as far as Paris is concerned and going to New York to listen to radios, read the baseball scores and join the breadline."[92] Within a few days, Harold Belshaw, with the help of Horatio Krans of the American University Union, secured an earlier reservation for the Farrells' return trip, this time on the Holland-American liner *Statendam*, sailing from Boulogne on 9 April.[93]

Jim scurried around to take care of loose ends and obligations. Dorothy began packing up. Jim picked up their luggage left with Madam Prévost and arranged with Henri to pay rent still owed. He met with Ed Bastian and Pierre to make sure they would keep in touch with him. He gave a load of his books, too bulky for his trunk, to the United States Students and Artists Club. He mailed a farewell letter to Don Sewarts, addressed to "Don Sewarts and the Club." He arranged with the American Express to take care of incoming mail. He paid some overdue bills, including almost a thousand francs to Le Home Joli. He caught up on his correspondence. He thanked Ezra Pound for all his help and asked that he return Jacob Schwartz's letters, "gems I'm very very anxious to preserve."[94]

Two days before they sailed, Jim and Dorothy went to a movie in the afternoon, then sat leisurely talking with Kathleen Coyle in a café on the boulevard Saint-Michel. "It was one of the first warm days of a new spring, and Paris was at its most charming. There was a full and flowing life passing before one along the sidewalk, the endless and kaleidoscopic crowd, the bumptious and unrepressed students, the peanut vendors, the rug merchants, that always fascinating life of a Paris street. . . . We sat there for a long time in the sun and sipped our drinks."[95] The next day, the Neagoes picked them up in their car and drove them to Fontenay-aux-Roses, where they and the Putnams spent the afternoon talking and riding about. Sam gave Jim a letter of introduction written to J. G. Grey, literary editor of the *New York Sun*. It introduced him as "a young wild-eyed Irish genius" with "all sorts of a future . . . and a punch to his style."[96]

Back at Le Home Joli in the evening, Jim found a message from Pierre. He read it to Dorothy. They looked at each other and laughed. He typed a quick note to the Putnams: "All day long my translator has been trying to get me. Gallimard, of NRF, broke down with big-heartedness and there was 1000 francs waiting for me at the NRF, and I didn't get the message until the office was closed. . . . How's that for a break? If I had only gotten back here in time, as I had a hunch to, and got the message, we be traveling forty bucks richer. Anyway, *c'est la vie*."[97]

Early the next morning, the Farrells, accompanied by Ed Bastian to see them off, left their hotel for the Gare du Nord to catch their boat train. "We had an open cab with the top down," Dorothy remembered, "and it was a beautiful day. We sat in the back and we rode through Paris to take the boat train. It was wonderful. We hated to leave Paris in a way because we loved it, but we knew we really had to. . . . He had two books on the way. It was time to go back. . . . And we'd lost the baby."[98]

On the way to the station, they told Ed their boat train left at 8:45. All the way there, he wrote home, "they enlarged on the awful effects if they missed their train: they would miss the boat, too, and then what would they do? When we arrived at the station, they *had* missed their train. . . . Talk of unconsciousness! Neither Jimmy nor Dorothy had seen that their tickets expressly said eight twenty-five; they had not checked up at all. . . . Will we catch our boat? Dorothy asked with perfect anguish."[99] American Aid agents lingering on the platform upbraided them. They hustled them onto another train luckily just leaving for Boulogne, and telephoned ahead that the Farrells would be late. At Boulogne, a dory took them to the *Statendam*, waiting in the harbor, with its railing lined with passengers wondering who the late VIPs were. "They held the boat for half an hour for two third-class passengers!" Dorothy marveled. "Wasn't that something?"[100]

The voyage back was stormy, and Dorothy was often seasick. Jim wrote to his sister Mary that the boat "pitches like holy Nell." But "Ocean voyaging goes good by me. I don't get seasick. I eat like a horse."[101] On the third-class level, Jim observed fellow passengers: the old Dutch lady who never bathed, Lithuanian orphan boys, Hollanders who disliked the Poles and Lithuanians. All of them, it seemed, saw America as a land with streets of gold.[102]

Sitting on deck with his diary at hand, he thought back over the past year. When they came to Paris, he had no way of knowing when, or even if, *Young Lonigan* would be published. Now he knew he would hold a copy in ten days. He liked to think that any artist's best answer to "the indignity of death" was the work he left to posterity. He wrote in his diary: "I can die now. *Young Lonigan* will be published." If it occurred to him that such a declaration was grandiose, he nevertheless must have known it was true to his feelings and somehow validated by the struggles they had lived through.[103]

In the cabin next to the Farrells lay Phyllis Russell, an American expatriate in Paris since the 1920s. She was on her way home, partially paralyzed from a stroke. Dr. Krans had arranged for the Farrells to look in on her and help her during the voyage. In his 1932 notebook, Jim noted that "brain fever" had kept her in the American Hospital for five months. In Paris, she had "hell-raised," he wrote. She had written under the name of Evans, and claimed to be a friend of Djuna Barnes and Janet Flanner. She had lived the life of a Hemingway character, Jim thought. Now without money, she feared being put into New York's Bellevue Hospital. At his own expense, Jim telegraphed her brother, who owned the Greenwich Village Inn on the Square, to meet her at the boat.[104]

On the night of 15 April, the *Statendam* anchored outside New York harbor off Sandy Hook. "I was coming back, I knew, to a suffering America," Jim wrote, "with millions out of work. . . . I would need to catch up with the change. I dreaded the necessity of having to work at a regular job eight hours a day far more than I dreaded being broke. . . . One always ate."[105] Dorothy was coming back knowing she must break the news to her family that she had had, and lost, a baby.[106]

The next morning, the *Statendam* docked at Hoboken, opposite West Twenty-third Street in Manhattan, on the other side of the Hudson

River. The Farrells got through customs in an hour, a copy of *Lady Chatterley's Lover* craftily hidden in Jim's trunk. On the dock, they hoped to be met by Jim Henle, or Evelyn Shrifte, or Walt Carmon, but no one came. With about ten dollars between them, Jim and Dorothy took a cab to the Cornish Arms Hotel on West Twenty-third Street and Eighth Avenue and rented a room for six dollars. Their first meal was at the Automat on Sixth Avenue across from Bryant Park.[107] They were back in New York one year after having embarked for Paris, and five days before *Young Lonigan* would be published.

Wambly Bald, writing in the *Paris Tribune*, noted the departure of the Farrells for the United States and, two weeks later, the appearance of "Jimmy Farrell's book" and the acceptance of "Helen, I Love You," by H. L. Mencken. Farrell, he wrote, was "an exponent of stockyards realism. Hardboiled as hell."[108]

Reflecting on his friendship with Farrell, Sam Putnam recalled that

> There was in Farrell a tenderness that was not that of a Hemingway in his tenderest moments. . . . A tenderness and a hope.
>
> Jimmy himself was one of the most humanly sympathetic persons I have ever known. I have never known anyone with a deeper feeling for the outcasts of life, or who was capable of being more unobtrusively helpful to them when he could be. I have always had to smile when I have heard it said that he has a hardness if not a contempt for the types that he portrays.[109]

Ed Bastian, writing to a Chicago friend a few days before the Farrells sailed for home, spoke of Jim and Dorothy as "these two admirable specimens of trans-Atlantic, anti-maternal daring."[110]

# Abbreviations

*The main body of Farrell's Paris memoirs is contained in six notebooks written between July 1971 and March 1972. In the list below, their cover titles are given following the abbreviations PN1 through PN6, the PN standing for Paris Notebook. Readers should be aware that a citation in the footnotes to any one of these six sources includes only the abbreviation for the notebook. The page and section numbering in the notebooks is too erratic to be cited without causing confusion and frustration. The reader also should know that the initial citation to a Paris notebook, with respect to a particular person, place, or event mentioned in the text of this book, also will include the citations to other Paris notebooks regarding that particular reference.*

| | |
|---|---|
| Bald | Wambly Bald |
| "Began" | "Since I Began," Farrell's autobiographical notebooks other than his six Paris notebooks |
| Boyle | Kay Boyle |
| "Call" | "The Call of Time," unfinished novel MS |
| CF | Clifton Fadiman |
| "Data" | "Data Abroad," Farrell MS |
| DB | Dorothy Butler |
| DF | Dorothy Farrell |
| "Distance" | "The Distance of Sadness," unfinished novel MS |
| EB | Edward Bastian |
| EP | Ezra Pound |
| Ford | Charles Henri Ford |
| "Friend" | "My Friend, Jean Paul," Farrell MS |
| "Innocents 1" | "Innocents in Paris," text 1, unfinished novel MS |
| "Innocents 2" | Innocents in Paris," text 2, unfinished novel MS |

| | |
|---|---|
| "Intro" | "Introduction Studs Lonigan," Farrell MS notebook |
| JS | Jacob Schwartz |
| JTF | James T. Farrell |
| JTF-MU | James T. Farrell Collection, Miami University King Library, Oxford, Ohio |
| JTF Papers | James T. Farrell Papers, University of Pennsylvania Van Pelt Library |
| LB | Laura Bastian |
| LS | Lloyd Stern |
| MB | Margaret Butler |
| "Memoir" | "James T. Farrell Pens a Paris Memoir," Farrell article |
| "Memories" | "Some Memories of Paris," Farrell MS |
| MF | Mary Farrell |
| MJF | Martin Joseph Freeman |
| "Notes" | "Notes-Studs," Farrell MS |
| "Paris" | "Paris Novel," Farrell MS |
| *PH* | *New York Herald Tribune*, Paris edition (*Paris Herald*) |
| PN | Paris notebook |
| PN1 | "Since I Began Completed July 1 [17?] 1971 Paris 1931–1932 by James T. Farrell Paris [illegible]" |
| PN2 | "Since I Began No. 2 by James T. Farrell Paris Experience [?] 1931–32 Completed Oct 14/71" |
| PN3 | "Autobiography Paris Notebook 3 by James T. Farrell Oct 14/71 N.Y. N.Y. Completed Nov 30/71" |
| PN4 | "Autobiography Paris Notebook 4 James T. Farrell Nov 30/71 N.Y. N.Y. Completed Feb 3 1973 [1972] N.Y. N.Y." |
| PN5 | "Paris Autobiography by James T. Farrell Feb 3/1972 N.Y. N.Y. Completed March 8/1972 4th [5th] Notebook N.Y. N.Y." |
| PN6 | "Paris Autobiography by James T. Farrell March 8 1972 N.Y. N.Y. Final Notebook of MSS Completed March 20, 1972 N.Y. N.Y." |
| *PT* | *Chicago Daily Tribune*, Paris edition (*Paris Tribune*) |
| RCB | Robert Carlton Brown |

| | |
|---|---|
| "Return" | "Return to Paris," Farrell MS |
| "Sceaux" | "Sceaux Re-Visited," Farrell MS |
| "Scenes" | "Some Scenes of My Paris Stories," Farrell MS |
| "Time" | "Paris Was Another Time," unfinished novel MS |
| TM | Theodore Marvel |
| WC | Walt Carmon |
| "Went Away" | "After Eddie and Marion Went Away," unfinished novel MS |
| "Young" | "When Time Was Young," unfinished novel MS |

# Notes

In the following notes, the abbreviation JTF-MU stands for The James T. Farrell Collection, Miami University King Library, Oxford, Ohio, and the abbreviation JTF-Papers stands for The James T. Farrell Papers in the University of Pennsylvania Van Pelt Library. The letters of Farrell and others to the author, photocopies of the relevant part of Edward Bastian's letters to family and friends in Chicago, and the author's interviews with James Farrell, Dorothy Farrell, and Edward Bastian that are cited below are located in the Miami University Farrell Collection. The interviews of Dorothy Farrell and the final interview of Edward Bastian are tape-recorded. Additional letters to or from Farrell and others that are cited are, unless otherwise specified, photocopies (found in the Miami University Farrell Collection) of letters in the University of Pennsylvania Farrell Papers. The location of Farrell's manuscripts used in this study is given in the first citation to them.

## Preface

1. James T. Farrell's unpublished novel, "Innocents in Paris," text 2, (hereafter, "Innocents 2"), 7, JTF-MU.

2. "Return to Paris," *New Leader* 32 (7 May 1949): 8 (hereafter, "Return"); "On Coming to Paris," JTF MS, JTF Papers (JTF-MU photocopy), n.d., 7.

## Chapter 1: Gearing Up for Paris: In Chicago and New York

1. James T. Farrell (hereafter, JTF) to the author, 9 Jan. 1976; Dorothy Farrell (hereafter, DF), interview by author (hereafter, interview), 22 Oct. 1992. In an autobiographical note written in 1932, Farrell stated: "I have done some bumming" ("James T. Farrell," in *Americans Abroad: An Anthology*

(hereafter, *Americans Abroad*), ed. Peter Neagoe (The Hague: Servire Press, 1932), [142].

2. JTF to author, 7 Jun. 1957; DF, interviews, 27 Jul. 1993, 8 Dec. 1994. Farrell wrote of the Slow Club in his novel *Lonely for the Future*. See also his unfinished novel "The Call of Time" (hereafter, "Call"), 1: 293, and 2: 127, JTF Papers (JTF-MU, photocopy).

3. JTF to Edward Bastian (hereafter, EB), 31 Aug. 1932.

4. JTF, interview, 14 Mar. 1957; JTF to author, 9 Jan. 1976.

5. "A Criticism of the University Library Department," *Daily Maroon*, 14 Dec. 1928, p. 3.

6. Farrell's unfinished novel "When Time Was Young" (hereafter, "Young"), 6, JTF Papers (JTF-MU, photocopy).

7. JTF to author, 31 Jul. 1975, 7 Jan. 1976, note postmarked 4 Jan. 1976; DF, interviews, 22 Oct. 1992, 8 Dec. 1994. Farrell tried without success to get Ruth Jameson's novel published. James Henle rejected it for Vanguard Press. See JTF to Lloyd Stern (hereafter, LS), 21 Feb. 1932, and JTF's fictional accounts of Jan Varsky and Janet Ross (Janowicz and Jameson) in "After Eddie and Marion Went Away" (hereafter, "Went Away"), 90–95, 98–104, JTF-MU.

8. JTF's unfinished novel "Paris Was Another Time," (hereafter, "Time"), 739, JTF Papers (JTF-MU, photocopy).

9. JTF, interview, 14 Mar. 1957.

10. JTF to author, 26 Jul. 1975.

11. "I read *Ulysses* for the first time early in 1928. A copy of this book was in the Rare Book Room of the University of Chicago Library. I was able to take it out on loan, and to keep it for several weeks. I read *Ulysses*, then, with great excitement" ("The World Is Today," n.d., written for the Alburn Bureau, an agency supplying unsigned editorials to many newspapers, JTF-MU).

12. JTF, interview by Matthew J. Bruccoli, in *Conversations with Writers II*, ed. Richard Layman (Detroit: Gale Research Co., 1978), 23–24; JTF to author, 26 Jul. 1975.

13. "Library Contest Shows Greater Interest by Men," *Daily Maroon*, 15 Nov. 1929, p. 4. Also see "Maroon Man Victor in Library Nucleus Contest," *Daily Maroon*, 14 Nov. 1929, p. 1.

14. "The University of Chicago Official Academic Record: James Thomas Farrell," JTF Papers (JTF-MU, photocopy); Maxine A. Sullivan to Cleo Paturis, 10 Jun. 1993, (JTF-MU, photocopy).

15. Dorothy Butler (hereafter, DB), "Modernism Marks American Exhibit at Art Institute," *Daily Maroon*, 9 Nov. 1928, p. 3.

16. See also (1) JTF's appreciation of Van Gogh's and Cézanne's paintings in an entry for 22 Feb. 1935 in "Notes by James T. Farrell/Volume One/1935," 435–37, JTF Papers (JTF-MU, photocopy); (2) "On Picasso and Van Gogh: Forms of Alienation," *Genesis West* 1 (winter, 1962–63): 114–22.

17. JTF, interviews, 27 Dec. 1955, 17 Feb. 1956.

18. M. R. Y., "Looking Back/Life Is Long, Art Short," *University of Chicago Magazine* (Dec. 1991): 48; "And Here Was Bohemia," *Chicago Sunday Tribune Magazine of Books*, (14 Mar. 1959): 6, 13.

19. Notices in the *Daily Maroon* for 9 and 16 Feb. 1928 publicize the opening and purpose of the Cube as a "laboratory theater." Throughout the year, the *Maroon* carried notices of plays and other performances there; JTF to author, 7 Jul. 1957.

20. Stanley Newman to author, 24 Apr. 1956. Newman became a distinguished anthropologist.

21. JTF to author, 7 Jun. 1957; DF, interviews, 22 Oct. 1992, 20 Oct. 1993. Examples of Matsoukas's writing are "Frozen Idols," *Daily Maroon Quarterly Review*, n.d., but late 1927, pp. 11–12; "Athenaeum," *Daily Maroon*, 24 Jan. 1928, p. 3; "The Literary Movement in Modern Greece," *Forge* [the campus poetry magazine] (winter 1928): 43–46. Sterling North, a contemporary of Matsoukas's and Farrell's at the university, satirized Matsoukas, called Demetrius Dardanus, in his novel *Seven Against the Years* (New York: Macmillan, 1939). See North to JTF, 29 Apr. 1942, JTF Papers (JTF-MU, notation), and North to author, 11 Mar. 1956.

22. JTF to author, 7 Jan. 1976; DF, interview, 8 Dec. 1994; "Call," 1: 267ff, 372–75. Notices of plays Mary Hunter directed at the Cube appear in the *Daily Maroon*. In October 1928 she directed Pirandello's *Six Characters in Search of an Author*, billed as the play's first Mid-west appearance. This production inspired Farrell to write an (unfinished) article on Pirandello as playwright, his first attempt at a major critical piece. In spring 1929, at Nick Matsoukas's urging, she pioneered within the university community the production of "an all Negro show of . . . three one act plays, about Negro life, with an all-Negro cast" ("Call," 1: 190) when she directed O'Neill's *The Dreamy Kid*, and Paul Green's *The Man Who Died at 12 O'Clock* and *The No 'Count Boy*." Mary Hunter later directed on Broadway. She played Marge in the television series "Easy Aces."

23. JTF, interviews, 17 Mar. 1957, 7 Jun. 1957, 23 Jul. 1960, 9 Jan. 1976; JTF to author, 23 Jul. 1960, 23 Aug. 1960; "Call," 211–20; JTF's unfinished novel "The Distance of Sadness" (hereafter, "Distance"), 106, JTF-Papers (JTF-MU, photocopy); *Poetry World* 1 (Aug. 1929): [4].

24. JTF, interviews, 14 Mar. 1957, 23 Jul. 1960; DF, interview, 2 Nov. 1994; JTF's unfinished novel, "Innocents in Paris," text 1 (hereafter, "Innocents 1"), 15, JTF-MU.

25. Dorothy Butler was born 6 March 1910 (DF, interview, 2 Nov. 1994). In Farrell's "Distance," p. 215, Merkle (Beatrice Timmins) comes to the household in 1911 as a servant and remains as a family member after the death of Mr. Healy (Mr. Butler) in the mid-1920s.

26. DF, interview, 20 Oct. 1993. Also see JTF to author, 7 Jun. 1957, and "Distance," 30–32. During an interview by the author on 15 March 1957, Farrell recalled that he wrote two papers for Dorothy; also see "Distance," 111–13. The first paper was on Bodenheim's verse and the other on Shelley's "Ode to the West Wind." Farrell was chagrined when the latter received only a C. A scene in "Distance," 24–29, depicts Bodenheim's conduct about this time at a party given in the Fifty-seventh Street art colony.

27. JTF, interview, 14 Mar. 1957. The descriptive details of Dorothy's appearance are from "Distance," 31. Perhaps because of her good looks and her childlike innocence of manner, Dorothy's friends often called her "Doralesque." George Brodsky, one of her undergraduate friends, met her again after almost fifty years, in Evanston's Calvary Cemetery at Farrell's final services in 1979. "I recognized Dorothy instantly," he wrote, "by the color of her hair (still titian) and her still unmistakable facial beauty. . . . I found Dorothy as ingenuous as I had known her at the University. There was still that same naiveté, the same gentle quality I remembered" (Brodsky to author, 3 Oct. 1997).

28. DF, interviews, 22 Oct. 1992, 20 Oct. 1993. Farrell's friend Ed Bastian, fluent in French, recalled that Farrell's French accent was "atrocious" (EB, interview, 9 Dec. 1992).

29. DF, interviews, 8 Dec. 1994, 11 Jan. 1995.

30. DF, interviews, 20 Oct. 1993, 8 Dec. 1994; "Distance," 21–22, 178–85. In later life, Dorothy acted in several Broadway and off-Broadway plays, including June Havoc's *Marathon '33* (DF, interview, 4 Oct. 1997).

31. DF, interviews, 22 Oct. 1992, 20 Oct. 1993.

32. John Roney is the model for Tom Gregory in Farrell's tale "Can All This Grandeur Perish?" (*Can All This Grandeur Perish? and Other Stories*

[New York: Vanguard Press, 1937], 3–24). In the tale, Tom begins his career working in a butter and egg store in an Irish district on Chicago's southwest side and becomes a multimillionaire. His standard advice to his many nieces is: Rise early in the morning and keep your feet on the ground.

33. DF, interview, 22 Jul. 1994.

34. Ibid.

35. DF, interviews, 22 Oct. 1992, 22 Jul. 1994; JTF, interview, 15 Mar. 1957.

36. JTF, interviews, 15 Mar. 1957, 7 Jun. 1957; "The Open Road" in *Guillotine Party and Other Stories* (New York: Vanguard Press, 1935), 13–32; "Distance," 69–72.

37. "The University of Chicago Academic Record: James T. Farrell"; Jones was a replacement for Robert Morss Lovett, earlier scheduled for the course. A profile of Jones and an account of Farrell's experience in the class are given in "Distance," 104–5, 109–10, 172–76.

38. DB to JTF, 8 Sept. 1929; DF, interview, 20 Oct. 1993.

39. DF, interview, 22 Oct. 1992.

40. JTF to author, 28 Jul. 1975, 7 Jan. 1976.

41. JTF to author, postmarked 7 Jan. 1976; DF, interviews, 22 Oct. 1992, 8 Dec. 1994.

42. JTF, interviews, 13 Mar. 1957, 15 Mar. 1957; JTF to author, 23 Jul. 1960, 31 Jul. 1975; DF, interview, 22 Oct. 1992.

43. "Distance," 79. On pages 129–34, Dorothy is shown in the store working behind the counter and lifting spending money from the cashier's till.

44. DF, interview, 22 Oct. 1992; JTF, "Paris Novel" (hereafter, "Paris"), 231, JTF Papers (JTF-MU, photocopy).

45. DB to JTF, 16 Sept. 1930; JTF to author, 23 Jul. 1960; JTF, interviews, 15–17 Mar. 1957.

46. JTF, typescript, "Memoirs of a Cub Campus Reporter Who Covered the St. Valentine's Day Massacre," JTF-MU; JTF to author, 7 Jun. 1957, 31 Jul. 1975, 11 Aug. 1975; "The World Around Me," n.d., editorial for the Alburn Bureau, n.d., probably 1957, JTF-MU; DF, interview, 20 Oct. 1993; Sterling North to author, 11 Mar. 1956. After seven months, Farrell was fired from his job ("I was once fired from a Hearst paper," in "James T. Farrell" in *Americans Abroad*, [142]).

47. *University of Chicago Magazine* (fall 1981): 46.

48. JTF to author, 23 Jul. 1960; Maxine H. Hunsinger to author, 30 Nov. 1992, JTF-MU. Farrell stated that Dorothy was dropped by the university because of failing grades. Also see "Young," 263, and "Call," 1: 295.

49. DF, interview, 22 Oct. 1992; JTF, interview, 15 Mar. 1957.

50. "Liberals in Chicago," *Plain Talk* 5 (Nov. 1929): 582–88; Clarence Darrow to JTF, 31 May 1929; J. U. Nicolson to JTF, 6 Jun. 1929; Jane Addams to JTF, 15 Jul. 1929; G. D. Eaton to JTF, 16 May 1929, 18 Jun. 1929, 15 Jul. 1929, 14 Oct. 1929; JTF to G. D. Eaton, 3 Jul. 1929, 17 Jul. 1929 (three versions); Evelyn Light to JTF, 21 May 1929, 23 Aug. 1929; JTF to author, 7 Jun. 1954; 29 Jan. 1976.

51. Vladimir Janowicz to JTF, 1 Jul. 1931; "Went Away," 90; "Time," 739, 741. PEN is the acronym for the international organization of poets, playrights, editors, essayists, and novelists.

52. Ford to JTF, 3 Mar. 1929, 30 Apr. 1929, 7 May 1929, 21 Jun. 1929, 9 Jul. 1929, 9 Oct. 1929; JTF to Ford, 18 Jul. 1929.

53. William Carlos Williams to Ford, as quoted by Ford in his letter of 9 Oct. 1929 to Farrell.

54. JTF to Ford, 18 Jul. 1929. In "Suggestions for a New Magic," *transition*, no. 3 [Jun. 1927], pp. 178–79, Eugene Jolas and Elliot Paul had stated with finality: "Realism in America has reached its point of saturation. We are no longer interested in the photography of events, in the mere silhouetting of facts, in the presentation of misery."

55. "Death Notices/Cunningham William P.," *Chicago Daily Tribune*, 12 Mar. 1929, p. 32; "Standard Certificate of Death," State of Illinois, Dept. of Public Health, 12 Mar. 1929.

56. JTF, interview, 15 Mar. 1957; JTF to author, 23 Jul. 1960; 29 Jan. 1976.

57. "Author's Note" prefacing "Studs" in *The Short Stories of James T. Farrell* (New York: Vanguard Press, 1955), 348.

58. Clifton Fadiman (hereafter, CF) to JTF, 19 Jun. 1929; Farrell's notebook "Introduction Studs Lonigan" (hereafter, "Intro"), completed 16 Feb. 1972, sec. ii, JTF Papers (JTF-MU, photocopy). This notebook narrates the history of the origin, composition, and publication of *Studs Lonigan*. Sections two through seven cover the first part of the story: from the time Farrell began working on his trilogy through the publication of *Young Lonigan* in 1932. Citation to specific passages by page numbers is uninformative, however, because the numbering is chaotic. Citations to it will be by section number. Sometimes the sequence of events given in the narrative is faulty: e.g., the times at which Farrell submitted his "Young Lonigan" manuscript to two New York publishers. Sometimes the memory of a detail is mistaken: e. g., the amount he was paid for his story "Studs." Nevertheless, the notebook is a comprehensive, useful account of the trilogy's creation.

59. JTF to CF, 24 Jun. 1929, 10 Jul. 1929; CF to JTF, 27 Jun. 1929, 10 Jul. 1929.

60. CF to JTF, 9 Aug. 1929.

61. JTF to author, 31 Dec. 1975, 9 Jan. 1976.

62. DB to JTF, 29 Aug. 1929; JTF to DB, 1 Sept. 1929.

63. JTF to DB, 3 Sept. 1929.

64. Robert Morss Lovett to JTF, 6 Sept. 1929; DB to JTF, 9 Sept. 1929; JTF to DB, 10 Sept. 1929.

65. William MacDonald (of the *Nation*) to JTF, 10 Sept. 1929; Amy Loveman to JTF, 16 Sept. 1929; JTF to author, 7 Jun. 1957, 9 Jan. 1976, 20 Aug. 1976 postmark.

66. JTF to DB, 17 Sept. 1929.

67. JTF to DB, 14 Sept. 1929, 15 Sept. 1929, 17 Sept. 1929; JTF to author, 9 Jan. 1976.

68. JTF to author, 7 Jun. 1957, 23 Jul. 1960, 9 Jan. 1976. Mary Hunter turned to Jim's friend James J. ("Jack") Sullivan, who married her in 1933. See Sullivan to JTF, 17 Sept. 1933.

69. "Call," 2: 195.

70. Ibid., 201.

71. As narrated about Eddie Ryan (Farrell) in "Young," 675.

72. W. J. Wiscott to JTF, 2 Jun. 1930; "Intro," sec. iii; typescript of "Since I Began" (hereafter, "Began"), titled "Autobiography," completed 17 Apr. 1970 [1971], 8, JTF Papers (JTF-MU photocopy). Farrell's date 1970 should be 1971. Hereafter the year 1971 will be used for citations to this notebook. "Since I Began" is Farrell's title for a series of autobiographical notebooks written over a period of years.

73. *Tambour*, no. 8 (1930): 36–40. See also JTF's brief undated manuscript titled "Autobiography," JTF-MU.

74. SP to JTF, 23 Apr. 1930; SP, *Paris Was Our Mistress* [hereafter, *Mistress*] (New York: Vanguard Press, 1947), 109. See also SP to JTF, 23 Jul. 1930; JTF to SP, 4 May 1930, 9 May 1930, 10 Feb. 1931; "Intro," sec. iii. For Titus, see PN1, PN4. For Putnam, see PN1–PN6.

75. JTF, interview, 15 Mar. 1957; Karen Rood, "Samuel Putnam," *American Writers in Paris, 1920–1939*, Dictionary of Literary Biography, vol. 4, ed. Karen Rood (Detroit: Gale Research Co., 1980), 333–43.

76. "The Truth about Fascism" in "Italica," *This Quarter*, no. 4 (Apr.–May–Jun. 1930): 563–65.

77. In 1926, Farrell received grades of A from Professor Rodney Mott in

Political Science 101, "Introduction to American Government," and from Professor Harold Lasswell in Political Science 103, "Comparative Government" ("The University of Chicago Official Academic Record: James Thomas Farrell"). His term paper for Professor Lasswell was on Mussolini's Fascism.

78. In this belief, Putnam may have echoed Ezra Pound, associate editor of Putnam's *New Review*. Farrell learned later that the American pragmatic philosopher Horace M. Kallen, a student of William James and George Santayana, while visiting Mussolini in the 1920s, was informed by the dictator that the instrumentalism of William James anticipated the thinking and strongarm action of Italian Fascists. In the fall of 1932, Pound translated and published in *Il Mare* Farrell's critical piece on *The Philosophy of the Present*, an influential book by the University of Chicago pragmatist George Herbert Mead. In Pound's preface, Farrell noted, the poet claimed "a kinship . . . between the thinking of Mead . . . and Fascist thinking. This was as false as Mussolini's claim of kinship with the thought of William James" ("Began," vol. 3, notebook completed 26 May 1976, 2970, 2981, 2983–84 [erratic numbering]). See "La filosofia del presente, di G. H. Mead," *Il Mare, Supplemente Letterario* 1 (12 Nov. 1932): 3. Published in Farrell's *Literature and Morality* (1947) as George Herbert Mead's *"Philosophy of the Present"*; JTF to EP, 18 Sept. 1932, 11 Nov. 1932; EP to JTF, 27 Oct. 1932.

79. The quotations in this paragraph are from SP, "A Paris Letter," *New York Sun*, 27 Feb. 1931, p. 32, "A Paris Letter," ibid., 3 Jul. 1931, p. 7, and *Mistress*, 225–28.

80. SP to JTF, 23 Apr. 1930, 23 Jul. 1930; JTF to SP, 4 May 1930, 9 May 1930; Slater Brown to JTF, 22 Feb. 1930, and n.d. (probably early Dec. 1930); JTF to Edward Titus, n.d. (probably late Feb. 1930); Edward Titus to JTF, 15 Jan. 1931, 17 Jan. 1931; SP, *Mistress*, 109; "Intro," sec. iii; JTF to Serge Fauchereaux, 28 May 1977.

81. 13 Jan. 1931. See also SP to JTF, 9 Dec. 1930, JTF to SP, 27 Dec. 1930.

82. "Call," 2: 214.

83. *Boarding House Blues* (New York: Paperback Library, 1961), 153.

84. JTF to author, 23 Jul. 1960; "Intro," sec. ii. See also Lloyd Stern to author, 16 Aug. 1975, 5 Sept. 1975, 9 Sept. 1975.

85. "Began," 2: 1, completed 17 Apr. 1971, pages double-numbered 21–22 and 96–97.

86. JTF to Sherwood Kohn, 10 Dec. 1960; JTF to Victor Weybright, n.d., tracing the development of *Studs Lonigan* from 1929 to 1935; "Intro," sec. ii.

87. JTF to SP, 31 Jan. 1931.

88. CF to JTF, 4 Feb. 1931. See CF to author, 15 Mar. 1956.

89. JTF to SP, 27 Mar. 1931; "Intro," sec. ii.

90. JTF to SP, 10 Feb. 1931.

91. JTF, interviews, 15 Feb. 1956, 17 Mar. 1957.

92. Harry Block to JTF, 12 Mar. 1931; Joseph Brewer to JTF, 24 Mar. 1931, 31 Mar. 1931, 6 Apr. 1931 (in April 1930, John S. Sumner had brought obscenity charges against Brewer & Warren for publishing Nathan Asch's *Pay Day*); JTF to SP, 27 Mar. 1931, 8 Apr. 1931; JTF to Martin J. Freeman (hereafter, MJF), 16 Apr. 1931; "Intro," sec. ii.

93. Ezra Pound (hereafter, EP) to SP, 16 Feb. [1931].

94. SP to JTF, 12 Mar. 1931.

95. SP to JTF, 14 Mar. 1931.

96. As expressed by Eddie Ryan (Farrell) in "Innocents," 2: 7.

97. JTF to SP, 21 Mar. 1931; Joseph Brewer to JTF, 31 Mar. 1931.

98. Vladimir Janowicz to JTF, 20 Apr. 1931.

99. "Innocents 1," 46–47.

100. DF, interviews, 22 Oct. 1992, 8 Dec. 1994.

101. DF, interview, 8 Dec. 1994.

102. JTF, interview, 17 Mar. 1957; JTF to author, 23 Jul. 1960, 8 Sept. 1969; JTF to MJF, 16 Apr. 1931.

103. "Thoughts on Chicago and Paris," JTF manuscript, JTF Papers (JTF-MU, photocopy).

104. DF, interview, 22 Oct. 1992.

105. JTF to author, 28 Jan. 1976.

106. JTF to author, 19 Mar. 1976.

107. JTF to SP, 28 Mar. 1931.

108. "Began," 2: 2, begun 17 Apr. 1971, pp. 279–82 (one of three numbering sequences for these pages); "Went Away," 92–94.

109. DF, interview, 22 Oct. 1992; JTF, interviews, 13–16 Mar. 1957.

110. DF, interviews, 22 Oct. 1992, 21 Aug. 1994; JTF, interviews, 17 Mar. 1957, 8 Sept. 1969; JTF to author, 23 Jul. 1960.

111. "Marriage License," State of Illinois, Cook County, Andrew B. Adams, County Clerk, 13 Apr. 1931; JTF to MJF, 16 Apr. 1931; DF, interview, 22 Oct. 1992.

112. DF, interview, 22 Oct. 1992.

113. Theodore Marvel (hereafter, TM) to author, 13 Mar. 1957, 14 Mar. 1957; DF, interview, 22 Oct. 1992. For vivid accounts of Farrell and his activ-

ities in New York in 1927–28, see Marvel's 1927 journal kept in the Chelsea YMCA, and Marvel's "Report to the Executive Secretary of the 23d St. Y.M.C.A., N.Y.C., from the Night Clerk," dated 2 Jan. 1928, JTF-MU photocopy.

114. DF, interview, 22 Oct. 1992.

115. JTF to author, 9 Jan. 1976; "Went Away," 1.

116. JTF MS, "Some Memories of Paris" (hereafter, "Memories"), JTF Papers (JTF-MU, photocopy); "Innocents 1," 16; "Innocents 2," 132; JTF, *The Dunne Family*, 100–1.

117. Isabel Simpson (hereafter, IS) to DF, 17 Apr. 1931, 23 Apr. 1931; JTF to James Henle (hereafter, JH), 27 May 1931; JTF, interview, 8 Sept. 1969; JTF to author, 9 Jan. 1976, 1 Sept. 1976; DF, interview, 10 Apr. 1996.

118. "Intro," sec. ii; JTF's brief undated MS titled "Autobiography," JTF-MU.

119. "Intro," sec. iii; typescript of "Began," vol. 2, no. 1, titled "Autobiography," completed 17 Apr. 1971, pp. doubly numbered 32–33 and 68–69; JTF to author, 9 Jan. 1976.

120. JTF to author, n.d. but received 13 Jan. 1976; typescript of "Began," titled "Autobiography," 2: 1, completed 17 Apr. 1971, 3; PN2.

121. Walt Carmon (hereafter, WC) to JTF, 17 Dec. 1929.

122. "Intro" sec. iii; typescript of "Began," vol. 2, no. 1, completed 17 Apr. 1971, 3–4.

123. JTF to MJF, 16 Apr. 1931; "Began," titled "Autobiography," vol. 2, no. 1, completed 17 Apr. 1971, pp. doubly numbered 32–33 and 33–34; "Intro," sec. iii; JTF to author, 9 Jan. 1976, 11 Jan. 1976.

124. JTF to author, 9 Jan. 1976; "Began," ibid, 7–8.

125. "Began," ibid, 8–9. On 28 April 1975, Cowley wrote to the author: "Jim Farrell is correct in his memory of meeting me for the first time, in my office at the *New Republic*. I liked him and thought he was taking an awful risk by going to Paris in the trough of the Depression. I probably suggested some people for him to look up, and Laurence Vail may have been one of them."

126. JTF to MJF, 16 Apr. 1931.

127. JTF to author, 25 Jan. 1976, 28 Jan. 1976.

128. JTF to JH, 19 Jun. 1931.

129. JTF to author, 11 Jan. 1976; WC to JTF, 15 Jun. 1931; JTF's untitled, undated manuscript on James Henle, JTF Papers (JTF-MU, photocopy).

130. JTF to author, 31 Jul. 1975, 9 Jan. 1976.

131. JTF to MJF, 16 Apr. 1931.

132. "Innocents 2," 2.

133. "Memories," 1–2; also see "Innocents 1," 16–17.

134. IS to DF, 23 Apr. 1931; DF, interview, 8 Dec. 1994; "Innocents 1," 12–13, 31–35, 68–70, 75–79.

135. "Innocents 2," 76; "Counting the Waves," in $1,000 a Week and Other Stories (New York: Vanguard Press, 1942), 177; IS to DF, 23 Apr. 1931.

136. DF, interview, 8 Dec. 1994; Cf. "Innocents 1," 39–41, 69–70; "Pennland Brings Many Voyagers to Europe Today," New York Herald Tribune, Paris edition (hereafter, PH), 26 Apr. 1931, p. 13.

137. Farrell changed the name from Nielsen to Thompson in the manuscript of his uncompleted novel "Innocents in Paris." See PN1.

138. "Liner Pennland Arrives with Many Passengers for Visits to Europe," PH, 27 Apr. 1931, p. 2. For Nielsen, see PN1.

139. "Memories," 2–5; "Innocents 2," 1–5; "Some Scenes of My Paris Stories" (hereafter, "Scenes"), JTF MS dated 20 Apr. 1968, p. 9, JTF-MU; PN1.

## Chapter 2: The Left Bank

1. "On Coming to Paris," 7, JTF MS, JTF Papers (JTF-MU, photocopy).

2. DF, interview, 22 Oct. 1992.

3. IS to DF, 10 May 1931, 18 May 1931, 23 Jun. 1931; DF, interviews, 26 Feb. 1996, 10 Apr. 1996.

4. Wambly Bald (hereafter, Bald), "La Vie de Bohème," Chicago Daily Tribune, Paris edition (hereafter, PT), 7 Apr. 1931, p. 4, and 21 Apr. 1931, p. 4. According to Farrell in his manuscript "Paris," 246–47, Peter Neagoe told him, presumably at a later time, that Putnam had planned to meet them, but then started drinking. In his autobiographical note in Neagoe's Americans Abroad, 322. Putnam stated: "[I] am in the habit of working 18 or drinking 96 hours a day." See PN1.

5. JTF to SP, 29 Apr. 1931.

6. DF, interview, 22 Oct. 1992. A full account of the d'Armenonville dance-hall episode is given in Farrell's "Innocents 2," pp. 18–25. See also PN2.

7. JTF to author, 20 Oct. 1975, 28 Dec. 1975, 31 Dec. 1975, 9 Jan. 1976; SP, Mistress, pp. 40–41; DF, interview, 22 Oct. 1992. Dorothy remembered Drake as a pleasant and "dapper . . . man about town." In his unpublished manu-

script "My Friend, Jean Paul," (hereafter, "Friend," JTF Papers [JTF-MU, photocopy]), Farrell characterized him as a "decent sort of chap . . . intelligent but intellectually unreliable," someone who wanted friends badly, but usually failed to make and keep them. He was inclined to get involved in literary feuds. His wife was ill, Farrell observed, and he was rumored to be involved with a rich American woman. Drake visited the Farrells from time to time as long as they were in Paris. See PN1.

8. Victoria Palace Hotel statement to "Monsieur Ferryl" for Apr. 29–May 2; "Scenes," 9; "Innocents 2," 29; PN1.

9. "Paris Was Another Time," a two-page fragment possibly from the longer MS of that title, JTF Papers (JTF-MU photocopy); JTF to Herbert Rosengren, 15 Jul. 1932; "Scenes," 8; "Innocents 2," 43–50. For Riva Putnam, see PN2–4.

10. DF interview, 22 Oct. 1992; also see "Paris," 213–15.

11. "Innocents 2," 51–52, 101–2.

12. SP, *Mistress*, 110.

13. "Innocents 2," 52.

14. Ibid.

15. PN4.

16. JTF to author, 1 Sept. 1961; DF, interviews, 22 Oct. 1992, 8 Dec. 1994; "Friend," 261–62; "Paris," 209, 260–61; "Return," 8. During his summer 1938 stay in Paris, Farrell again talked with Eve Adams, by then even more of a Paris institution, and again he was captivated by the beauty of the Saint-Germain-des-Prés tower (JTF to JH, 9 Jun. 1938).

17. "[Bernard in] Paris," 8–15, JTF-Papers (JTF-MU, photocopy). In "Notebook–Novel–Am Ex Company," 94, in an entry for 13 Feb. 1933, Farrell reported a conversation with J. G. Grey, book-review editor of the *New York Sun*, for whom Farrell had written reviews: "Grey said—[']Religion must have hurt you terribly when you were young.['] Well in a sense it did. I'm still a left-handed Catholic" JTF Papers (JTF-MU, photocopy). Several times in conversations with the author, Farrell referred to himself as "a left-handed Catholic."

18. DF, interview, 11 Jan. 1995.

19. "Innocents 2," 53.

20. SP, *Mistress*, 109–10. Also see SP's "A Manifesto for One," in "The Bear Garden," *New York Sun*, 7 May 1932, p. 8, and his "A Paris Letter," ibid, 26 Jun. 1931, p. 25. There he states that while in America he was "living in a cultural vacuum." His "oxygen tank" there was "the tradition of a non-insu-

lar, non-hermetic, internationally radiating Mediterranean culture." Already he has selected Paris as the city "in which I prefer to die. . . . In Paris, one may walk the streets in pain and misery; yet there is always the thought, 'Anyway, I'm in Paris, and not somewhere else.'"

21. "Innocents 2," 47.

22. JTF, interview, 16 Mar. 1957. For *cartes de travail*, see PN1.

23. DF, interviews, 8 Dec. 1994, 10 Apr. 1996; "Paris," pp. 209, 218. The two women continued to see each other after both had returned to the States, and following Sam's death, Dorothy visited Riva, who was living in Philadelphia.

24. DF, interview, 22 Oct. 1992.

25. *The Letters of Ezra Pound: 1907–1941*, ed. D. D. Paige (New York: Harcourt, Brace, 1950), 233. For Pound, see PN2. For McAlmon, see PN2.

26. JTF, Jim Farrell Pens a Paris Memoir" (hereafter, "Memoir"), *Panorama*, (syndicated magazine), *Chicago Daily News* (23 Oct. 1967): 7; Don Brown, "Ezra Pound Back in Paris, Urges Revival of Pamphleteering to Save U.S. Intellect," *PT*, 10 May 1931, pp. 1, 3.

27. DF, interview, 22 Oct. 1992. Also see JTF to author, 19 Mar. 1976.

28. Cecil Desmond Bernard Harmsworth became the second baron of Egham in 1939. Following an early career as a newspaperman and publisher, he studied painting at the Académie Julian in Paris. He was best known for his portraits, which were widely exhibited in France, England, and the United States as late as 1988 (*Who's Who*, 1990, p. 785).

29. JTF to author, n.d. but received 12 Sept. 1960, and 19 Mar. 1976; EP to JTF, n.d; JTF to Serge Fauchereaux, 28 May 1977; DF, interview, 22 Oct. 1992; Peter Quennell, "A London Letter," *New York Sun*, 8 Jan. 1932, p. 30. Pound probably was referring to Harmsworth in a newspaper interview at this time when he said: "As for pamphleteering, I dare say a young Englishman now living in Paris may beat the American publisher to it" ("Ezra Pound Finds Flaws in a Number of U.S. Institutions Dealing with Learning and Finance," [*PT*, 14 May 1931, p. 9]). For Harmsworth, see PN6.

30. EP to JTF, n.d.; JTF to author, 20 Oct. 1975.

31. Possibly the next time the two men met face to face was in 1945, when Farrell visited Pound, then an inmate at the government's Washington, D.C. St. Elizabeth's Hospital, where Farrell's brother Jack, a psychiatrist, was a staff member. According to Farrell, Pound complained that President Roosevelt had disrupted the effort Pound and "his group" had been making to bring about desirable change in Italy. Farrell asked him who were the mem-

bers of his group and what changes did they have in mind. Pound, Farrell wrote, mentioned only one group member, Odon Por [author of the book *Fascism*, 1923]. Their aim, Pound stated, was to rid the Italian government of Count Ciano, Mussolini's son-in-law, whom Il Duce would later execute ("Began," vol. 3, completed 26 May 1976, pp. 2942–45), JTF Papers (JTF-MU photocopy).

32. JTF to EP, n.d.; "Memoir," 7.

33. "In the Latin Quarter," *PH*, 4 Jan. 1932, p. 2.

34. Writing to Harry Levin shortly before his death, Farrell stated that he regretted never having looked Joyce up while in Paris, "partly out of shyness, and partly not to waste his time, with the further partial motivation that I didn't want to give the impression that I was a younger writer going to him for aid, help, praise, or in discipleship—although I admired him tremendously, and had been much influenced by his writing, more so than by that of Dreiser. Had I known him, I doubt that I could truly have liked the man" (JTF to Harry Levin, 19 Jul. 1979).

35. Jacob Schwartz (hereafter, JS) to JTF, 12 Nov. 1931.

36. EP to JTF, n.d.

37. Edward Bastian, a Chicago friend of the Farrells who arrived in Paris that summer, observed: "My impression was . . . that he spent his time reading and writing, and going about trying to make useful literary acquaintances" (EB, interview, 9 Dec. 1992); see also "Time," 1.

38. Helen Lathrop to JTF, 24 Sept. 1931.

39. "Paris," 212.

40. DF, interview, 22 Oct. 1992.

41. One of Gillespie's more intelligible (and latently humorous) *transition* pieces was "Expatracination," his response in a symposium asking "Why Do Americans Live in Europe?" Explaining why he preferred to live outside America, Gillespie wrote: "(a) because in Europe I find MeaningScurry in their Organise-Self-Divert—hours loll here all simmer-rife-Expect-lush-stat, GET is less necessary. (b) because of the absence of Tight-blank faces here (European Maturity seems of the in-touch-YouthPulse ripe sort). (c) Liquor-Gamme abroad somewhat breatheier. (d) abroad, as if transplanted to an ideating DreamStanceIndef, the me-expatriate remenvisages America-the-Spectacle, init-sensing its cosmintegrality, critifocaspecting its Univeering probably for a first time, (local Econs are *so* intrude-mussuppy.)" (*transition*, no. 14 [fall 1928]: 103–4). For Gillespie, see PN3.

42. JTF, interview, 16 Mar. 1957; Bald, "La Vie de Bohème," *PT*, 9 Jun.

1931, p. 5. Linc and the Farrells later knew each other in New York City. When he was looking for a job there, Dorothy introduced him to Slim Brundage, the Farrells' acquaintance from Jack Jones's Dill Pickle Club in Chicago, who was then at the College of Complexes in New York (DF, interview, 22 Oct. 1992).

43. JTF, interview, 14 Mar. 1957; JTF to author, 12 Sept. 1960, 1 Sept. 1961, 10 Jan. 1976. See JTF's "Data Abroad" (hereafter, "Data"), an undated JTF MS written about 1 Dec. 1957, JTF-MU.

44. JTF to author, 12 Sept. 1960, n.d. but received 1 Sept. 1961, and 10 Jan. 1976; JTF to Serge Fauchereaux, 28 May 1977; JTF's manuscript "Notes—Studs" (hereafter, "Notes"); JTF to Noah Fabricant, 8 Aug. 1932. "Slob," the first of Farrell's tales to be published, appeared in Ford's little magazine *Blues* in June 1929. Among Morris's novels are *Liberty Street* (a Literary Guild selection), *The Bombay Meeting, The Paper Wall, The Road to Spain, Such a Pretty Village*, and the best-selling *The Chicago Story*.

45. "Paris," 214–15.

46. JTF to Meyer Schapiro, 22 Apr. 1947; JTF, *My Baseball Diary* (New York: A. S. Barnes, 1957), 235.

47. In the *PT*: "Fred Lindstrom Smashes Ankle," 11 Jul. 1931, p. 9; "Lott, Van Ryn Win Wimbledon Doubles Crown," 5 Jul. 1931, p. 1; "Lott, Van Ryn Smear Britons in Davis Cup," 19 Jul. 1931, pp. 1, 9; "Goodwillie Wins 100 Yard Dash," 19 Jul. 1931, p. 9. Goodwillie, a neighborhood boy, had gone to the University of Chicago High School ("U. High") and became a star track-man, baseball player, and all-around athlete.

48. WC to JH, 2 May 1931, 13 May 1931; JH to WC, 12 May 1931; WC to JTF, 13 May 1931; JH to JTF, 14 May 1931; "Intro," sec. v. For Henle, see PN2–4.

49. "Montparnasse Publisher Undertakes Book Forecasting Modern Trend of Literature," *PT*, 15 May 1931, p. 3; JTF to TM, 15 Sept. 1931; JTF to JH, 4 Oct. 1931; notation near the final page of JTF's Paris address book, JTF Papers (JTF-MU photocopy); JTF to author, 20 Oct. 1975.

50. The amount is specified in JTF's Paris address book; DF, interviews, 22 Oct. 1992, 21 Jul. 1994; "Paris," 208, 217. For Althouse, see PN2.

51. JTF to author, 20 Oct. 1975; DF, interviews, 22 Oct. 1992, 22 Jul. 1994. Major sources of the Farrells' income while in Paris are recorded in Jim's address book and various letters and cables to them. Advances from James Henle: $600. From Mrs. Butler: between $500 and $700. Earnings from writings: $60. Small gifts or loans from Edward Bastian, Martin J. Freeman, Felix Kolodziej, Vladimir Janowicz, Irving Goodman, the Paris taxicab driver

Bazin. A loan from the Reverend Harold Belshaw: two hundred francs a week for eight weeks in March and April, 1932; financial help in returning home from the American Aid Society. See JTF's Paris address book; JTF to author, 8 Sept. 1969.

52. TM to JTF, 8 May 1931, 28 May 1931, 4 Jun. 1931; Paul Rosenfels to JTF, 26 May 1931; Frances Strauss to JTF, 13 Jun. 1931.

53. DF, interview, 22 Oct. 1992; "Innocents 2," 75.

54. JTF to author, 31 Jul. 1975; SP's autobiographical sketch in Neagoe's *Americans Abroad*, 322. For Pirandello, see PN2, PN5.

55. "Author Buys Interest in 'The New Review,'" *PH*, 10 Dec. 1931, p. 3. For Neagoe, see PN2, PN4, PN6.

56. JTF to author, 12 Sept. 1960; DF, interview, 22 Oct. 1992; "Innocents 2," 72; SP, *Mistress*, 230. PN2, PN4, PN6. Among Neagoe's later works were *Winning a Wife and Other Stories* and the novels *Easter Sun* and *There Is My Heart*.

57. Hazel Rowley, chapter "La Parisienne" in *Christina Stead* (New York: Henry Holt, 1994), 101–40 passim. For Stead, see PN2.

58. JTF to author, 31 Jul. 1975, 20 Aug. 1976; DF, interviews, 22 Oct. 1992, 10 Apr. 1996; "Data," 12.

59. DF, interview, 22 Oct. 1992. PN2, PN4.

60. "Paris," 247–52; "Intro," sec. iv; Paul Avrich, *Anarchist Voices: An Oral History of Anarchism in America* (Princeton, N.J.: Princeton University Press, 1995), 66–68. Javsicas was a successful businessman, the president of the Javsicas Mahogany Company in New York City. In 1943, he published *Shortage of Victory: Cause and Cure*, a study of tyrannical totalitarian regimes. He was the witness at Jim and Dorothy's second marriage in 1955, and he and Jim remained friendly until Farrell's death in 1979.

61. JTF to Serge Fauchereaux, 28 May 1977; JTF to author, 12 Sept. 1960; "Data," 12.

62. "Notes on Contributors," *New Review* 1 (Feb./Mar./Apr. 1931): 68.

63. "Innocents 2," 134. For Bodenheim, see PN2.

64. "Paris," 220–23.

65. SP, *Mistress*, 102.

66. Bald, "La Vie de Bohème," *PT*, 17 Jun. 1931, p. 4.

67. "Paris," 262–63.

68. JTF, interview, 14 Mar. 1957; DF, interview, 21 Aug. 1994; "Time," 18–19; "Paris," 225–27, 239–42. According to Farrell, Menken became a

wealthy Chicago real-estate operator and Ginny eventually suffered a permanent mental breakdown (JTF, interview, 15 Mar. 1957).

69. JTF, interview, 20 Oct. 1975; JTF to author, 10 Aug. 1976; JTF to WC, 27 May 1931; "Paris," 235–36; PN2–3.

70. JTF to author, 9 Sept. 1959, 31 Jul. 1975, 20 Oct. 1975, 28 Jul. 1976; JTF, interview, 14 Mar. 1957; DF, interview, 22 Oct. 1992; JTF to Richard Parker, 5 Mar. 1957; JTF to Serge Fauchereaux, 28 May 1977; "Time," 143. Handler became a *New York Times* foreign correspondent in Bonn and elsewhere. He and Farrell kept in touch later in the United States. The Kahns and the Handlers frequently visited the Farrells during their Paris year. For Handler, see PN6. For Kahn, see PN2.

71. JTF, interview, 15 Mar. 1957; "Paris," 225–45.

72. SP to JTF, 22 May 1931.

73. JTF to MJF, 20 Jun. 1931; DF, interview, 22 Oct. 1992; Henri Prévost's statement specifying the Farrells' rental period. The street now is named rue Jean Mascré.

## *Chapter 3: Sceaux*

1. JTF's revised autograph manuscript "Sceaux Re-Visited" (hereafter, "Sceaux"), passim, JTF-Papers (JTF-MU, photocopy).

2. Ibid., 1–2; JTF interview, 15 Mar. 1957.

3. IS to DF: 8 Jun. 1931, 17 Jun. 1931, 7 Aug. 1931, 19 Aug. 1931, 12 Sept. 1931; "Cermak Is Firm in Vow to Clean up City's Gangs," *PT*, 21 May 1931, p. 1.

4. JTF to WC, 27 May 1931. Three weeks later, JTF wrote to his friend Tom Freeman: "Don't go much the Parisian literary atmosphere, but am not in it, so it does not affect me" (JTF to MJF, 20 Jun. 1931).

5. DF, interviews, 15 Mar. 1957, 22 Oct. 1992.

6. JTF to Riva Putnam, n.d.

7. Receipt dated 25 Aug. 1931 for rental payment to the Prévosts; "Return," 8; DF, interviews, 22 Oct. 1992, 8 Dec. 1994; *The Dunne Family*, 135. For Madame and Henri Prévost, see PN2–6.

8. DF, interview, 22 Oct. 1992.

9. Ibid.

10. JTF to author, 28 Jul. 1976; DF, interviews, 22 Oct. 1992, 8 Dec. 1994.

11. Matthews Eliot, "What the Writers Are Doing," *PT*, 14 Jun. 1931, p. 5.

12. Under "Notes on New Contributors" in the *New Review* for Aug./
Sept./Oct. 1931, p. [126], Putnam wrote: "James T. Farrell comes from
Chicago and writes about his native 'back o' the yards' district. He is a shin-
ing example (luminous by his aloneness) of literary sincerity in America. A
University of Chicago man by background, he is still in his early twenties. At
the moment, he is residing in the suburbs of Paris." Yet, if Putnam wrote the
*Tribune* item, as a Chicagoan he should have known Farrell was not from the
stockyards neighborhood. Forty-five years later, Kay Boyle repeated the error.
She believed that Farrell told her he worked in the stockyards. See Kay Boyle
(hereafter, Boyle) to author, 10 Apr. 1976. The belief that Farrell was a tough,
uncouth individual from a tough neighborhood has been a common mis-
conception.

13. JTF, interview 15 Mar. 1957; "Sceaux," passim; JTF to JH, 9 Jun. 1938;
Dorothy, interview, 27 Oct. 1997.

14. "Sceaux," 3.

15. DF, interview, 22 Oct. 1992.

16. Farrell tells the story of Heinz in his tale "Fritz," published in *When
Boyhood Dreams Come True* (New York: Vanguard Press, 1946), 140–53. For
Mullender, see PN2, PN4, PN6.

17. JTF to JH, 9 Jun. 1938. JTF, interview, 16–17 Mar. 1957; JTF to author,
20 Oct. 1975; DF, interview, 22 Oct. 1992. In his minibiography in Peter Neagoe's *Americans Abroad*, 322, Putnam stated: "Fascist in politics (hold the
*Tessera d'onore*) and respect the Communists highly." Also see JTF's 1932
diary entry for May 28. The Putnams returned to the United States in 1933
and Sam was hard pressed to earn a living. In mid-1934, he wrote to Jim: "You
may have heard that I have gone red as hell. When you've practically carried
the banner with your family for a year, you do get that way. The John Reed
Club even has decided that I'm orthodox and eligible to membership" (SP
to JTF, 24 Jul. 1934). The year before, his article "Red Days in Chicago"
(*American Mercury*, 30 [Sept. 1933]: 64–71) traced his "Red affiliation" in the
early 1920s. He was a Syndicalist at heart, and Big Bill Haywood of the IWW
was his hero. But the Wobbly movement disintegrated and "Communism
seemed to be the only other thing in sight, and I was soon taking orders from
the Third International." In Europe during the late 1920s, his sympathies
veered toward Italian Fascism. Benito Mussolini became his second and
"the only other" hero in his life.

18. SP, "A Paris Letter," *New York Sun*, 21 Nov. 1931, p. 27.

19. DB to JTF, 16 Sept. 1930; DF, interview, 22 Oct. 1992; PN2. For Saint-

Blaise, see PN3–4. Farrell remembered him as "a peppery and witty little man, but also very kind and sympathetic. He knew that we were poor and did not charge us for his services. He was reported to have delivered the Queen of Belgium and was a very distinguished French obstetrician. He had known Marcel Proust and is mentioned in *A la recherche du temps perdu*. As I look back on it, we must have seemed like American waifs to him and yet there was nothing patronizing in the man's sympathy . . . his gentleness is something that I will never forget" (JTF to Serge Fauchereaux, 28 May 1977).

20. JTF, interview, 15 Mar. 1957; Dorothy Butler to JTF, 16 Sept. 1930; DF, interview, 22 Oct. 1992; JTF to author, 13 Sept. 1960; JTF's 1931–32 notebook, titled "Journal," p. 2, JTF Papers (JTF-MU photocopy). Twenty years after their first separation, Jim and Dorothy remarried in 1955. They separated for a second time in 1958. Thereafter, in some of his letters and unpublished fiction, Farrell sometimes depicted their relationship pre-dating their first separation in a way unfavorable to Dorothy, and expressed doubts about their compatibility almost from the beginning. Considerable contemporary evidence supports the belief that their bonds remained strong beyond their year in Paris and well into the 1930s.

21. DF, interviews, 22 Oct. 1992, 22 Jul. 1994, 8 Oct. 1994; PN3–4; EB to his mother, Laura Bastian (hereafter, LB), 2 Sept. 1931; JTF to author, 20 Oct. 1975, 11 Aug. 1976; "Time," 83–112 passim. Judy Klein was born in October, a Downs syndrome baby. This led to the breakup of the Kleins's marriage. They returned to the United States before the Farrells did, and at Nathan's insistence Judy was institutionalized in Paris. She died there in 1955. Klein remarried and returned to business. Fanny remained single. She and Dorothy kept in touch.

22. In the *PT*: "Joseph Stella's Work to Go on Exhibition," 14 Jun. 1931, p. 2; "Joseph Stella Hits Note New to Paris in Current Show," 17 Jun. 1931, p. 2; "American Art Show to Open Tomorrow in Paris Gallery," 17 Jan. 1932, p. 2; "Paris Brevities," 18 Jan. 1932, p. 4; JTF to author, 12 Sept. 1960.

23. Published in 1933 by Houghton Mifflin as *Storm Beach*.

24. JTF to author, 12 Sept. 1960; JTF's 1933 diary, 28 Jan. 1933 entry, JTF Papers (JTF-MU photocopy). In the *PT*: Bald, "La Vie de Bohème," 6 Jan. 1931, p. 4; Bald, "La Vie de Bohème," 14 Apr. 1931, p. 4; Harold Ettlinger, "What the Writers Are Doing," 17 Apr. 1931, p. 4; Matthews Elliot, "What the Writers Are Doing," 20 Jun. 1931, p. 9; Bald, "La Vie de Bohème," 5 Jan. 1932, p. 4.

25. "Memoir," 7. For the Fischers, see PN3, PN5–6.

26. "Diego Rivera," *Thought* 10 (21 Jun. 1958): 15. See also DF, interview, 22 Oct. 1992; "Memoir," 7; JTF to Serge Fauchereaux, 28 May 1977; JTF to author, n.d. but received 12 Sept. 1960.

27. Farrell's untitled review of the book in the *New York Sun*, 19 Nov. 1932; "Memoir," 7; "Diego Rivera," 15; "Data," 12.

28. In *PT*: "Marathon Dance Packs 'Em in as 20th Day Starts," 8 Jul. 1931, p. 5; "Doctor at Marathon Dance Threatens Suit; Charges Against Participants Cause Stir," 13 Jul. 1931, p. 3; Herol Egan, "The Once Over," 16 Jul. 1931, p. 9; "Ho Hum! Marathon Dancers Near End; Rest Periods Cut," 20 Jul. 1931, p. 3; Bald, "La Vie de Bohème," 7 Jul. 1931, p. 4; DF, interview, 22 Oct. 1992. *La Liberté* denounced the marathon as cruel exploitation playing to the brutal instincts of the spectators. It charged that the Paris receipts were three million francs, whereas the winners were paid only twenty-five thousand francs. See "Paris Paper Attacks Marathon Dance Here as Brutal, Repugnant," *PH*, 9 Jul. 1931, p. 3.

29. For the United States Students and Artists Club, see PN3. For the Reverend Belshaw, see PN3, PN5–6.

30. JTF to author, 31 Jun. 1975, 20 Oct. 1975; for Sewarts, Squires, Catherine, and Rausch, see PN3–5; DF, interview, 22 Oct. 1992; "Time," 19–24, 118–26. Each year, the club sponsored social gatherings in Paris hotel settings, featuring prominent singers and musicians, with dancing and refreshments following. See "Paris Brevities," *PT*, 31 Oct. 1931, p. 4. An estimated five thousand U.S. students were in Paris in 1931. American residents in Paris already had raised money to construct a greatly expanded student social center, to be known as the American Students' Club. Later, it was built farther down the boulevard Raspail, adjacent to the Marie-Thérèse Hospital on land formerly part of the Chateaubriand estate. See "American Students' Social Center Opposed in Aim to Develop Site in Montparnasse," *PT*, 22 Jul. 1931, pp. 1–2; Jacques Hillairet, *Dictionnaire Historique des Rues de Paris*, 2d. édn., vol. 2 (Paris: Les Éditions de Minuit, 1964), 320–21, nos. 10 and 261 under "RASPAIL."

31. Maurice Rausch came to Paris after having broken up with the American ballet dancer Stafino. He returned to America and Stafino in 1932.

32. "Time," 19–20, 66 (the second page of that number in the sequence).

33. JTF to author, 29 Jul. 1975, 9 Sept. 1979 postmark. Other readings included Julien Green's *The Closed Garden*, Raymond Radiguet's *The Devil in the Flesh*, Irving Babbitt's *Rousseau and Romanticism*, Benjamin Hampton's

*History of the Movies*, and unspecified works by Dashiell Hammett, Kathleen Coyle, Djuna Barnes, Ben Hecht, and Lawrence Drake.

34. Harper published three of Knoblock's mysteries—one in 1931 and two in 1932—as well as his *A Winter in Mallorca* (1934). For the Knoblochs, see PN5.

35. JTF to author, 1 Sept. 1960, 20 Oct. 1975; Kenneth Knoblock to JTF, n.d.; DF, interview, 11 Jan. 1995; EB, interview, 9 Dec. 1992; EB to LB, 31 Dec. 1931. In 1937, Knoblock supported Farrell's fight against the attempted suppression of *A World I Never Made* (Kenneth Knoblock to JTF, 23 Jan. 1937).

36. PN2; Farrell discovered this when reading *Out of the Night* by Richard J. H. Krebs (Jan Valtin pseud.). See pp. 185–93 of Valtin's book. Ginny Menken's family relationship with the Russian commisar Mikhail Borodin may explain Rue Menken's acquaintance with Ginsburg. Farrell never learned whether Heinz Mullender and Rudy, Ginsburg's architectural assistants, also were involved in espionage. JTF to author, n.d. but received 12 Sept. 1960 and 1 Sept. 1961, and 20 Oct. 1975; DF, interview, 22 Oct. 1992; "Notes," 2.

37. Desmond Harmsworth to JTF, 25 May 1931; JTF to author, 25 Jul. 1961, 19 Mar. 1976.

38. EP to JTF, 23 Jun. 1931; Matthews Eliott, "What the Writers are Doing," *PT*, 14 Jun. 1931, p. 5.

39. JTF to WC, 27 May 1931.

40. JH to JTF, 14 May 1931; JTF to JH, 27 Jun. 1931, 4 Jul. 1931; JTF to SP, 1 Sept. 1931; For YL revisions, see PN2–3; "Intro," sec. v. Following Henle's suggestion, Farrell wrote and inserted a new chapter one introducing the Lonigan family at home before they go to Studs's and Frances's graduation exercises. It precedes the original chapter one, now chapter two, that opens with Father Gilhooley's graduation address. He deleted the gang-shag scene at Iris's apartment and published it twenty-five years later as "Boys and Girls" in *A Dangerous Woman and Other Stories* (1957). Before leaving for Paris, Farrell had deleted from his manuscript an episode he later published as "Curbstone Philosophy" in *Can All This Grandeur Perish? and Other Stories* (1937). He also deleted the episode about Davey Cohen after Iris had put him out of her home before Davey could take part in the gang-shag. In 1931, he published that deletion as "Jewboy" in Sam Putnam's *New Review* (Aug./Sept./Oct. 1931), 21–26. Eventually, he extensively revised "Jewboy"

and reinserted it into *Young Lonigan* as subsection i of chapter seven. This enabled him to treat the gang-shag scene indirectly through Davey's thoughts and imagination.

41. JTF to JH, 27 May 1931; "Intro," sec. v.

42. Amy Loveman to JTF, 15 May 1931, 29 May 1931; Frances Strauss to JTF, 30 Jun. 1931, 17 Jul. 1931; JTF to SP, n.d., 1 Sept. 1931; JTF to JH, 19 Jun. 1931; SP to JTF, 22 Aug. 1931; SP to Slater Brown, 22 Aug. 1931; Slater Brown to SP, 26 Aug. 1931.

43. Farrell's brother Jack, his sister Mary, Lloyd Stern, and Vladimir Janowicz heard Putnam lecture at the Fifty-seventh Street art colony (Lloyd Stern to JTF, 31 Jan. 1932; Vladimir Janowicz to JTF, 22 Oct. 1931). Stern wrote Jim that he and others among Jim's Chicago friends heard Putnam talk up Farrell while he was in the city. Janowicz mentioned in his letter that he had heard Dorothy was pregnant. Farrell told the author that he believed Putnam may have leaked that news in Chicago.

44. JTF to SP, 19 Jun. 1931; JTF to SP, n.d.; JTF to JH, 19 Jun. 1931; Boris J. Israel to JTF, 21 May 1931; H. L. Mencken to JTF, 1 Jun. 1931; JTF to Whit Burnett, 4 Jul. 1931.

45. Brown was a prolific writer in numerous genres, among them the novel, poetry, pulp fiction, detective stories, and popular history. In 1931, he published three books of his poems and was working on his 1932 *Let There Be Beer* (Joseph M. Flora, "Bob Brown" in *American Writers in Paris, 1920–1939*, ed. Karen Lane Rood [Detroit: Gale Resarch Co., 1980], 60–64).

46. Robert Carlton Brown (hereafter, RCB) to JTF, 3 Jun. 1931; Brown's "Appendix" to *Readies for Bob Brown's Machine* (Cagnes-sur-Mer: Roving Eye Press, 1931), 172, 185; PN5; Bald, "La Vie de Bohème," *PT*, 19 May 1931, p. 4. The machine was constructed by Brown's Cagnes neighbor Ross Saunders. It presented texts passing before the reader's eyes on a moving tape unrolled by an electric motor at reader-controlled speeds. Its model would be completed in a month. The texts were streamlined and fragmented, with so-called useless or superfluous words removed. Replacing conventional punctuation marks were arrows, dots, percentage marks, slant bars, equals marks, diamonds, parentheses, and other experiments in typography, all of which, Brown believed, would promote rapid reading through "quicker and vivider images than the threadbare words of the plodding pundits." Examples from *Readies* are (1) a section of Laurence Vail's "Always Gentlemen" reading: "bosomstroke onda bitches sinnocent arsetimes sliper lick cuntadino interuts Tipsindignation oral screwples," with arrows placed between the

phrases, and (2) William Carlos Williams's humorous, tongue-in-cheek "Readie Poem": "Grace - face: hot - pot: lank - spank: meat - eat: hash - cash: sell - well: old - sold: sink - wink: deep - sleep: come - numb: dum - rum: some - bum."

47. RCB to JTF, 3 Jun. 1931, 12 Jun. 1931, 19 Jun. 1931, 30 Jun. 1931; JTF to RCB, 6 Jun. 1931, two undated letters (but written June 1931).

48. RCB to JTF, 30 Jun. 1931.

49. RCB to JTF, 7 Jan. 1932, also see 3 Jun. 1931, 12 Jun. 1931, 19 Jun. 1931, 30 Jun. 1931, 1 Jul. 1931; JTF to RCB, 6 Jun. 1931, two undated letters (but written June 1931). *Readies* sold for fifty francs or two dollars.

50. JTF to JH, 7 Jan. 1931.

51. Arthur Moss, "Around the Town," *PH*, 30 Jan. 1932, p. 3.

52. Bald stated that Putnam originated the idea for this anthology and gave the task of compiling it to Neagoe, his associate on the *New Review* (Bald, "La Vie de Bohème," 20 Dec. 1932, p. 4).

53. JTF to Peter Neagoe (hereafter, Neagoe), n.d. (but written in June), 8 Jul. 1931, 3 Aug. 1931 (two letters), 5 Aug. 1931, 7 Aug. 1931, 21 Aug. 1931; Neagoe to JTF, 16 Jun. 1931, 5 Aug. 1931, 27 Oct. 1931; Vladimir Janowicz to JTF, 1 Jul. 1931. Neagoe offered to pay contributors fifty francs a page and to divide the proceeds from sales among contributors on a profit-sharing basis, an offer he was unable to honor. See Bald, "La Vie de Bohème," *PT*, 12 Oct. 1931, p. 4; Bald, "La Vie de Bohème," *PT*, 23 Sept. 1931, p. 4.

54. JTF to Neagoe, n.d.; Neagoe to JTF, 16 Jun. 1931; JTF to author, 12 Sept. 1960, 3 May 1976; "Time," 735; "Paris," 245.

55. SP, *Mistress*, 232; SP to JTF, 22 Aug. 1931; JTF to JH, 25 Aug. 1931.

56. JTF to author, 15 Aug. 1975; Henry Poulaille to JTF, 13 Jun. 1931, 14 May 1947; JTF to George Brodsky, 25 Feb. 1932. A major work by Poulaille is *Nouvel Age Litteraire* (1930), a massive commentary treating individual authors, movements, and genres. One lengthy section is on "Littérature Prolétarienne." For Lhôte and Poulaille, see PN2.

57. JTF to Serge Fauchereaux, 28 May 1977; JTF to author, n.d. but received 12 Sept. 1960, and 15 Aug. 1975; "Data," 12.

58. Henri Barbusse to JTF, 12 Jun. 1931; EB to LB, 2 Sept. 1931; PN3–4; Jacques Duclos and Jean Fréville, *Henri Barbusse* (Paris: Éditions Sociales, 1946), 17; JTF to author, 15 Aug. 1975.

59. DF, interview, 8 Dec. 1994; EB to LB, 4 Feb. 1932.

60. JTF to Evelyn Shrifte, 7 Oct. 1931; "Paris," 208; "Intro," sec. iv; PN1; Matthews Elliot, "What the Writers Are Doing," *PT*, 14 Jun. 1931, p. 5. Baker,

the author of *Cooperative Enterprises* (1937), became Farrell's good friend. Evelyn Shrifte published many of Farrell's books after she purchased Vanguard Press from Henle and became its president in 1952.

61. JH to JTF, 8 Jun. 1931; Frances Strauss to JTF, 13 Jun. 1931; WC to JTF, 15 Jun. 1931; PN2.

62. JTF to JH, 19 Jun. 1931, 22 Jun. 1931, 26 Jun. 1931.

63. JTF to RCB, 5 Jul. 1931.

64. JTF, "Afternoon in Paris," *Thought* 16 (18 Apr. 1964): 11.

65. P. 110.

66. TM to JTF, 4 Jul. 1931, 6 Jul. 1931; MJF to JTF, 14 Jul. 1931.

67. IS to DF, 7 Jul. 1931, 19 Aug. 1931, 25 Aug. 1931; DF, interview, 26 Feb. 1996.

68. JH to JTF, 30 Jun. 1931. See also JH to JTF, 12 Jun. 1931.

69. DF, interview, 22 Oct. 1992.

70. JTF to JH, 27 May 1931, 22 Jun. 1931; PN to JTF, 16 Jun. 1931.

71. JTF to RCB, n.d.

72. JTF to JH, 22 Jun. 1931. For JTF on sociology, see PN3.

73. Riva Putnam to JTF, 27 Jun. 1931, 11 Jul. 1931; JTF to Riva Putnam, 4 Jul. 1931.

74. DF, interview, 22 Oct. 1992; PN3.

75. "Parisians Swarm Out and Provincials Flock in as City Begins Three-Day National Festival," *PT*, 13 Jul. 1931, p. 1. In the *PH:* "Paris Prepares for Celebrations on Bastille Day," 12 Jul. 1931, p. 3 and "Streets Filled with Whirling Dancers as Paris 'Lets Go' for Bastille Day," 13 Jul. 1931, pp. 1, 3.

76. JTF to Herbert Rosengren, 15 Jul. 1932.

77. JTF to Riva Putnam, 17 Aug. 1931; Christina Stead to JTF, n.d.

78. "Magnificent Show for Bastille Day Defies Weather," *PT*, 15 Jul. 1931, pp. 1, 3.

79. EB to LB, 24 Jul. 1931; Paul Rudnick to JTF, 25 Apr. 1931; Frederick Schuman to JTF, 14 Feb. 1976; Paul Rudnick to author, 21 Jul. 1976; JTF to author, 20 Oct. 1975, 28 Jul. 1976, 26 Aug. 1976; Frederick L. Schuman to author, 14 Feb. 1976; Schuman to JTF, 14 Feb. 1976; DF, interviews, 22 Oct. 1992, 20 Oct. 1993. Rudnick became a well-known astronomer and astrophysicist.

80. JH to JTF, 30 Jun. 1931; JTF to JH, 16 Jul. 1931, 17 Jul. 1931; JTF to Mary Farrell, n.d.

81. JTF to JH, 19 Jun. 1931; JH to JTF, 30 Jun. 1931; JTF to author, 7 Jan. 1976.

82. WEF to JTF, 5 Jul. 1931, 29 Jul. 1931, 8 Sept. 1931; John Farrell to JTF, 21 Jul. 1931.

83. TM to JTF, 8 May 1931; Frances Strauss to JTF, 5 Oct. 1931, 26 Nov. 1931, 30 Dec. 1931; Heinz Mullender to JTF, 16 Nov. 1931, 30 Nov. 1931, 21 Dec. 1931; WEF to JTF, 8 Sept. 1931; James J. ("Jack") Sullivan to JTF, 15 Sept. 1931; Ruth Jameson to JTF, 4 Feb. 1932.

84. Vladimir Janowicz to JTF, 26 Aug. 1931, 22 Oct. 1931, 14 Dec. 1931.

85. JTF to author, 15 Aug. 1961.

86. After his return to New York in April 1932, Farrell wrote to his friend Dr. Noah Fabricant: "Everybody is going proletarian, sociological, etc., and they have now gotten a lot of shibboleths like social significance, which they tack onto everything that is written. It seems to me that the pattern of the story is very old and very deeply rooted in the human organism, and that people like the story for its own sake" (JTF to Dr. Noah Fabricant, 8 Aug. 1932).

87. JTF to JH, 14 Aug. 1931, 21 Sept. 1931; JTF to Richard Johns, 25 Sept. 1931.

88. DF, interview, 22 Oct. 1992. For JTF's composition of "The Madhouse," later retitled *Gas-House McGinty*, see PN4–5.

89. JTF to Theodore Marvel, 15 Sept. 1931. "In the early fall," Farrell recalled, "I had in something like ten days, written the first draft of my second novel, *McGinty*, and had mailed it off to the United States in order to get a contract and an advance of money which I badly needed. . . . I remember how happy and confident I had been . . . working from morning on into the night until I was too tired to continue" ("Sceaux," 4). In 1955, he believed he worked all day every day for ten days or two weeks before he completed his manuscript. ("The Tommy Collins Stories," JTF Papers [JTF-MU photocopy], dated 9 Jun. 1955); also see "Return," 8.

90. DF, interview, 22 Oct. 1992; JTF to JH, 19 Jun. 1931, 16 Jul. 1931, 17 Jul. 1931, 14 Aug. 1931, 13 Sept. 1931; JTF to MJF, 1 Aug. 1931; JH to JTF, 30 Jun. 1931, 3 Aug. 1931; JTF to author, 7 Jan. 1976.

91. JTF MS "The History of Studs' Death Consciousness," JTF Papers (JTF-MU, photocopy), 1.

92. "Special Introduction to the Avon Edition of Gas-House McGinty," *Gas-House McGinty* (New York: Avon, 1950), n.p.

93. "Return," 8.

94. "On the American Express Novel to be Titled 'The Madhouse,'" n.d. Also see "Journal," JTF's 1931–32 notebook, 37–38, a Jun. 14 entry. Written while he was still revising *Gas-House McGinty* in New York, this entry ex-

plains that he tried to approach his literary material without preconceptions, whereas Marxists demanded "cast-iron preconceptions, which means 'You know the Marxian meaning of a thing before the fact.' . . . My method permits one to register the feelings of the day. The Marxian method fails to permit one to make this registration as successfully."

95. JTF to JH, 15 Sept. 1931; see also JTF to Whit Burnett, 15 Sept. 1931; JTF to SP, 1 Sept. 1931.

96. Edwin Seaver's *The Company* (1930) is a series of sketches, each focusing on a representative episode in the lives of eleven persons who work in the office of the Universal Illuminating Company. Unlike *Gas-House McGinty*, the interaction depicted between the characters in the company's office is relatively momentary and minor.

97. JH to JTF, Aug. 1931; John Howard Lawson, "Preface," *Processional: A Jazz Symphony of American Life in Four Acts* (New York: Thomas Seltzer, 1925), i–ix; JTF to JH, 14 Aug. 1931.

98. JH to JTF, 3 Aug. 1931.

99. Dorothy recalled that they were stopped by the Paris police near the Cluny Museum (DF, interview, 22 Oct. 1992).

100. Riva Putnam to JTF, 27 Jun. 1931; JTF to Riva Putnam, 5 Jul. 1931; Henri Prévost's residency statement for the Farrells; DF, interviews, 22 Oct. 1992, 8 Dec. 1994.

101. JTF to MF, 17 Aug. 1931; JTF to RCB, n.d.; JTF to JH, 18 Oct. 1931; DF, interview, 22 Oct. 1992; "Friend," 18–19, 30–31.

102. "Friend," 31. Farrell here misdates his effort to get the *cartes d'identité*. For JTF on Pierre-Jean Robert, see PN3–6.

103. DF, interview, 22 Oct. 1992.

104. RCB to JTF, 3 Jun. 1931, 1 Jul. 1931; JTF to RCB, 5 Jul. 1931; DF, interviews, 22 Oct. 1992, 21 Aug. 1994; JTF to Riva Putnam, n.d.; Sarajo Caron Krumgold to JTF, n.d.; JTF to author, 11 Jul. 1976. After the death of Paul Caron, Sarajo's first husband and Farrell's friend, she married Joseph Krumgold, a writer and director at Hollywood's Paramount Studios.

105. JTF to EB, 24 Aug. 1931; EB to LB, 26 Aug. 1931; DF, interview, 22 Oct. 1992. Farrell's story "Mendel and His Wife" is his fictional portrait of the Menkens. It was published in *Can All This Grandeur Perish? and Other Stories* (1937), 3–24.

106. Kenneth and Adaline Knoblock to JTF and DF, 27 May 1932.

107. Farrell envied Ed Bastian for his opportunity to study with Mathiez and read about the French Revolution. His own interest in that subject was

later deepened by his reading of Mathiez's *The French Revolution* and *After Robespierre* (JTF to author, 28 Jul. 1976). Farrell's story "An American Student in Paris" is based on Ed Bastian's year in Paris (*Childhood Is Not Forever* [New York: Doubleday, 1969], 133–65).

108. EB, interviews, 6 Oct. 1975, 21 Oct. 1975, 9 Oct. 1992. PN3–6. In later life, Bastian edited *Business Week*, fought in the Second World War, completed his graduate work, taught for ten years in the Humanities Division of the University of Chicago College, and then, until retirement in 1975, at Earlham College.

109. DF, interview, 8 Dec. 1994.

110. JTF to MJF, 1 Aug. 1931.

111. DF, interviews, 22 Oct. 1992, 8 Dec. 1994, 26 Feb. 1996; EB to LB, 5 Aug. 1931; IS to DF, 23 Jun. 1931, 17 Jul. 1931, 19 Aug. 1931, 8 Sept. 1931, 11 Dec. 1931.

112. EB, interview, 9 Dec. 1992.

113. Frances Strauss to JTF, 31 Jul. 31; JTF to EB, 11 Aug. 1931, 13 Aug. 1931, 17 Aug. 1931, n.d. postcard; EB to LB, 12 Aug. 1931, 19 Aug. 1931; EB to Philip Kinsley, 18 Aug. 1931.

114. EB to LB, 19 Aug. 31.

115. Ellen Julia (Ella) Daly to JTF, n.d. In this letter, as in all other transcripts, the spelling is as in the original. See also WEF to JTF, 31 Aug. 1931.

116. Margaret Butler (hereafter, MB) to DF, 20 Aug. 1931. After Maggie Butler learned of the marriage, Ted Marvel wrote to Jim about his visit to her. He found her in "a convalescent stage after the overwhelming shock you gave her." He believed that just before she received Dorothy's letter, she learned the truth from "the Greek who owns the grocery and delicatessen on the corner," who learned it from the Farrells' friend Mary Hunter, who learned it from a university professor. See TM to JTF, 1 Sept. 1931; JTF to TM, 15 Sept. 1931. For Maggie Butler, see PN3–4, PN6.

117. "'Tribune' Staff Does Its Bit for Third Issue of 'New Review,'" *PT*, 17 Aug. 1931, p. 2.

118. Bald, "La Vie de Bohème," *PT*, 19 Aug. 1931, p. 4.

119. Harold Ettlinger, "What the Writers Are Doing," *PT*," 1 May 1931, p. 4.

120. JTF to Nancy Cunard, 26 Aug. 1931; Helen Rosenfels to JTF, 1 Nov. 1931. For Cunard, see PN4.

121. DF, interview, 22 Oct. 1992.

122. EB to LB, 2 Sept. 1931.

123. JTF to EB, 8 Sept. 1931; EB to LB, 2 Sept. 1931; EB to Albert C. Hess, 3 Sept. 1931; EB to Philip Kinsley, 3 Sept. 1931; EB, interview, 9 Dec. 1992.

124. EB to Walter J. Hipple, 2 Sept. 1931.

125. JTF to EB, 8 Sept. 1931; EB, interview, 9 Dec. 1992.

126. Whit Burnett to JTF, 13 Sept. 1931, 6 Oct. 1931; H. L. Mencken to JTF, 5 Sept. 1931; H. L. Mencken to WC, 22 Oct. 1931; Richard Johns to JTF, 8 Sept. 1931; JTF to Richard Johns, 25 Sept. 1931; Lincoln Kirstein to JTF, 15 Sept. 1931, 14 Oct. 1931.

127. JTF to EP, 12 Oct. 1931; EP to JTF, 16 Oct. 1931, postcard.

128. Sarajo Caron Krumgold to JTF, 19 Sept. 1931; JTF to JH, 14 Aug. 1931, 4 Oct. 1931.

129. JTF to RCB, 13 Sept. 1931.

130. JTF to JH, 13 Sept. 1931.

131. JTF, "Return," 8; "Data," 12.

132. JTF to JH, 13 Sept. 1931; JTF to TM, 15 Sept. 1931; JTF to author, 18 Jan. 1976.

133. JTF to JH, 13 Sept. 1931.

134. JTF to TM, 15 Sept. 1931.

135. JTF to JH, 4 Oct. 1931; see also JTF to TM, 15 Sept. 1931; JTF to Richard Johns, 25 Sept. 1931.

136. JTF to JH, 15 Sept. 1931, 21 Sept. 1931.

137. DF, interview, 22 Oct. 1992; EB, interview, 9 Dec. 1992.

138. JH to JTF, 28 Sept. 1931; JH to WC, 28 Sept. 1931; Frances Strauss to JTF, 29 Sept. 1931; JTF to EB, 30 Sept. 1931.

139. JTF to Helen and Lawrence Townley, 10 Oct. 1931; JH to JTF, 28 Sept. 1931; JTF to JH, 4 Oct. 1931; JTF to Evelyn Shrifte, 7 Oct. 1931.

140. JTF to Evelyn Shrifte, 7 Oct. 1931; Paul Avrich, *Anarchist Voices*, 58–59. In later life, Pauline Turkel was managing editor of *The Psychoanalytic Quarterly*. For Evelyn Shrifte and Pauline and Nat Turkel, see PN4.

141. JTF's 1934 diary for Feb. 2, p. 74, JTF Papers (JTF-MU photocopy); "Began," begun 17 Apr. 1971, 4.

142. "Return," 8. In the *PT*: "Two More Strikers Die in Kentucky Coal Mine War," 1 Sept. 1931, p. 1; "Jobless Problem Serious, Chicago Bishop Declares," 2 Sept. 1931, p. 2; "Market Again Drops, Bringing Crisis Nearer," 9 Sept. 1931, p. 1; "England Abandons Gold Basis," 21 Sept. 1931, p. 1; "Increase in Idle Adds to Growing Woes of G.O.P.," 26 Sept. 1931, p. 1; "Hoover Silent on U.S. Attitude toward Silver," 5 Oct. 1931, pp. 1, 3; "Danger of Inflation Is Seen by French in Hoover's Proposal," 8 Oct. 1931, p. 1.

143. JTF to EB, 5 Oct. 1931.

144. EB, interview, 9 Dec. 1992.

145. EB to Walter J. Hipple, 5 Oct. 1931.

146. DF, interview, 22 Oct. 1992.

147. Death notice of Julia Daly, *Chicago Daily Tribune*, 3 Oct. 1931, including the statement: "Grandmother of James T. Farrell of Paris, France"; "Return," 8; PN4.

148. "Return," 8.

149. James J. Sullivan to JTF, 15 Sept. 1931; JTF to author, 15 Dec. 1975.

150. JTF to JH, 4 Oct. 1931. Dorothy met Titus only once—on a Paris street leading two greyhounds that he said belonged to his son Horace. She found him to be friendly and pleasant. See DF, interview, 22 Oct. 1992.

151. Cable, DF to MB, 3 Oct. 1931: "Send flowers Daly 2023 E. 72 St. sign card Jimmie grandmother dead mailing cost"; JTF to JH, 4 Oct. 1931.

152. Ellen Julia (Ella) Daly to JTF, 4 Oct. 1931, 6 Oct. 1931; Helen Farrell Townley to JTF, 5 Oct. 1931; WEF to JTF, n.d.; JTF to Helen and Lawrence Townley, 10 Oct. 1931; Lloyd Stern to JTF, n.d.; Joseph Cody to JTF, n.d.

153. Au Bon Marché sales slips for 12, 13, and 16 Oct. 1931; EB to LB, 14 Oct. 1931.

154. JTF to SP, 10 Oct. 1931.

155. JTF to SP, 1 Sept. 1931.

156. JTF to EB, 14 Oct. 1931, 31 Oct. 1931; DF, interview, 22 Oct. 1992; EB to LB, 4 Nov. 1931; Heinz Mullender to JTF, 16 Nov. 1931, 30 Nov. 1931.

157. JTF to JH, 18 Oct. 1931; "Friend," 2–3. PN3, PN5–6.

158. Pierre-Jean Robert to JTF, 22 Oct. 1931.

159. JTF to JH, 24 Oct. 1931.

160. EB, interview, 6 Oct. 1975.

161. JTF to Neagoe, 7 Nov. 1931. For Fernandez, see PN4–5.

162. JTF to JH, 24 Nov. 1931.

163. JTF to EB, 31 Oct. 1931.

164. JTF to MJF, 7 Nov. 1931. See also JTF to Neagoe, 7 Nov. 1931; EB to LB, 4 Nov. 1931, 12 Nov. 1931, 25 Nov. 1931.

165. IS to DF, 19 Oct. 1931, 20 Nov. 1931, 21 Dec. 1931; EB, interview, 9 Dec. 1992.

166. JTF to JH, 4 Oct. 1931, 7 Oct. 1931, 18 Oct. 1931, 24 Oct. 1931, 31 Oct. 1931; JTF to MJF, 14 Oct. 1931; WC to JTF, 16 Sept. 1931; JTF to MF, 5 Nov. 1931; JTF to EP, 12 Oct. 1931, 21 Nov. 1931; EP to JTF, n.d., postcard.

167. Walt Carmon wrote Farrell on 16 September 1931 that he was so

swamped with work that in all fairness he felt Farrell should get a new agent. He suggested Maxim Lieber. Farrell came to an agreement with Lieber in October. See JTF to Richard Johns, 25 Sept. 1931; JTF to JH, 4 Oct. 1931, 24 Oct. 1931.

168. JTF to JH, 4 Oct. 1931, 31 Oct. 1931. Krumgold became a successful screenwriter, director, and producer for the major Hollywood film companies and, later on, for television. Among his eight published books were the award-winning novels about the maturation of adolescents . . . *And Now Miguel* (1953), *Onion John* (1959), and *Henry 3* (1967).

169. Alexander F. Schlosser to JTF, 18 Oct. 1931; JTF to Lloyd Stern, 30 Oct. 1931; JTF to JH, 31 Oct. 1931, 1 Nov. 1931, 6 Nov. 1931; JTF to EB, 31 Oct. 1931, 4 Nov. 1931; JTF to MJF, 7 Nov. 1931; EB to JTF, 3 Nov. 1931.

170. JTF to JH, 31 Oct. 1931.

171. JTF to JH, 24 Oct. 1931, 31 Oct. 1931, 24 Nov. 1931, 2 Dec. 1931.

172. JTF to JH, 9 Nov. 1931 (one of two letters of this date to JH).

173. JTF to Desmond Harmsworth, 17 Oct. 1931; Desmond Harmsworth to JTF, 18 Nov. 1931; JTF to JH, 21 Nov. 1931.

174. JTF to JH, 4 Oct. 1931, 6 Nov. 1931; JH to JTF, 30 Oct. 1931, 20 Nov. 1931; JTF to MF, 5 Nov. 1931; JTF to MJF, 7 Nov. 1931.

175. JH to JTF, 30 Oct. 1931; JTF to MJF, 7 Nov. 1931; "Began," vol. 2, no. 1, completed 17 Apr. 1971, 80, 101–11 (erratic numbering).

176. JTF to Neagoe, 7 Nov. 1931; JTF to MJF, 7 Nov. 1931.

177. H. L. Mencken to JTF, 21 Oct. 1931.

178. JTF to JH, 9 Nov. 1931.

179. JH to JTF, 20 Nov. 1931.

180. Neagoe to JTF, 23 Nov. 1931. Neagoe's reference is to Theodor Hendrik van de Velde's *Ideal Marriage — Its Physiology and Technique.*

181. JTF to JH, 9 Nov. 1931; JH to JTF, 14 Nov. 1931; JTF to Carl Sandburg, n.d.; Carl Sandburg to JTF, 17 Dec. 1931.

182. "Friend," 18.

183. Boyle to author, 10 Sept. 1976. For Kay Boyle and Laurence Vail, see PN5.

184. DF, interview, 22 Oct. 1992; JTF to author, 18 Apr. 1976.

185. JTF to SP, 17 Nov. 1931; DF, interview, 22 Oct. 1992.

186. "Innocents 1," 3–4; "Friend," 10.

187. JTF to EB, 15 Nov. 1931.

188. JTF to JH, 9 Nov. 1931.

189. JTF to JS, 8 Nov. 1931; JS to JTF, 12 Nov. 1931. Schwartz mentioned to Farrell: "I asked Henderson 'Well why don't you print Farrell if he's so

good?' but I never got a definite answer—it's so English—to be evasive—but I guess your hootch is too strong for them." Titus was the husband of Helena Rubinstein, although they were separated. He was wealthy. Farrell confirms in his PN1 that many Montparnassians called him "Tight-Ass" or "Mr. Rubinstein . . . as though he had at his command, all of Helena Rubinstein's fortune and resources, but that he was withholding this wealth from needy artists . . . who were his betters."

190. JTF to EB, 15 Nov. 1931, 17 Nov. 1931; JTF to JH, 16 Nov. 1931; JTF to JS, 15 Nov. 1931; JS to JTF, 19 Nov. 1931.

191. JTF to EB, 17 Nov. 1931.

192. Cablegram, DF to MB, 14 Nov. 1931.

193. MB to JTF, 14 Nov. 1931. In Farrell's MS "Went Away," 126–31, Marion Healy's (Dorothy Butler's) mother gives Eddie's (Jim's) mother ten dollars as she leaves Mrs. Healy's apartment. On 18 October, Isabel Simpson wrote to Dorothy that Maggie, although upset by the marriage, was virtually reconciled to it and secretly glad. In a letter of 20 Nov., Isabel told Dorothy that Maggie had Jim's mother and his aunt Ella over for tea, further evidence, Isabel believed, that she was becoming reconciled to Dorothy's marriage. Isabel reported that Maggie liked her guests but thought that Mrs. Farrell, Jim's mother, was too religious, even though witty. Isabel advised Dorothy to tell everyone of the marriage, including her uncle and aunt Roney. "James is so highly spoken of by anyone and everyone that your mother really feels that you are in very good hands."

194. MB to DF, n.d.

195. JTF to EB, 17 Nov. 1931.

196. DF to MB, 24 Nov. 1931; JTF to MB, 24 Nov. 1931.

197. JTF to JH, 16 Nov. 1931, 24 Nov. 1931; JTF to EB, 17 Nov. 1931; JTF to EP, 21 Oct. 1931; "Return," 8; "Thoughts on Returning to Paris," JTF MS, JTF Papers (JTF-MU, photocopy).

198. JTF to JH, 24 Nov. 1931; JTF to EB, 17 Nov. 1931.


## Chapter 4: Sean

1. IS to DF, 21 Dec. 1931.

2. "Innocents 1," 1–4; DF, interview, 22 Oct. 1992.

3. EB to LB, 2 Dec. 1931; JTF to JH, 6 Nov. 1931; JH to JTF, 20 Nov. 1931; JTF to EB, 10 Dec. 1931.

4. JS to JTF, 1 Dec. 1931; JTF to EB, 2 Dec. 1931, 10 Dec. 1931.

5. JTF to JS, 6 Jan. 1932.

6. EB to LB, 2 Dec. 1931, 9 Dec. 1931, 19 Dec. 1931.

7. JTF to Riva Putnam, n.d., but written 10 Dec. 1931.

8. JTF to EB, 10 Dec. 1931, 13 Dec. 1931.

9. JTF to Riva Putnam, n.d., but written 10 Dec. 1931; JTF to EB, 10 Dec. 1931; JTF to JH, 17 Dec. 1931; EB to LB, 19 Dec. 1931; JTF, "Friend," 31, 33; JTF, "Soap," *Guillotine Party and Other Stories* (New York: Vanguard Press, 1935), 3–12.

10. DF, interview, 22 Oct. 1992. For Sean's birth, see PN4.

11. "Return," 8.

12. "Friend," 31–32.

13. JTF to Riva Putnam, n.d., but written 10 Dec. 1931.

14. "Friend," 31.

15. EB to LB, 19 Dec. 1931, 31 Dec. 1931; DF, interview, 22 Oct. 1992; JTF to MJF, 6 Jan. 1932. For Sean's death, see PN4.

16. William E. DeCourcy, U.S. consul, "Report of the Death of an American Citizen," American Foreign Service, 19 Dec. 1931; Bernard J. Lane, embaumer, receipt to JTF, 16 Dec. 1931; Dr. Boeffe de Saint-Blaise, statement, 28 Dec. 1931 and 18 Feb. 1932; JTF to Serge Fauchereaux, 28 May 1977.

17. JTF to SP, 17 Dec. 1931.

18. EB to LB, 19 Dec. 1931, 21 Jan. 1932.

19. DF, interview, 22 Oct. 1992.

20. JTF to Riva Putnam, 13 Dec. 1931; JTF to Kay Boyle, 13 Dec. 1931.

21. "Friend," 33–34.

22. "A new girls' club has been organized near Edgar-Quinet. It is called The Sphinx and about 30 girls may be found there. It is an interesting place, and modern husbands are sending their wives to this lively center for special domestic instruction" (Bald, "La Vie de Bohème," *PT*, 9 Jun. 1931, p. 5). Sam Putnam remembered that "invitations to the *'grande ouverture'* were . . . sent out to practically everyone in the sixth *arrondisement*, and we were supposed to bring our wives! . . . a characteristic Gallic touch . . . it was very much as if the café du Dôme and the café Sélect had merged and moved to another location." The Sphinx was "a most respectable institution of its sort, conducted under municipal supervision and known to the French by the charming euphemism *maison close*" (*Mistress*, 90–92).

23. "The Girls at the Sphinx," *An American Dream Girl* (New York: Vanguard Press, 1950), 58–62. For JTF at the Sphinx, see PN5.

24. Ibid, 62–63; "Friend," 34–37.

25. DF, interview, 22 Oct. 1992.

26. "In the Latin Quarter," *PH*, 14 Dec. 1931, p. 11. Farrell is named there as "the young Chicago writer now coming into prominence."

27. PN4, pp. 214–18. On pages 652–53 of volume one of his unfinished novel "Equal to the Centuries" JTF Papers (JTF-MU photocopy), Farrell recorded Eddie Ryan's musings about his baby's death one year after it occurred. Then visiting Marion's (Dorothy's) family in Chicago, Eddie recognizes that he and Marion "had been hurt" by the loss, she more than he. But now "he could say it had been a blessing in disguise. . . . If the baby had lived . . . he would have been placed in a position of dependency on her family. Wouldn't this have been intolerable? . . . If the baby had lived, they would have had to return to America sooner and he would have had to get a job. What kind of job? . . . Where? New York? Chicago? Would he have been able to publish *Loudmouth Cannon* [the novel's equivalent of *Gas-House McGinty*]? . . . He did not want another baby . . . he had suggested to Marion shortly after their return from Paris that she go to a birth control center and get fitted for a pessary. She had. He had no thought of becoming a father."

28. H. L. Mencken to JTF, 6 Dec. 1931; JH to JTF, 3 Dec. 1931 (one of two letters of that date from Henle), 11 Dec. 1931.

29. JTF to EB, 22 Dec. 1931; JTF to JH, 23 Dec. 1931; EB to LB, 31 Dec. 1931.

30. JS to JTF, 17 Dec. 1931, 7 Jan. 1932.

31. In mid-1931, Collier had won the prize offered by Edward Titus to the best young English poet whose poems had appeared in *This Quarter*; Alf to JS, 11 Dec. 1931; JTF to EP, 9 Jan. 1932; JTF to author, 25 Jul. 1961.

32. Boyle to JTF, 15 Dec. 1931.

33. JTF to JS, 6 Jan. 1932; JS to JTF, 7 Jan. 1932; JTF to JH, 7 Jan. 1932.

34. JTF to EP, 6 Jan. 1932, 9 Jan. 1932.

35. EP to SP, Friday, n.d.; JTF to EP, 6 Jan. 1932, 9 Jan. 1932.

36. JTF to JH, 24 Nov. 1931, 2 Dec. 1931.

37. Pierre-Jean Robert to JTF, 23 Dec. 1931; JTF to RCB, 11 Jan. 1932; JTF to MF, 12 Jan. 1932; EB to LB, 31 Dec. 1931.

38. "Friend," 16–17.

39. JTF to Riva Putnam, n.d., but written 23 Dec. 1931; JTF to MF, 12 Jan. 1932; Boyle to author, 10 Apr. 1976; JTF to author, 19 Apr. 1976.

40. EB to LB, 2 Apr. 1932. For Bazin, see PN5.

41. Farrell usually welcomed "Irish" book review assignments. From 1929

through Feb. 1934, he reviewed almost twenty books about Irish culture or by Irish authors, including Liam O'Flaherty, Thurston Macauley, George Moore, Frank O'Connor, Maurice O'Sullivan, and James Joyce.

42. PN5; JTF to author, 20 Oct. 1975; JTF, interview, 17 Mar. 1957. Farrell also had read Mary Colum's literary criticism, which, he stated, showed "an aggressiveness of manner and vocabulary. . . . She wrote badly. She thought as badly as she wrote. Her writing was a matter of citation which far outran assimilation." PN5.

43. EB to LB, 9 Dec. 1931; JTF to EB, 22 Dec. 1931.

44. In PH: "In the Latin Quarter," 29 Dec. 1931, p. 3, and "'New Review' Group Hosts to Gathering of Artists, Writers," 2 Jan. 1932, p. 3.

45. JTF to JH, 17 Dec. 1931, 8 Jan. 1932; JH to JTF, 28 Dec. 1931; EB to LB, 31 Dec. 1931; JTF to EB, 5 Jan. 1932.

46. JTF to RCB, 11 Jan. 1932; RCB to JTF, 17 Jan. 1932; also see RCB to JTF, 12 Jan. 1932; DF, interview, 22 Oct. 1992.

47. Boyle to author, 10 Apr. 1976.

48. JTF to MF, 12 Jan. 1932.

49. JTF to author, 18 Apr. 1976.

50. JTF to author, 19 Apr. 1976.

51. JTF to RCB, 31 Dec. 1931; JTF to EB, 5 Jan. 1932; JTF to JH, 5 Jan. 1932, 7 Jan. 1932; IS to DF, 4 Feb. 1932, 15 Feb. 1932.

52. Arthur Moss, "Around the Town," PH, 2 Jan. 1932, p. 2.

53. Boyle to author, 10 Apr. 1976. This procedure occurred later. It is related in Farrell's story "Soap," which possibly is the source of Boyle's recollection.

54. "'New Review' Group Hosts to Gathering of Artists, Writers," PH, 2 Jan. 1932, p. 3; "Paris Autobiography," JTF-Papers (JTF-MU photocopy), notebook completed 8 Mar. 1972, 377–82.

## Chapter 5: Final Days

1. George Brodsky to JTF, 9 Mar. 1932. Kathleen Coyle agreed with Brodsky's view. On 3 August 1932 she wrote to Farrell: "You are essentially an American writer and your place is there. . . . I mean that you are, deep down at your roots, in touch with the American consciousness, that your value as an artist lies there."

2. JTF to JH, 13 Mar. 1932; JTF to RCB, 11 Jan. 1932, n.d., but probably 12

Jan. 1932; RCB to JTF, 12 Jan. 1932, 17 Jan. 1932; JTF to MF, 12 Jan. 1932; JTF to MJF, 18 Jan. 1932; JTF to George Brodsky, 25 Feb. 1932. In Apr. 1932 Farrell commented in a biographical note: "I . . . belong to no expatriate literary movements, so-called, and am in no sense of the word an expatriate" ("James T. Farrell," *Americans Abroad*, [142]).

3. JTF to William Targ, 6 Jan. 1932, 11 Jan. 1932. In 1942, Targ, then an editor at World Publishing Company in Cleveland, arranged with Farrell to publish a forty-nine-cent hardcover edition of *Gas-House McGinty*, which quickly sold more than 135,000 copies. This led Targ and Ben Zevin, head of World, to put out similar reprint editions of the three Studs Lonigan novels and then the Danny O'Neill novels, all of which sold extremely well. See JTF to author, 9 Apr. 1975.

4. JTF to EP, 11 Jan. 1932.

5. EB to Albert C. Hess, 22 Jan. 1932.

6. Edward Titus to JTF, 8 Feb. 1932.

7. LS to JTF, n.d.

8. EP to SP, n.d., postcard probably written 4 Jan. 1932; JTF to MJF, 6 Jan. 1932; JTF to EP, 6 Jan. 1932; JTF to MF, 12 Jan. 1931.

9. "Paris Brevities," *PT*, 14 Jan. 1932, p. 4; Horatio S. Krans to JTF, 5 Feb. 1932; PN6.

10. RCB to JTF, 7 Jan. 1932; JTF to RCB, 11 Jan. 1932.

11. JTF to JH, 8 Jan. 1932; JTF to MJF, 18 Jan. 1932.

12. JTF to JH, 11 Jan. 1932, 16 Jan. 1932; Alexander L. Schlosser to JTF, 4 Feb. 1932; JTF to Alexander L. Schlosser, 16 Feb. 1932; JTF to MF, 12 Jan. 1932.

13. JTF to MJF, 18 Jan. 1932.

14. LS to JTF, 8 Feb. 1932.

15. RCB to JTF, 12 Jan. 1932.

16. EB to LB, 21 Jan. 1932, 29 Jan. 1932.

17. JTF to EP, 6 Jan. 1932, 17 Feb. 1932; JTF to JH, 11 Jan. 1932; JTF to RCB, 11 Jan. 1932; JTF to MJF, 18 Jan. 1932; "Friend," 210.

18. JTF to JH, 8 Jan. 1932, 11 Jan. 1932; JTF to EP, 17 Feb. 1932; JTF to MF, 12 Jan. 1932; EB to LB, 21 Jan. 1932; JTF to RCB, 11 Jan. 1932.

19. EP to JTF, 3 Feb. [1932]. Farrell readily admitted the influence of *A Portrait* upon his writing. "I believe until this day I favor that among Joyce's books," he stated shortly before his death (JTF interview with Matthew J. Bruccoli, in *Conversations with Writers II*, ed. Richard Layman, 24).

20. JTF to JH, 11 Jan. 1932, 18 Feb. 1932; JTF to EP, 6 Jan. 1932, 17 Feb.

1932; EP to JTF, 3 Feb. 1932; RCB to JTF, 12 Jan. 1932; Desmond Harmsworth to JTF, 23 Feb. 1932.

21. JTF to EP, 17 Feb. 1932; "Ernest Hemingway Features First Crosby Edition," *PH*, 28 Dec. 1931, p. 5; "Mrs. Crosby Tells of New Plans for Book Publishing," *PT*, 23 Jan. 1932, p. 3; Bald, "La Vie de Bohème," *PT*, 2 Feb. 1932, p. 4.

22. JTF to MJF, 18 Jan. 1932.

23. EB to LB, 21 Jan. 1932.

24. JTF to JH, 8 Jan. 1932, 18 Feb. 1932; JTF to EB, 21 Jan. 1932; Le Home Joli billing statement, 17–29 Mar. 1932; "Time," 16–18, 58–63; EB to Albert C. Hess, 22 Jan. 1932.

25. EB to LB, 29 Jan. 1932.

26. EB to LB, 29 Jan. 1932, 5 Feb. 1932.

27. DF, interview, 22 Jul. 1994.

28. "Began," vol. 2, no. 1, completed 17 Apr. 1971, renumbered pp. 252–53. Coincidentally, in 1932, when the Farrells lived at Truly on the Square in Greenwich Village, the Cohens again lived above them. Jim learned that Larry was a Museteite and a revolutionist and that Jane was a firebrand radical who had difficulty keeping a job because she loved to march in picket lines and join antipolice demonstrations ("Began," vol. 2, no. 2, begun 17 Apr. 1971, doubly numbered pp. 81–84, 254–57).

29. "Time," 43–49.

30. Farrell's tale "Soap" in *Guillotine Party and Other Stories:* 3–12; "Time," passim.

31. EB to LB, 29 Jan. 1932; "Time," 68–75.

32. DF, interview, 22 Oct. 1992. Sam Putnam may have been thinking of this time when he wrote: "They came about as near starving as anyone could" (*Mistress,* 108). In response to a reader's criticism of the antics of café-going Montparnasse artists, Wambly Bald wrote an affective essay on Parnassian poverty. A brief excerpt:

> Tales of slow starvation are old and homely. . . . You will often find among your despised Parnassians better examples of pride and courage than are exhibited by the whimpering stockholders. The general tendency in these parts, believe it or not, is to conceal one's embarrassment. . . . These artists and poets of Montparnasse, who cling to the slippery surface of survival, should not all be deposited in a bogus classification. Many of them, most of them perhaps, clutch their weary muses hour after hour, day after day, in skimpy hall bedrooms and badly ventilated studios while nervous

landlords annoy them for back rent. If, now and then, some of them get lost in play and raise hell at the Dôme, as they did on Bastille Night, and annoy their neighbors, let us not leap at conclusions. ("La Vie de Bohème," 26 Jul. 1932, p. 4)

33. DF, interview, 22 Oct. 1992.

34. "Time," 192.

35. "Paris Shivers in Blanket of Snow, with Cold Wave Due to Continue," *PT*, 11 Feb. 1932, p. 1.

36. JTF to author, 20 Oct. 1975; EB to LB, 12 Feb. 1932; "Data," 12; "Notes," 2; "Time," 1–15; JTF to Bruce Parrain, 25 May 1933; PN6.

37. "Time," 76; PN5.

38. "Time," 76–80; "Return," 8.

39. "Time," 81–82.

40. JTF to author, 20 Oct. 1975; Horatio S. Krans to JTF, 17 Feb. 1932; cablegram from Paris, dated 10 Feb. 1932, 8:19 A.M.

41. MB to JTF, n.d., probably 11 or 12 Feb. 1932.

42. JTF to JH, 12 Feb. 1932. Dorothy Farrell related the following to the author: While Jim was house-bound, she went to see Fanny Klein. There she met a Mrs. Horowitz, a neighborhood friend of Fanny's who knew Gertrude Stein. The three women were soon on their way to Stein's apartment in the rue de Fleurus. Dorothy remembered that several men—painters, she believed—were there, as well as Robert McAlmon, the only person she knew. He put his arm around her shoulders, took her up to Gertrude Stein, and introduced her. Stein soon dismissed her: their conversation was limited to Dorothy's explanation that she was living in Paris with her husband, a young American writer. She spent most of her time there looking at Picasso paintings on the walls, and she recalled that Gertrude Stein served little round cakes and not sandwiches (DF, interview, 22 Oct. 1992).

43. *New Review* 1 (Aug./Sept./Oct. 1931): 138. Putnam's translation was published by Dutton in 1932.

44. "Paris Theatres," *PH*, 16 Nov. 1931, p. 2; "News of the Theatres," *PH*, 23 Nov. 1931, p. 7; "Paris Brevities," *PT*, 30 Jan. 1932, p. 4; "News of the Theatres," *PH*, 4 Apr. 1932, p. 2..

45. "Pirandello to Hear Play Read Americans," *PH*, 8 Feb. 1932, p. 3; "News of the Theatres," *PH*, 15 Feb. 1932, p. 7; Putnam, *Mistress*, 62. See also in the *New Review* 1 (Feb./Mar./Apr. 1931): Willard Widney, "Records/Notes on New Jazz," 60–61, and "Notes on Contributors," 69. Putnam sketches the Widneys under the names of Steve and Emily Braden in *Mistress*, 92–93.

46. Felix Kolodziej to JTF, 19 Mar. 1932. For the Pirandello reading and the Widneys, see PN5.

47. DF, interview, 22 Oct. 1992.

48. "Time," 185–86, 189.

49. LS to JTF, 1 Mar. 1932.

50. "Time," 148, 173–86; JTF to Florence W. Bowers, 1 May 1939; JTF, "A Tribute to Kathleen Coyle," *News of Books and Authors* [E. P. Dutton trade paper] 1 (May–Jun. 1939): 1, 3–4; PN5.

51. "Time," 181. In Farrell's "Paris Was Another Time" Coyle is the basis for the character Celia Kearney. In a letter to the author postmarked 17 Dec. 1975, Farrell remarked: "I took liberties imagining a past for her."

52. PN5.

53. JTF to EB, 17 Feb. 1932; Kathleen Coyle to JTF and DF, 24 Feb. 1932; JTF to JH, 7 Mar. 1932; "Time," 189–92, 204–7; EB to LB, 26 Feb. 1932, letter written and double-dated 2 and 4 Apr. 1932. Kathleen Coyle and the Farrells continued an overseas friendship by correspondence for several years. Farrell tried to help her place a novel with Vanguard Press and to get movie rights for another novel (Kathleen Coyle to JTF, 18 May 1932, 3 Aug. 1932, 4 Nov. 1936).

54. "Return," 8; EB to LB, 21 Mar. 1932.

55. JTF to George Brodsky, 25 Feb. 1932. See also George Brodsky to author, 3 Feb. 1976, 6 Nov. 1979. Brodsky had published poetry in Chicago, and in 1932 he was working on a massive history of novels about the First World War that he did not complete. Later he established his successful Chicago firm, George Brodsky Advertising, Inc.

56. JTF to Brodsky, 25 Feb. 1932, 20 Apr. 1932, and 16 May 1932; Brodsky to JTF, 7 Mar. 1932.

57. Fanny's story served Farrell as the basis for his tale "Scrambled Eggs and Toast," *The Life Adventurous and Other Tales* (New York: Vanguard, 1947), 76–82.

58. EB to LB, 26 Feb. 1932, 5 Mar. 1932; Pierre-Jean Robert to JTF, 1 Mar. 1932; in *PT*: "Albert Mathiez, Noted Historian, Dies Suddenly," 27 Feb. 1932, p. 4; "Late Professor Mathiez Debunked Reputation of Revolutionary Hero," 6 Mar. 1932, p. 4. JTF to author, 10 Jan. 1976.

59. EB to LB, 14 Mar. 1932; DF, interview, 22 Oct. 1992; in *PT*, "Briand, 11 Times Premier, Dies," 7 Mar. 1932, p. 1, and "Friends, Foes of Briand Join in Final Rites," 12 Mar. 1932, pp. 1, 2. JTF, "An American Student in Paris," *Childhood Is Not Forever*, 149.

60. Albert M. Newman to SP, 5 Mar. 1932; SP to Newman, 8 Mar. 1932.

61. Published by Bobbs-Merrill in 1933.

62. Writing to Henle on March 13, Farrell stated that Newman began the book as a defense of capitalism, visited Russia, changed his mind, and decided his book should be on an "economy for use."

63. JTF to JH, 13 Mar. 1932. For Newman, see PN6.

64. "Time," 133–39.

65. Ibid, 140–46.

66. In "Time," Eddie thinks of Marion: "Yes, he did love her. . . . Yet he often wished to go to bed with other girls. He kept looking at French women on the streets of Paris and he would fill up with desire. . . . But he was locked in monogamy. . . . Eddie was certain that if he had slept with Frances as many times as he had with Marion, he would have had eyes for Marion. Sleeping with the same woman did not wear well with him. He couldn't prove it but he didn't think that it did with any man" ("Time," 233, 734).

67. RCB to JTF, 12 Mar. 1932; JTF to JH, 13 Mar. 1932.

68. IS to DF, 5 Apr. 1932, 12 Apr. 1932; Western Union Telegraph Company receipt for one hundred dollars, dated 30 Mar. 1932, for a cablegram from MB to DF.

67. JTF to Albert Newman, 29 Mar. 1932.

70. JTF to EP, 7 Apr. 1932; JTF to JH, 31 Mar. 1932.

71. In *Guillotine Party and Other Stories*, 33–45.

72. DF, interview, 22 Oct. 1992.

73. The final legal guillotining in France occurred 17 June 1939. A decree forbidding public executions was issued 24 June 1939 (Barbara Levy, *Legacy of Death* [Englewood Cliffs, New Jersey, 1973], 244–45).

74. EB, interview, 9 Dec. 1992.

75. Ibid.

76. JTF to JH, 7 Mar. 1932; Milton Abernethy to JTF, 4 Mar. 1932. Abernethy published an excerpt from *Young Lonigan* in the 5 May 1932, number of *Contempo*.

77. "Indecorous But Good, Four Unusual Tales Feature New Story," *PT*, 14 Mar. 1932, p. 2.

78. WEF to JTF, 28 Feb. 1932.

79. PN1, PN5. In answer to the query "'Did Joyce influence you technically?'" Farrell stated:

"Oh yes. . . . In Paris in early 1932 or late '31 I was rereading *Ulysses*, and at the time I was working on *Gas-House McGinty*. I had my first book, *Young Lonigan*, accepted. Originally I'd planned the *Lonigan* as one book, and it grew into three books. To start, I'd planned for it to end with his death in his young manhood. When I reread the Night Town scene I thought to describe his death as—that suggestion, of course, came from the Night Town scene of his dying consciousness—a grand fantasy of the day of judgment. That's how I came to the title, *Judgment Day*. In preparation for that I added a chapter to *Gas-House McGinty*—I believe it's chapter seven—of McGinty's dreams. Finally the Lonigan books grew into three volumes; and I wrote that scene, but it wouldn't fit the book after Studs in *Judgment Day* receives the last sacraments of the church. The scene would have been out of proportion. I never could get it published separately." (JTF, interview by Matthew J. Bruccoli, *Conversations with Writers II*, 23–24)

Farrell published those portions of his depiction of Studs's dying consciousness that escaped burning in his 1946 apartment fire. See "Fragments from the Unpublished Death Fantasy Sequence of 'Judgment Day,'" *Tri-Quarterly* 1 (winter 1965): 127–38. Slightly revised versions are in the 1979 Vanguard Press and the Literary Guild Press editions of *Studs Lonigan*.

80. JTF to JH, 13 Mar. 1932.

81. "Introduction" to *Gas-House McGinty*, Tower Books edition (Cleveland and New York: World, 1942), 13–14.

82. "*Gas-House* was only one part of an enormous manuscript, and there was another entire novel, with Willie Collins the leading character. . . . In between, there was a shorter section, revised into 'Omar James'" (JTF to author, 15 Aug. 1961).

83. See the JTF MS "The History of Studs' Death Consciousness" and "The Tommy Collins Stories," JTF Papers (JTF-MU, photocopy). At some time in the fall of 1932, hurting for money in New York and with Henle's acquiescence, Farrell decided to publish section one, already accepted by Henle, by itself as *Gas-House McGinty*. He could then rather quickly complete *The Young Manhood of Studs Lonigan* and get a contract and an advance on it. His *McGinty* MS was in Henle's hands 1 November, Farrell corrected proofs early in December, and the novel appeared in February 1933. "Omar James" was published in Farrell's *To Whom It May Concern and Other Stories* (New York: Vanguard Press, 1944), 119–38. But large portions of sections two and three of his Express Company manuscript were destroyed in his 1946 apartment fire. However, he salvaged about a dozen short stories, ten from section three (JTF to author, 2 Jul. 1969; JTF to MJF, 6 Jun. 1932, 20 Aug. 1932, 2 Nov. 1932; JTF to LS, 28 Jul. 1932; JTF to MF, 18 Oct. 1932, 4 Dec. 1932; JTF to SP, 29 Nov. 1932).

84. Frederic Thrasher, "Introduction" to *Young Lonigan* (New York: Vanguard Press, 1932), xi; for Thrasher, see PN3.

85. JTF to Frederic Thrasher, 15 Mar. 1932.

86. JH to JTF, 1 Apr. 1932.

87. "Intro," sec. vii.

88. Desmond Harmsworth to JTF, n.d., 29 Mar. 1932, 12 Apr. 1932; JTF to SP, 1 Apr. 1932.

89. Bald, "La Vie de Bohème," 23 Feb. 1932, p. 4; 8 Mar. 1932, p. 4.

90. The American Aid Society in Paris screened "hundreds of applications for aid . . . received daily" and annually helped hundreds of the most needy: "Those who ask for transportation, those wanting employment, the needy who are too old to help themselves, stranded students, stranded seamen and deserted wives" ("American Groups Here to Launch Appeal for Aid Society, Broke after Bank Failure," *PT*, 18 Jan. 1931, p. 1). For the scope of the society's activity, see also in *PT*: "Aid Society Sent 25 Back to U.S.," 8 Jan. 1931, p. 8; "American Aid Society Helped 109 of 142 Applicants in January," 13 Feb. 1931, p. 2.

91. JTF to JH, 31 Mar. 1932; JTF to SP, 1 Apr. 1932; JTF to EB, n.d.

92. JTF to MJF, 31 Mar. 1932; JTF to EP, 7 Apr. 1932.

93. "Return," 8; JTF to EB, 6 Apr. 1932; EB to LB, 13 Apr. 1932.

94. JTF to EB, n.d., but probably 2 Apr. 1932, 6 Apr. 1932; JTF to SP, 1 Apr. 1932; statement from Le Home Joli for Mar. 17 to 29; EB to LB, written 2 and 4 Apr. 1932; Kenneth and Adaline Knoblock to JTF and DF, 27 May 1932; JTF to EP, 7 Apr. 1932.

95. JTF to Florence W. Bowers, 1 May 1939.

96. SP to J. G. Grey, 7 Apr. 1932; DF, interview, 8 Dec. 1994.

97. Pierre-Jean Robert to JTF, 8 Apr. 1932; JTF to SP and Riva Putnam, 8 Apr. 1932.

98. DF, interview, 22 Oct. 1992.

99. EB to LB, 13 Apr. 1932; "Statendam to Sail Today for New York," *PT*, 9 Apr. 1932, p. 2.

100. DF, interview, 22 Oct. 1992.

101. JTF to MF, 13 Apr. 1932.

102. "Journal" (JTF's 1931–32 notebook), p. 11, 16 Apr. 1932.

103. "A Special Message to Subscribers from James T. Farrell," introduction to *Young Lonigan* (Franklin Center, Pennsylvania: Franklin Library, 1979), n.p.

104. "Journal," 6–9, 14 Apr. 1932 entry; "Began," vol. 2, no. 1, completed 17

Apr. 1971, 46–51 (erratic numbering); DF, interview, 22 Oct. 1992. JTF to author, n.d., but postmarked 11 Mar. 1976 (two letters of this postmark). In New York, Dorothy and Jim talked to Phyllis Russell's brother at the Greenwich Village Inn and learned that she was being looked after. In Farrell's tale "After the Sun Has Risen," Agatha Stallings is the character modeled on Phyllis Russell. See $1,000 a Week and Other Stories, 86–97.

105. "Began," vol. 2, no. 1, completed 17 Apr. 1971, 5–6, 7–8 (erratic numbering).

106. DF, interview, 20 Oct. 1993.

107. "Began," vol. 2, no. 1, completed 17 Apr. 1971, 16–44 (erratic numbering).

108. Bald, "La Vie de Bohème," PT, 19 Apr. 1932, p. 4; 10 May 1932, p. 4.

109. SP, Mistress, 110–11.

110. EB to Phillip Kinsley, 4 Apr. 1932.

# Bibliography

*The following list is of works cited in the text and notes. The dates give date of first publication.*

## Publications by James T. Farrell

"After the Sun Has Risen." In *$1,000 a Week and Other Stories*, 86–97. New York: Vanguard Press, 1942.

*American Dream Girl, An*. New York: Vanguard Press, 1950.

"American Student in Paris, An" In *Childhood Is Not Forever*, 133–65. New York: Doubleday, 1969.

"Author's Note." Preface to "Studs" in *The Short Stories of James T. Farrell*, 348. New York: Vanguard Press, 1955.

*Boarding House Blues*. New York: Paperback Library, 1961.

"Boys and Girls." In *A Dangerous Woman and Other Stories*, 25–30. New York: Vanguard Press, 1957.

"Can All This Grandeur Perish?" In *Can All This Grandeur Perish? and Other Stories*, 3–24. New York: Vanguard Press, 1937.

*Can All This Grandeur Perish? and Other Stories*. New York: Vanguard Press, 1937.

"Casual Incident, A" In *Calico Shoes and Other Stories*, 140–47. New York: Vanguard Press, 1934.

*Childhood Is Not Forever*. New York: Doubleday, 1969.

"Counting the Waves." In *$1,000 a Week and Other Stories*, 173–91. New York: Vanguard Press, 1942.

"Criticism of the University Library Department, A" *Daily Maroon*, 14 December 1928: 3.

"Curbstone Philosophy." In *Can All This Grandeur Perish? and Other Stories*, 212–22. New York: Vanguard Press, 1937.

*Dangerous Woman and Other Stories, A.* New York: Vanguard Press, 1957.

"Diego Rivera." *Thought* 10 (21 June 1958): 15.

*Doll's Journey, The,* by Ellen and Adam Fischer, untitled review of. *New York Sun,* 19 November 1932, n.p. [copy of the needed edition unavailable].

*Dunne Family, The.* Garden City, New York: Doubleday, 1976.

"La filosofia del presente, di G. H. Mead." *Il Mare, Supplemente Letterario* 1 (12 November 1932): 3. ["George Herbert Mead's *Philosophy of the Present.*" In *Literature and Morality,* 177–81. New York: Vanguard Press, 1947].

"Fragments from the Unpublished Death Fantasy Sequence of 'Judgment Day.'" *Tri–Quarterly* 1 (winter 1965): 127–38.

"Fritz." In *When Boyhood Dreams Come True,* 140–53. New York: Vanguard Press, 1946.

*Gas-House McGinty.* New York: Vanguard Press, 1933.

"Girls at the Sphinx, The." In *An American Dream Girl,* 58–63 New York: Vanguard Press, 1950.

"Guillotine Party." In *Guillotine Party and Other Stories,* 33–45. New York: Vanguard Press, 1935.

*Guillotine Party and Other Stories.* New York: Vanguard Press, 1935.

"Half Way from the Cradle." *Earth* 1 (June 1930): 1–3, 14.

"Helen, I Love You!" *American Mercury* 26 (July 1931): 267–71. Revised and reprinted in *Calico Shoes and Other Stories,* 3–14. New York: Vanguard Press, 1934.

"Honey, We'll Be Brave." In *Calico Shoes and Other Stories,* 99–139. New York: Vanguard Press, 1934.

"In the Park." *Tambour* 8 (1930): 36–38.

"Introduction," *Gas-House McGinty,* Tower Books edn., 13–14. Cleveland and New York: World, 1942.

"James Farrell." *New York Herald Tribune Book Review,* 12 October 1972: 14.

"James T. Farrell." In *Americans Abroad: An Anthology,* edited by Peter Neagoe, [142]. The Hague: Servire Press, 1932.

"Jeff." In *Readies for Bob Brown's Machine,* edited and with an appendix by Robert Carlton Brown, with a preface by Hilaire Hiler, 16–25. Cagnes-sur-Mer: Roving Eye Press, 1931. Revised and reprinted as "Big Jeff," In *Guillotine Party and Other Stories,* 46–53. New York: Vanguard Press, 1935.

"Jewboy." *New Review* 1 (August/September/October 1931): 21–26. Revised and reprinted in *Young Lonigan*, chapter 7, part 1. New York: Vanguard Press, 1932.

"Jim Farrell Pens a Paris Memoir." *Panorama* (syndicated magazine). In *Chicago Daily News*, 23 December 1967: 7.

"John Dewey's Philosophy." *Saturday Review of Literature* 6 (12 July 1930): 1194.

*Judgment Day*. New York: Vanguard Press, 1935.

*Literature and Morality*. New York: Vanguard Press, 1947.

*Lonely for the Future*. New York: Doubleday, 1966.

"Looking 'Em Over." In *Calico Shoes and Other Stories*, 37–56. New York: Vanguard Press, 1934.

"Meet the Girls." In *Calico Shoes and Other Stories*, 264–303. New York: Vanguard Press, 1934.

"Mendel and His Wife." In *Can All This Grandeur Perish? and Other Stories*, 3–24. New York: Vanguard Press, 1937.

"Merry Clouters, The" *This Quarter* 5 (October-December 1932), 373–89. Revised and reprinted in *Guillotine Party and Other Stories*, 82–107. New York: Vanguard Press, 1935.

"Modernism Marks American Exhibit at Art Institute." *Daily Maroon*. 9 November 1928: 3.

*My Baseball Diary*. New York: A. S. Barnes, 1957.

"My Friend the Doctor." *Tambour* 8 (1929): 38–40.

*Note on Literary Criticism, A*. New York: Vanguard Press, 1936.

"Omar James." In *To Whom It May Concern and Other Stories*, 119–38. New York: Vanguard Press, 1944.

"On Picasso and Van Gogh: Forms of Alienation." *Genesis West* 1 (winter 1962–63): 114–22.

*$1,000 a Week and Other Stories*. New York: Vanguard Press, 1942.

"Open Road, The." In *Guillotine Party and Other Stories*, 13–32. New York: Vanguard Press, 1935.

"Return to Paris." *New Leader* 32 (7 May 1949): 8.

"Saturday Night." In *The Life Adventurous and Other Stories*, 83–136. New York: Vanguard Press, 1947.

"Scarecrow, The." In *Calico Shoes and Other Stories*, 15–36. New York: Vanguard Press, 1934.

*Short Stories of James T. Farrell, The*. New York: Vanguard Press, 1937.

"Slob." *Blues* 1 (June 1929): 114–16.

"Soap." In *Americans Abroad: An Anthology*, ed. Peter Neagoe, 143–48. The Hague: Servire Press, 1932. Revised and reprinted in *Guillotine Party and Other Stories*, 3–12. New York: Vanguard Press, 1935.

"Special Introduction to the Avon Edition of Gas-House McGinty." In *Gas-House McGinty*, Avon edn., n.p. New York: Avon, 1950.

"Special Message to Subscribers from James T. Farrell, A." The introduction to *Young Lonigan*, n.p. New York: Franklin Library, 1979.

"Spring Evening." In *Can All This Grandeur Perish? and Other Stories*, 138–50. New York: Vanguard Press, 1937.

"Studs." *This Quarter* 3 (July/August/September), 187–95. Revised and reprinted in *Guillotine Party and Other Stories*, 295–305. New York: Vanguard Press, 1935.

*Studs Lonigan: A Trilogy.* New York: Vanguard Press, 1935.

"Sylvester McGullick." In *Readies for Bob Brown's Machine*, edited and with an appendix by Robert Carlton Brown, with a preface by Hilaire Hiler, 16–25. Cagnes-sur-Mer: Roving Eye Press, 1931.

"Thirty and Under." *New Freeman* 1 (2 July 1930): 373–374.

*To Whom It May Concern and Other Stories.* New York: Vanguard Press, 1944.

*When Boyhood Dreams Come True.* New York: Vanguard Press, 1946.

*World I Never Made, A.* New York: Vanguard Press, 1936.

*Young Lonigan.* New York: Vanguard Press, 1932.

*Young Manhood of Studs Lonigan, The.* New York: Vanguard Press, 1934.


## James T. Farrell's Manuscripts
## Exclusive of Correspondence

Manuscript sources are (1) photocopies in the Miami University Farrell Collection made from originals in the Farrell Archives, Van Pelt Library, University of Pennsylvania: JTF Papers (JTF-MU photocopy); (2) originals in the Miami University Farrell Collection, Oxford, Ohio: (JTF-MU).

"After Eddie and Marion Went Away." JTF Papers (JTF-MU photocopy).

"Autobiography." A brief undated MS. JTF-MU.

"Autobiography Paris Notebook 3 by James T. Farrell Oct. 14/71 N.Y. N.Y. Completed Nov. 30/71": JTF Papers (JTF-MU photocopy).

"Autobiography Paris Notebook 4 James T. Farrell Nov. 30/71 N.Y. N.Y. Completed Feb. 3 1973 [1972] N.Y. N.Y." JTF Papers (JTF-MU photocopy).

"The Call of Time." JTF Papers (JTF-MU photocopy).

"Chamber of Horrors" [title of a projected but unpublished short-story collection].

"Data Abroad." JTF-MU.

Diary, 1933. JTF Papers (JTF-MU photocopy).

Diary, 1934. JTF Papers (JTF-MU photocopy).

"The Distance of Sadness." JTF Papers (JTF-MU photocopy).

"Equal to the Centuries." JTF Papers (JTF-MU photocopy).

"Harry and Barney." JTF Papers.

Untitled article on Henle, James. JTF Papers (JTF-MU photocopy).

"The History of Studs' Death Consciousness." JTF Papers (JTF-MU photocopy).

"Innocents in Paris," texts 1 and 2. JTF-MU (typescript revised by JTF).

"Introduction Studs Lonigan." JTF Papers (JTF-MU photocopy).

"Journal" [1931–32 notebook]. JTF Papers (JTF-MU photocopy).

"McGinty King of Ireland." JTF Papers.

"Madhouse, The" [provisional title for *Gas-House McGinty*].

"Memoirs of a Cub Campus Reporter Who Covered the St. Valentine's Day Massacre." JTF Papers (JTF-MU photocopy).

"My Friend, Jean Paul." JTF Papers (JTF-MU photocopy).

"Notebook and Diary for 1930." JTF Papers (JTF-MU phocotopy).

"Notebook-Novel-Am Ex Company." JTF Papers (JTF-MU photocopy).

"Notes by James T. Farrell/Volume One/1935." 22 February 1935 entry on Van Gogh and Cézanne, 435–37. JTF Papers (JTF-MU photocopy).

"Observations of American Life and Literature." JTF Papers.

"On Coming to Paris." JTF Papers (JTF-MU photocopy).

"On the American Express Novel to Be Titled 'The Madhouse.'" JTF Papers (JTF-MU typescript).

"[Bernard in] Paris." JTF Papers (JTF-MU photocopy).

Paris address book. JTF Papers (JTF-MU photocopy).

"Paris Autobiography." JTF Papers (JTF-MU photocopy).

"Paris Autobiography by James T. Farrell Feb. 3/1972 N.Y. N.Y. Completed March 8/1972 4th [5th] Notebook N.Y. N.Y." JTF Papers (JTF-MU photocopy).

"Paris Autobiography by James T. Farrell March 8 1972 N.Y. N.Y. Final Note-boook of MSS Completed March 20, 1972 N.Y. N.Y." JTF Papers (JTF-MU photocopy).

"Paris Novel." JTF Papers (JTF-MU photocopy).

"Paris—The Psychopathic Ward of America." JTF Papers.

"Paris Was Another Time." JTF Papers (JTF-MU photocopy).

"Sceaux Re-Visited." JTF Papers (JTF-MU photocopy).

"Since I Began," vol. 2, no. 1, completed 17 April 1971. JTF Papers (JTF-MU photocopy).

————, vol. 2, no. 2, begun 17 April 1971. JTF Papers (JTF-MU photocopy).

————, vol. 3, completed 26 May 1976. JTF Papers (JTF-MU photocopy).

"Since I Began Completed July 1 [17?] 1971 Paris 1931–1932 by James T. Farrell Paris [illegible word]," JTF Papers (JTF-MU photocopy).

"Since I Began No. 2 by James T. Farrell Paris Experience [?] 1931–32 Completed Oct. 14/71." JTF Papers (JTF-MU photocopy).

"Some Memories of Paris." JTF Papers (JTF-MU photocopy).

"Some Scenes of My Paris Stories." JTF-MU.

"Their Little Moments of Glory" [original title of "Saturday Night"].

"These Chicagoans." [provisional title for Farrell's first short-story collection].

"Thoughts on Chicago and Paris." JTF Papers (JTF-MU photocopy).

"The Tommy Collins Stories." JTF Papers (JTF-MU photocopy).

"Thoughts on Returning to Paris." JTF Papers (JTF-MU photocopy).

"The World Around Me." Editorial for the Alburn Bureau, a syndication agency, on his job as campus reporter. JTF Papers and JTF-MU.

"The World Is Today." Editorial for the Alburn Bureau, a syndication agency, on Joyce's *Ulysses*. JTF Papers and JTF-MU.

"When Time Was Young." JTF Papers (JTF-MU photocopy).

## Farrell's Correspondence

The text and notes cite letters in Farrell's correspondence (either to or from him) with the following individuals. Citation of individual letters—writer, recipient, date, and source—may be found in the notes.

Abernethy, Milton                    Kolodziej, Felix

Addams, Jane
Bastian, Edward
Block, Harry
Bowers, Florence W.
Boyle, Kay
Branch, Edgar M.
Brewer, Joseph
Brodsky, George
Brown, Robert Carlton
Brown, Slater
Burnett, Whit
Butler, Dorothy
Butler, Margaret
Carmon, Walt
Cody, Joseph
Cowley, Malcolm
Coyle, Kathleen
Cunard, Nancy
Daly, Ellen Julia
Darrow, Clarence
Eaton, G. D.
Fabricant, Noah
Fadiman, Clifton
Farrell, John Anthony
Farrell, Mary Elizabeth
Farrell, William Earl
Fauchereaux, Serge
Ford, Charles Henri
Harmsworth, Desmond
Henle, James
Israel, Boris J.
Jameson, Ruth
Janowicz, Vladimir
Johns, Richard
Kirstein, Lincoln
Knoblock, Adaline
Knoblock, Kenneth
Kohn, Sherwood

Krans, Horatio S.
Krumgold, Sarajo Caron
Lathrop, Helen
Levin, Harry
Light, Evelyn
Loveman, Amy
Lovett, Robert Morss
MacDonald, William
Marvel, Theodore
Mencken, H. L.
Mullender, Heinz
Neagoe, Peter
Newman, Albert M.
Nicolson, J. U.
North, Sterling
Parker, Richard
Parrain, Bruce
Poulaille, Henry
Pound, Ezra
Putnam, Riva
Putnam, Samuel
Robert, Pierre-Jean
Rosenfels, Helen
Rosenfels, Paul
Rosengren, Herbert
Rudnick, Paul
Sandburg, Carl
Schapiro, Meyer
Schlosser, Alexander
Schuman, Frederick L.
Schwartz, Jacob
Stead, Christina
Stern, Lloyd
Strauss, Frances
Sullivan, James J.
Targ, William
Titus, Edward
Thrasher, Frederic M.

## Correspondence Other Than Farrell's

Alf to Jacob Schwartz
Bastian, Edward to Laura Bastian
Bastian, Edward to Albert C. Hess
Bastian, Edward to Walter J. Hipple
Bastian, Edward to Philip Kinsley
Boyle, Kay to Edgar M. Branch
Butler, Margaret to Dorothy Farrell
Carmon, Walt to James Henle
Cowley, Malcolm to Edgar M. Branch
Henle, James to Walt Carmon
Hunsinger, Maxine H. to Edgar M. Branch
Mencken, H. L. to Walt Carmon
Newman, Albert M. to Samuel Putnam
Newman, Stanley to Edgar M. Branch
North, Sterling to Edgar M. Branch
Pound, Ezra to Samuel Putnam
Putnam, Samuel to Pascal Covici
Putnam, Samuel to J. G. Grey
Putnam, Samuel to Ezra Pound
Rudnick, Paul to Edgar M. Branch
Schuman, Frederick L. to Edgar M. Branch
Simpson, Isabel to Dorothy Farrell
Sullivan, Maxine to Cleo Paturis
Williams, William Carlos to Charles Henri Ford

## Selected Secondary Bibliography

Bald, Wambly. "La Vie de Bohème," column in the *Chicago Daily Tribune* (Paris edn.) April 1931–July 1932.

Bastian, Edward. Interviews by the author. 6 October 1975, 22 October 1975, 9 December 1992. JTF-MU.

Brown, Robert Carlton, ed. *Readies for Bob Brown's Machine*. Cagnes-sur-Mer: Roving Eye Press, 1931.

Bruccoli, Matthew. "James T. Farrell," interview. In *Conversations with Writers II*, ed. C. E. Frazer Clark Jr. Detroit: Gale Research Co., 1978.

*Chicago Daily Tribune* (Paris edn.). January 1931–May 1932.

Fischer, Ellen and Adam. *A Doll's Journey*. London: Desmond Harmsworth Press of Bloomsbury, 1932.

Flora, Joseph M. "Bob Brown." In *American Writers in Paris, 1920–1939*, ed. Karen Rood. Vol. 4 of *Dictionary of Literary Biography*. Detroit: Gale Research Co., 1980.

Ford, Hugh. *Published in Paris: A Literary Chronicle of Paris in the 1920s and 1930s*, Collier Books edn., New York: Macmillan, 1988.

———, ed. *The Left Bank Revisited: Selections from the Paris Tribune 1917–1934*. University Park and London: Pennsylvania State University Press, 1972.

Fritz, Mark. "Peter Neagoe." In *American Writers in Paris, 1920–1939*, ed. Karen Rood. Vol. 4 of *Dictionary of Literary Biography*. Detroit: Gale Research Co., 1980.

Hillairet, Jacques. *Dictionnaire Historique des Rue de Paris*, 2d. édition. Paris: Éditions de Minuit, 1964.

Lawson, John Howard. *Processional: A Jazz Symphony of American Life in Four Acts*. New York: Thomas Seltzer, 1925.

Mellen, Joan. *Kay Boyle: Author of Herself*. New York: Farrar, Straus & Giroux, 1994.

Neagoe, Peter, ed. *Americans Abroad: An Anthology*. The Hague: Servire Press, 1932.

*New Review*. 1, no. 1 (February/March/April 1931), 2, no. 5 (April 1932).

*New York Herald* (Paris edn.). January 1931–May 1932.

*New York Sun*. Samuel Putnam's column "A Paris Letter," 1931–32, secs. "Books and Bookmen" and "Books."

Newman, Albert M. *Enough for Everybody*. Indianapolis: Bobbs-Merrill, 1933.

Putnam, Samuel. *Paris Was Our Mistress: Memoirs of a Lost and Found Generation*. New York: Viking Press, 1947.

Rood, Karen L. "Samuel Putnam." In *American Writers in Paris, 1920–1939*, ed. Karen L. Rood. Vol. 4, *Dictionary of Literary Biography*. Detroit: Gale Research Co., 1980.

Rowley, Hazel. *Christina Stead*. New York: Henry Holt, 1994.

Seaver, Edwin. *The Company*. New York: Macmillan, 1930.

Thrasher, Frederic L. Introduction to *Young Lonigan: A Boyhood in Chicago Streets*. New York: Vanguard Press, 1932.

University of Chicago. "The University of Chicago Official Academic Record: James Thomas Farrell."

# Index

Beach, Sylvia, 3, 20

Beckett, Samuel, 80, meets the Farrells, 40

*Béjazet* (Racine), 120

*Belle Eveillée, La* (Franc-Nohain), 120

Belshaw, Rev. Harold: aids the Farrells, financially, 165–66 n. 51, 236–37; —, locating apartment for, 124; —, obtaining return passage for, 141–42; description and status, 58; as peacemaker, 77–78

Berkman, Alexander, 45; meets Farrell, 109

*Bird of God: The Romance of El Greco* (Virginia Hersch), 56

Black Manikin Press, 30

Blake, William (Wilhelm Blech), 44–45

Blech, Wilhelm. *See* Blake, William

Bliven, Bruce, 13

*Blues*, publishes Farrell's "Slob," 11, 12

Bodenheim, Maxwell: and the Farrells in Chicago, 5–6, 7, 154 n. 26; in Paris, 46–47

Bontempelli, Massimo, 15

Borodin, Mikhail, 77

*Boston* (Sinclair), Farrell reads, 58

*Bostonians, The* (James), Farrell reads, 58

Boyd, Ernest, 25

Boyle, Kay, 63, 77, 107; Farrell reads, 2; gives baby clothes to Dorothy, 99; gives Christmas reception, 115–16; on Farrell's background and description, 116, 168 n. 12; on Farrell's fiction, 111, 122; meets Farrell, 112; visits the Farrells, 117

Brewer and Warren Publishers, 19, 24

Brewer, Joseph, on *Young Lonigan*, 19, 29, 24

Briand, Aristide, death of, 134

Brodsky, Bella Rubinson (Mrs. George), 133

Brodsky, George, 119; as businessman and writer in Chicago, 188 n. 55; characterizes Dorothy, 154 n. 27; elicits Farrell's view of Farrell's writing, 132–33; urges Farrell's return to U.S., 118–19

*Brothers Karamazov, The* (Dostoyevsky), in Farrell's "library nucleus," 4

Brown, Anna (Farrell's fictional character based on Dorothy), 17

Brown, Robert Carlton (Bob), 65, 67, 83–84, 93, 115, 119; helps Dorothy get baby clothes, 99; invites Farrells to Cagnes-sur-Mer, 76, 112, 115; offers Farrell sales commissions, 120; praises Farrell's writing, 122; publishes Farrell's "Jeff" and "Sylvester McGullick," 62–63; on *Readies for Bob Brown's Machine*, 61–62; recommends American Aid Society, 127; returns to U.S., 141; selections from *Readies*, 172–73 n. 46. *See also Readies for Bob Brown's Machine*

Brown, Slater, 61; aids Farrell, 25; informs Farrell of publication of "Studs," 17, 24

Brundage, Slim, 8, 164–65 n. 42. *See also* Dill Pickle Club

Bug House Square, 22

Burgess, Ernest, 98

Burnett, Whit, 61, 83. *See also Story*

*Business Weekly*, Paris edition, 31

Butler, Dorothy (later Mrs. James T. Farrell): as actress and dancer, 6, 154 n. 30; affair with Farrell, 2, 8–9, 18–19; birth, youth, and schooling, 6–7, 154 n. 25; incentive and plan to go to Paris, 20–22; marriage, 23; meets Farrell, 5–6; withdraws from University of Chicago, 10, 155 n. 48. *See also* Farrell, Dorothy Butler

Butler, Margaret (Maggie) (mother), 5, 20–21, 22, 23–24, 93, 102; cables Dorothy money, 101, 129, 136, 165–66 n. 51; characterized, 8–9; on Farrell's family, 101, 181 n. 93; on the Farrells' marriage, 80, 101, 177 n. 116, 181 n. 193; learns of *Young Lonigan* contract, 66; love for Dorothy and Farrell, 130; promissory notes to, 102; urges the Farrells' return to U.S., 129–30

Butler, Patrick (father): dies, 8, 154 n. 25; leaves money to Dorothy, 8, 22

Butler, Virginia (sister), 5, 23

Calverton, V. F., 14

*Coup d'État, the Technique of Revolution* (Malaparte), Farrell reads, 54

Courbet, Gustave, 4

Covici, Pascal, 19. *See* Covici, Friede publishers

Covici, Friede publishers, 18, 19

Coward, McCann publishers, 18, 25

Cowley, Malcolm, meets and helps Farrell, 25, 62, 160 n. 125

Coyle, Kathleen: aids Farrell, 131–32; bids farewell to Farrells, 142; characterizes Farrell's art, 184 n. 1; Farrell reads, 170–71 n. 33; transatlantic friendship with Farrell, 188 n. 53

Crane, Hart, 88; Farrell reads, 2

Croly, Herbert (*The Promise of American Life*), 79

Crosby, Caresse, and Crosby Continental Editions, 123

Cube, the (little theater): Bodenheim at, 6–7, 46; characterized, 5; Dorothy at, 5–7, 26; Farrell at, 5–7, 22, 46

Cunard, Nancy, 37; meets with Farrell, 81; Dorothy on, 81

Cunningham, William (Studs) (model for William [Studs] Lonigan): dies, 11; Farrell attends his wake, 11

Curie, Marie, 48

*Daily Maroon* (University of Chicago student newspaper), 10, 78; publishes Dorothy's and Farrell's "Modernism Marks Exhibit at Art Institute," 4, 153 n. 15; publishes item on Farrell's "library nucleus," 4, 152 n. 13

Daly, Ellen Julia (Ella) (aunt), 2, 7; on the Farrells' marriage, 79–80

Daly, Julia Brown (grandmother), 2; dies, 90–91, 179 n. 147, 179 n. 151; on the Farrells' marriage, 79–80; *Young Lonigan* dedicated to, 66

Daly, Richard Thomas (Tom) (uncle), 2, 90; on the Farrells' marriage, 79–80

Dangerfield, George, 24

Darrow, Clarence, 8; Farrell's correspondence and interview with, 10

Daumier, Honoré, 4

*De Grasse* (steamer), 70

Depression, Great: in America, xi, 22, 50–51, 88–89; in France, xi, 22, 89, 128

Desmond Harmsworth Press of Bloomsbury, 37, 95, 100. *See also* Harmsworth, Desmond

*Devil in the Flesh* (Raymond Radiguet), Farrell reads, 170–71 n. 33

Dewey, John, 6, 8; denigrated by Roger Ginsburg, 59; influences Farrell, 54

*Diamond Lil* (Mae West), Farrell and Dorothy see, 8

Dill Pickle Club, Farrell and Dorothy at, 8, 22, 98

*Distinguished Air (Grim Fairy Tales)* (McAlmon), Farrell reads, 36

*Doll's Journey, The* (Ellen and Adam Fischer): characterized, 57; Farrell reviews, 170 n. 27

Dos Passos, John, 123; and *Gas-House McGinty*, 85

Dostoyevsky, Fyodor, 4

Douglas, Paul, Farrell interviews, 10

Drake, Lawrence (formerly Samuel Pessin), 42, 96, 124; Farrell on, 162–63 n. 7; Farrell reads, 170–71 n. 33; meets Farrell, 31; seeks to publish Farrell, 86, 87

*Dreamy Kid, The* (O'Neill), 153 n. 22

Dreiser, Theodore, 25; influences Farrell, 164 n. 34

*Dubliners* (Joyce), Farrell reads, 3

Duncan, Isadora, *see* Isadora Duncan Dancers

Dunham, Katherine, 6

Dutton publishers, 131

*Earth*, publishes Farrell's "Half Way from the Cradle," 14

"Easy Aces" (TV series), Mary Hunter acts in, 153 n. 22

Eaton, G. D., 12

Egham, 2nd Baron of, Cecil Desmond Bernard Harmsworth. *See* Harmsworth, Desmond

Eliot, Mathews, on Farrell's arrival in Sceaux, 52

Emerson, Ralph Waldo, Farrell reads, 83

Farrell, James Thomas
  *Chronology: (cont.)*
    rejection of "Studs" by *Modern Monthly*, 14; 1930 literary activities, 14, 16–18; wins support of Sam Putnam and Ezra Pound, 14–20, *passim*; political views of, 15–16, 53–54, 89–90; publication of "Studs," 16–17; U.S. publishers' rejection of *Young Lonigan* manuscript, 18, 19, 24; resolves to leave for Paris with Dorothy, 20–22; marries Dorothy Butler, 23–24; in New York City in 1931, 23–26; submits *Young Lonigan* to Vanguard Press, 26; en route to Paris with Dorothy, 26–28;
    first days in Paris, 29–34; meets Riva and Sam Putnam, 31, 34–35; meets Ezra Pound, 36; meets Robert McAlmon, 36, 39; meets Desmond Harmsworth, 36–37; explores Paris, 38–40; café friends and acquaintances, 39–40, 46–47; social activities, with Riva and Sam Putnam, 43–44, 46; —, with Anna and Peter Neagoe, 44, 46; —, with Christina Stead, 44–45; —, with Irma and Gabriel Javsicas, 45; —, with Leopold Survage, 46; —, with Maxwell Bodenheim, 46–47; meets Virginia and Reuben Menken, 47–48;
    moves with Dorothy to Sceaux, 48; residence and first days in Sceaux, 49–50; first guests, 53–54; social activities, with Fanny and Nathan Klein, 55–56, 82; —, with Virginia and Lee Hersch, 55–56; —, with Ellen and Adam Fischer, 55–57; —, with Adaline and Kenneth Knoblock, 58–59, 113–14; first visits to U.S. Students and Artists Club, 115; at the dance marathon, 57–58; visits Roger Ginsburg, 59; revises *Young Lonigan*, 60–61, 67–68, 70; publishes in *Readies*, 61–63, 83; publishes in *Americans Abroad*, 63; publishes in *New Review* ("Jewboy"), 63–64, 81, 83; other efforts to publish, 64; visits

    Fontainbleau, 64–65; gets Vanguard contract for *Young Lonigan*, 65; dedicates *Young Lonigan* , 66; opposes literary censorship, 67–68, 96–98 (*also see* censorship: and Farrell's fiction); and sociologists, 68, 85–86, 97, 140–41; celebrates Bastille Day, 68–70; submits *Young Lonigan* to Vanguard Press, 70
    and the genesis of *The Madhouse* (tentative title for *Gas–House McGinty*), 70–72; clarifies his long-range literary plans, 73; composes *The Madhouse*, 73–75, 82; obtains *cartes d'identités*, 75–77; gets a new lease agreement, 77; scuffle with Rue Menken, 77–78; welcomes Ed Bastian to Paris, 78–79; discloses his marriage to his family, 79–80; and Nancy Cunard, 81; submits *The Madhouse* to Vanguard Press, 84; composes volumes 2 and 3 of *The Madhouse*, 85, 86, 93–94, 95, 103, 111–12, 120, 138–39; proposes a book titled *Chamber of Horrors*, 86, 87, 96;
    gets advance on *The Madhouse*, 87; meets Pauline and Nat Turkel, 88; exchange rate worries, 154; mourns death of Julia Daly, 90–91; plays with Hilary Putnam, 91; Gallimard as potential publisher of French *Young Lonigan*, 92, 104, 112, 112–13, 122, 127–28, 131–32, 143; reads Vanguard proof of *Young Lonigan*, 94; plans *The Young Manhood of Studs Lonigan*, 94–95; and Harmsworth as potential publisher of an English *Young Lonigan*, 95–96, 122, 141; opposes publishing *Young Lonigan* as a limited edition, 96–98; and Jacob Schwartz as potential publisher, 100, 104, 110–11; final days in Sceaux, 100–102;
    returns to Paris with Dorothy, 102; takes Dorothy to American Hospital, 105; Sean Farrell's birth, 105; Sean's death, 106–7; —, effect on Farrell, 107–8, 183 n. 27; with Kay Boyle and Laurence Vail, 112,

Farrell, James Thomas (*cont.*)

*Excerpts from novels:*

"Fragments from the Unpublished Death Fantasy Sequence of 'Judgment Day,'" 189–90

"McGinty King of Ireland" (unpublished), 110

"Young Lonigan," 138, 189 n. 76

*Novelette:*

"My Friend Jean Paul" (unpublished), 122

*Short Stories:*

"Accident," 110

"After the Sun Has Risen, 191–92 n. 104

"Calico Shoes," 11

"Casual Incident, A," 83, 104

"Fritz," 92

"Guillotine Party," 137

"Harry and Barney" (unpublished), 25–26, 71

"Helen, I Love You," 145

"Honey, We'll Be Brave," 36

"Jeff," 62

"Jewboy," approved by Pound, 19, 119; approved by Schwartz, 100; approved by Targ, 119; published in *New Review*, 52, 63–64, 80–81; reputation in Los Angeles, 83–84

"Looking 'Em Over," 36

"McGinty King of Ireland" (unpublished), 110

"Meet the Girls," 36, 100, 119

"Merry Clouters, The," 42, 110

"Saturday Night" (first titled "Their Little Moments of Glory"), 96

"Scarecrow, The," 36; approved by Pound, 19, 119; rejected by Neagoe, 63, 67; rejected by Mencken, 97

"Scene," 11

"Slob," 1, 11, 12, 112

"Soap," 44, 126; accepted by Neagoe, 63

"Spring Evening," 138

"Studs," accepted and published by Putnam, 14, 16–17, 24; rejected by Calverton, 14; writing of, 5, 11

"Sylvester McGullick," accepted and published by Brown, 62–63

"Their Little Moments of Glory" (published as "Saturday Night"), 116, 119

*Sketches:*

"In the Park," 14

"My Friend, the Doctor," 14

*Poems:*

"Happy Sunday," 9

"Sacrament of Marriage, The," 5

*Articles:*

"Criticism of the University Library Department, A," 2

"filosofia del presente, di G. H. Mead, La," 158 n. 78

"George Herbert Mead's *Philosophy of the Present*'"158 n. 78

"Half Way from the Cradle," 14

"John Dewey's Philosophy," 14

"Liberals in Chicago," 10, 12, 98

"Modernism Marks American Exhibit at Art Institute" (with Dorothy), 153 n. 15

"Observations of American Life and American Literature" (unpublished), 119

"On Picasso and Van Gogh: Forms of Alienation," 153 n. 16

"Paris—the Psychopathic Ward of America" (unpublished), 119

"Thirty and Under," 14, 18

*Autobiographical notes:*

"Author's Note," 156 n. 59

"James T. Farrell," 151 n. l

"World Is Today, The" 152 n. 11

Farrell, John Anthony (Jack) (brother), 23, 70, 72, 81, 90, 101; publishes "One of the Many" in *Readies*, 62–63; supplies information for *Gas-House McGinty*, 71

Farrell, Joseph Edward (Joe) (brother), as express company employee, 14

Farrell, Mary Daly (mother), 8; visits Maggie Butler, 101, 181 n. 193

Farrell, Mary Elizabeth (sister), 4, 23, 70, 112, 121, 143

Farrell, Sean Thomas Butler (son), 111, 112, 115, 121; born, 105; death and burial, 106–7

Farrell, William Earl (Earl) (brother): as express company employee, 74; on the Farrells' marriage,

Isadora Duncan dancers, Farrell and Dorothy see, 8

James, Henry: Farrell reads, 58; Pound's allusions to, 19, 36
James, William: Mussolini on, 158 n. 78; Putnam on, 15
Jameson, Ruth. *See* Janowicz, Ruth Jameson
Janowicz, Ruth Jameson: on the Depression in Chicago, 72; Farrell aids, 152 n. 7; in Paris, 3, 10–11; publishes in *transition*, 3
Janowicz, Vladimir, 72; aids the Farrells, 165–66 n. 51; advises the Farrells on Paris 17; in Paris, 3, 10–11
Javsicas, Gabriel (Gabby): sketch of, 45, 166 n. 60; on Sean's death, 109–10
Javsicas, Irma: Farrell visits, 45; sketch of, 45
Johns, Richard, 83
Jolas, Eugene, 11, 16; rejects literary realism, 156 n. 54
Jonathan Cape Smith, publishers, 18. *See* Cape and Smith
Jones, Jack, 8. *Also see* Dill Pickle Club
Jones, Llewellen, Farrell's English instructor, 8
Jones, W. Tudor, 59
Jordan, Harry (city editor, *Chicago Herald-Examiner*), 10
*Journal of Sociology*, Farrell on, 68
Joyce, James, 79, 100; alleged liking for Farrell's tales, 37; influences Farrell, 3–4, 123, 139, 152 n. 11, 164 n. 34, 185 n. 19, 189–90 n. 79; Farrell reads his books, 3

Kahn, S. Henry (correspondent for trade papers), meets and visits with the Farrells, 47, 53, 167 n. 70
Kahn, Mrs. S. Henry, meets and visits with the Farrells, 47, 53, 167 n. 70
Kallen, Horace M., 53, 158 n. 70
Karnow, David (correspondent), meets the Farrells, 40
*Katharsis*, 69
Kathleen (Farrell's fictional character based on Dorothy Farrell), 46, 47
Kirstein, Lincoln, 83, 108

Klein, Fanny, 137, 186; in American Hospital with Dorothy, 55; bears Judy, 92; later life in U.S., 169 n. 21; social activities with Farrells, 55–56, 82, 133
Klein, Judy: birth, 92; later life in Paris, 169 n. 21
Klein, Nathan, 86, 92, 137; background and status, 55–56; later life in U.S., 169 n. 21; social activities with Farrells, 55–56, 82, 133
Knoblock, Adaline, 124–25, 133, 142; background, 58–59; social activities with the Farrells, 58–59, 113–14, 137
Knoblock, Kenneth, 124–25, 133; background and sketch of, 116; social activities with the Farrells, 58–59, 113–14, 137
Kolodziej, Felix, 23; aids the Farrells, 165–66 n. 51
Krans, Horatio S., aids the Farrells, financially, 120, 129; helps Farrells obtain passage home, 142; aids Phyllis Russell, 144
Kropotkin, Peter, 26
Krumgold, Joseph, considers *Young Lonigan* for movie script, 94; sketch of and writings, 176 n. 104, 180 n. 168
Krumgold, Sarajo Caron, 94, 176 n. 104; on "Jewboy," 83; on the Menkens, 77. *See also* Caron, Sarajo

La Follette, Suzanne, 49
*Lady Chatterley's Lover* (Lawrence): Farrell reads, 58; Farrell smuggles, 133, 145
Lanson, Ed (Farrell's fictional character based on Paul Caron), 17
Laski, Harold, 45
Lasswell, Harold (Farrell's instructor in Political Science), 98, 157–58 n. 77
Lawrence, D. H. See *Lady Chatterley's Lover*
Lawson, John Howard, 75
Le Grand, Maurice (pseud. Franc-Nohain), 120
Lewisohn, Ludwig, meets the Farrells, 40, 114

Ramuz, Charles Ferdinand, meets the Farrells, 64

Rausch, Maurice, 92, 105, 133, 135–36, 170 n. 31, ; meets the Farrells, 58

*Readies for Bob Brown's Machine* (Brown), 117, 123; described and characterized, 62–63, 172–73 n. 46; Farrell on, 119; influences *Gas-House McGinty* , 83–84; publishes "Jeff," 62; publishes "One of the Many," 62–63; publishes "Sylvester McGullick," 62–63; selections from, 172–73

Reavey, George, 80; meets the Farrells, 40

"Red Days in Chicago" (Putnam), 168 n. 17

Reitman, Ben, 28, 109

Renoir, Pierre Auguste, 4

Revolution of the Word, The, in *transition*, 16

Rivera, Diego, 56

Robert (Farrell's autobiographical character in "Paris Novel"), 39, 41, 46, 47

Robert, Pierre-Jean, 102, 104, 106, 113, 114, 119, 132, 137, 142; gets *cartes d'identités* for Farrells, 76–77; gives Farrell shoes, 128–29; political views, 76, 89; at the Sphinx with Farrell, 108–9; and *Young Lonigan*, as Gallimard's agent for, 92, 112; —, praise of, 92; —, as translator of, 113, 122

Robeson, Paul, Farrell and Dorothy hear recital of, 8

Rolvaag, Ole, 8

Roney, Grace (Mrs. John) (Dorothy's aunt), 10, 20, 80; affection for Dorothy, 7; sees Dorothy in Paris, 79

Roney, John (Dorothy's uncle), 10. 20. 80; affection for Dorothy, 7; aids Dorothy, 8, 9; business and background, 7, 154–55 n. 32

Roney, Marian (Dorothy's cousin), 7

*Roosevelt, U.S.S.,* 142

Root, Waverly, meets the Farrells, 40

Rose, Sam, 12

Rosenfels, Paul, aids Farrell, 23

Rosengren, Herbert, 69

Rosenwald, Julius, Farrell interviews, 10

Ross, Harold, 57

*Rousseau and Romanticism* (Babbitt), Farrell reads, 170–71 n. 33

Rudnick, Jessie, visits the Farrells in Sceaux, 70, 78

Rudnick, Paul, visits the Farrells in Sceaux, 70, 78

Rudy (German student of architecture), 47, 53, 59; political views, 171 n. 36

Russell, Phyllis: model for Agatha Stallings in "After the Sun Has Risen," 191–92 n. 104; in New York City, 191–92 n. 104; on the *Statendam*, 144

Russell, Bertrand, 4, 8

Ryan, Eddie (Farrell autobiographical character), 3, 13–14, 127; contrasts Paris and Chicago, 32, 35; desires Catherine, 58, 136; on Marion Healy (Dorothy), 26–27, 125; on Paris, 17, 131

Sacco, Nicola, 26; influences Farrell, 88

Sage, Maeve, 105

Sage, Robert, 105

Saint-Blaise, Boeffe de, 55; on cause of Sean's death, 106; Dorothy on, 55, 105; Farrell on, 106, 168–69 n. 19; forgives payment, 200

Saint-Germain-des-Prés tower, appeal to Farrell, 33, 34, 162 n. 16

Salemson, Harold, 3, 14, 19. See *Tambour*

*Sanctuary* (Faulkner), Farrell reads, 58

Sandburg, Carl, 8; and *Young Lonigan* proof, 98

Santayana, George, 158 n. 78

Sapir, Edward, 4

*Saturday Review of Literature,* 12–13, 61; publishes Farrell's "John Dewey's Philosophy," 14

Saunders, Ross, 62

*Sawdust Caesar* (George Seldes), 84

Sceaux: compared to Chicago, 50–51; Dorothy's feeling for, 51; importance to Farrells, 49–50; pavillon described, 51–52

Titus, Edward, 55, 94, 96, 100, 104, 119; accepts "The Merry Clouters," 42, 110; aids the Farrells, 90; and *Contemporaries 1931*, 42; on Farrell's short stories; 14; meets Dorothy, 179 n. 150; meets Farrell, 30–31; reputation, 180–81 n. 189; and "Studs," 16–17

"Today Is Friday" (Hemingway), Farrell acts in, 6–7

Tolstoy, Lev Nikolaevich, 26

*Tonight We Improvise* (Pirandello): Pirandello reads publically, 30–31; Putnam translates, 44, 130

*Torrents of Spring, The* (Hemingway), 123

Townsend, Eric, 69

*transition* (Paris), 40, 105; Farrell on, 2, 119, 139; Farrell's submissions to, 3, 11; influences Farrell, 2, 3; Putnam's relation to, 16

"Triplexicated Illustratification of Go-Getters" (McAlmon), Farrell on, 63

Trotsky, Leon, Farrell reads, 58

"Truth about Fascism, The" (Putnam), 15

Tschann, Louis (bookstore owner), 39

Turbyfill, Mark, 6

Turkel, Nat, friendship with Farrells, 87–88

Turkel, Pauline," friendship with the Farrells, 87–88; sketch of, 87–88, 178 n. 140

Uasia. *See* Slow Club, the

*Ulysses* (Joyce), 79; Farrell reads, 3–4, 152 n. 11; Farrell re-reads, 124–25; influences *Gas-House McGinty*, 139, 189–90 n. 79; influences *Judgment Day*, 189–90 n. 79

United States Students and Artists Club, 124, 134, 141; activities and history of, 170 n. 30; Farrells at, 58, 106, 125–26; Farrells' farewell to, 142; Farrell's scuffle with Menken in, 77–78

*Under Fire* (*Le Feu*, Barbusse), 64

University of Chicago, xx, 15; Dorothy at, 6–7, 8, 10; Farrell at, 2–4, 8; Farrell in Linn's class at, 11; Farrell's study of political science and Fascism at, 15–16, 157–58 n. 77

Vail, Laurence, 62, 77, 111, 112, 160 n. 125, 172–73 n. 46; social activities with Farrells, 112, 115–16, 117

van de Velde, Hendrik, 98, 180 n. 180

Van Doren, Irita, 13

Van Gogh, Vincent, 4

Vanguard Press, 26, 61, 63, 65, 96, 104, 120; accepts, *Gas-House McGinty*, 87; —, *Young Lonigan*, 47; advance payments to Farrell, 65, 79, 87, 114–15; contract for *Gas-House McGinty*, 87; contract for *Young Lonigan*, 65; Farrell on, 65; publishes *Gas-House McGinty*, 190 n. 83; publishes *Young Lonigan*, 145. *See also* Henle, James; *Young Lonigan*; and *Gas-House McGinty*

Vanzetti, Bartolomeo, 26; influences Farrell, 88

Veblen, Thorstein, 26

Velásquez, Diego, 4

Walsh, Ernest, 3

Washington Park neighborhood, 2, 12

West, Mae, Farrell and Dorothy see in "Diamond Lil," 8

Widney, Mary: as hostess at Pirandello reception, 130–31; Putnam's sketch of, 187 n. 45

Widney, Willard: hosts Pirandello reception, 130–31; Putnam's sketch of, 187 n. 45

Williams, William Carlos: contributes to *Readies*, 172–73 n. 46; on Farrell's "Scene," 11

Wolfe, Thomas, Farrell reads, 58

*Woman under Glass, Saint Teresa of Avila* (Virginia Hersch), 56

"Work in Progress" (Joyce), Farrell reads, 3

Yeats, William Butler, 4